FREEDOM OF THE SKIES

FREEDOM OF THE SKIES

OF THE

SKIES

ADVENTURE AROUND THE WORLD IN A LIGHT AIRCRAFT

— MARGI MOSS —

Airlife
England

Copyright © 1997 Margi Moss

First published in the UK in 1997
by Airlife Publishing Ltd

Portuguese language edition
first published by Editora Globo S.A., Brazil in 1995
under the title *A Volta por Cima*

British Library Cataloguing-in-Publication Data
   A catalogue record for this book
   is available from the British Library

ISBN 1 85310 906 1

Typeset by Hewer Text Composition Services, Edinburgh
Printed in England by Livesey Ltd, Shrewsbury

Airlife Publishing Ltd
101 Longden Road, Shrewsbury, SY3 9EB, England.

Contents

FOR MY FATHER

Mais les vrais voyageurs sont ceux-là seuls qui partent
Pour partir; coeurs légers, semblables aux ballons,
De leur fatalité jamais ils ne s'écartent,
Et, sans savoir pourquoi, disent toujours: Allons!

Charles Baudelaire, *Le Voyage*

Abbreviations

AGL	Above Ground Level
AOPA	Aircraft Owners and Pilots Association
Avgas	Aviation gasoline
CAA	Civil Aviation Authority
CAVOK	Ceiling and Visibility OK
CITES	Convention on International Trade in Endangered Species
DAC	Department of Civil Aviation
DME	Distance Measuring Equipment
ETA	Estimated Time of Arrival
ELT	Emergency Locator Transmitter
FAI	Fédération Aéronautique Internationale
FIR	Flight Information Region
FL	Flight Level
GMT	Greenwich Mean Time
GPS	Global Positioning System satellite navigator
HF	High Frequency radio
IFR	Instrument Flight Rules
ILS	Instrument Landing System
ITCZ	Inter-Tropical Confluence Zone
MAF	Mission Aviation Fellowship
NDB	Non-Directional Beacon
NOTAM	Notice to Airmen
ONC	Operational Navigational Chart
RVR	Runway Visual Range
SAR	Search and Rescue
SatNav	Satellite Navigator
VFR	Visual Flight Rules
VHF	Very High Frequency
VOR	VHF Omnidirectional Range

Acknowledgements

Gérard and I would like to thank the unsung hundreds who helped us during our voyage, people who showed us spontaneous kindness even though many times we did not even have the chance to learn their names. With a simple hallo, a word of advice, a smile or a warm handshake, they contributed towards blessing our flying visits to the distant corners of this marvellous planet with the joy of discovery.

We apologise to our families for the moments of tension and worry which we caused them. Together, we learned that danger is both fleeting and surmountable, that it is an important part of life and even enriches it.

The whole team at Indústria Aeronáutica Neiva S.A. (Botucatu, São Paulo), where the plane was manufactured, were extremely helpful, enthusiastic and generous with their time, both before and after the trip. Our friends Stan and Rosie Haynes took us to Santos Dumont airport on a rainy day in June 1989 and stood there, waving wistfully at the sky, until the small plane disappeared into stormy clouds. And there they were, smiling, at the same airport on a sunny day in February 1992 when we returned. Arnold Gibbons, in Rarotonga, kept us going during many tense hours as we flew over the solitary waters of the Pacific; the echo of his voice over the radio was our lifeline. Special thanks to Hélio de Almeida who encouraged us to make a book, and Eliana Sá of Editora Globo in Brazil and Alastair Simpson of Airlife in England, who rose to the challenge of publishing it. Much gratitude also to my mother Margery and Sabastian Segriff, who waded through the manuscript and gave sound advice.

I am especially indebted to my beloved husband Gérard. If he had not insisted, I would never have boarded this flight. Finally, I take my hat off to valiant *Romeo*, who behaved like an angel throughout, tackling all manner of skies and landing strips with calm resignation.

We are grateful to the following people and institutions:
Brazil: Aeroclube do Brasil, Ken Baxter, Carlota Camargo, José Bonifácio de Castro, Fernando Cortes, Philippe & Janine Desmeules, Embraer, Lena M. Guimarães, Marco Antônio Montenegro, Hugo Moss, Neiva, Albano Pinto.
Sénégal: Christian & Nicole Virmaud.
Burkina Faso: Aéroclub de Ouagadougou, Dominique & Myriam Vignon.
Ivory Coast: Jean-Louis & Carmen Butticaz.
Gabon: Patrick & Martine Crouzet, Martine Marchal.

Kenya: Claire Colpoys, CMC Aviation, Tony & Myrtle Granger-Brown, Debbie Marvin, Brian McCoun, Mick & Jane Wilson-Smith.
Tanzania: Antônio Luz, M.A.F. (Dodoma), Charles Mzena.
Zimbabwe: Mark & Carol Bates, Fields Aviation, Pierre & Antoinette Jaunet, Dawes & Virginia Malton, Peter & Janet Marchussen, Spencer Tigere.
South Africa: Billy Saad.
Mozambique: Paulo Muxanga, Rex & Dana Potter.
Nepal: Andrew & Dorrie Brass, Tika Ram Puri, G.P. Rimal.
Thailand: Ko Kyaw, Hervey Oei, Robert Schmidt, Thai Flying Club.
Singapore: Ted & Susie Nation, Jack & Betty Oei, Singapore Flying Club.
Malaysia: Lelis & Ivone Fachini, Douglas Leong, Penang Flying Club, Jorge & Monica Reis, Royal Selangor Flying Club, Kandasamy Sandanam.
Brunei: Julia Forsyth, Mike Puleston.
Indonesia: Man Ali, Dar & Berna Bone, Philip & Marian Holley, Bernie Krause, Mission Aviation Fellowship.
Australia: Trevor & Judi Breed, Pete & Ali Dawson, Edward & Marie-Hélène Gilly, Toby & Leiticia Grey, Peter Hoad (Regalair), Ken Martin, Edwin Murphy, John, Sheilagh & Gail Nolan-Neylan, Eric Savage, Dick & Pip Smith, Marie Varnier, David & Helen Walford, Clive West, John Weymouth.
Solomon Islands: Adjit, David Friend, Charles & Mefanwy Humphries, Athol & Verity Smith-Loretz.
Vanuatu: Claude Mitride, Norman & Elaine Sanson, Brian Smith.
Fiji: Rick & Do Cammick, Shane Devery, Sunflower Airlines Ltd.
Tonga: Cecil & Tu'ifua Crocker, S.T. Lava & Tangakina Faleola, Seletuti Falevai, Peter Goldstern, TuiPolutu & Savieti Lea.
Western Samoa: Aggie Grey's Hotel, Alfred, Fala, Pita & Roy (Faleolo), Heini Sanft, Viiga Herman & Tania of Polynesian Airlines, Gene Witham.
Cook Islands: Arnold & Rosie Gibbons, Sacha Vukasinovic (The Rarotongan).
French Polynesia: Aéroclub de Tahiti, Air Moorea, Euthyme Carlson, Léon Chanel, François & Amélie Dantzer, Daniel Delile, Ron Falconer, Dominique Jarreau & Mireille Jeanne, Lan-Chile, Roy McKibbon & Desirée Posse-Brazda on the yacht *Finesse*, Jacques Maechler, Reia Matehau, Rino Matehau, Daniel Roy, Royal Papeete Hotel, Tobia & Titine Tane, Marc Teixeire.
Easter Island: All those on duty in Mataveri Control Tower on 16 and 22 January 1992.
Chile: Hotel Carrera, Eneas Grisolia, Taxpa, Ernesto Zieleniewicz.
Argentina: Rick Jarvie, Timen.

Technical Data

Aircraft Registration: PT-RXE

Aircraft Type: Embraer 721 D – Sertanejo (1985). Six-seater single-engine with retractable gear.
Manufacturer: Indústria Aeronáutica Neiva, Botucatu, São Paulo.
Engine: Lycoming six-cylinder, 300 horsepower.
Propeller: Hetzell, three-blade, variable pitch.

Standard endurance: eight hours (385 litres).
Standard range: 1,000 nautical miles (1,850 km).
Fuel consumption: average of 45–50 litres Avgas (100–130 octanes) per hour at cruising speed.
Oil consumption: one litre per ten hours' flying time.

Instruments: standard IFR equipment, including two Nav/Coms with ILS approach, two ADFs, electrical horizon coupled auto-pilot and stormscope. Extra equipment included an ICOM HF transceiver, an EGT six-cylinder analyser and a Magnavox 4102 Satnav at the beginning of the trip, substituted later by the more reliable Magellan GPS (Global Positioning System).

Major legs across the oceans:

South Atlantic
Fernando de Noronha (Brazil) / Ilha do Sal (Cape Verde): 1,356 nautical miles (2,510 km) in 12 hours (headwinds).
Endurance: 15 hours (1,950 nautical miles – 3,600 km).
Usable fuel: 385 litres in the wing tanks plus two additional tanks inside the cabin with 150 and 180 litres.

South Pacific
Totégégie (Mangareva, Polynesia) / Easter Island (Chile): 1,420 nautical miles (2,600 km) in 11 hours, 40 minutes (tailwinds).
Easter Island (Chile) / Robinson Crusoe Island (Chile): 1,625 nautical miles (3,010 km) in 11 hours, 10 minutes (tailwinds).
Endurance: 18 hours (2,450 nautical miles – 4,530 km) because no refuelling is available on Robinson Crusoe Island, 415 miles from Santiago.
Usable fuel: 385 litres in the wing tanks, plus two additional tanks inside the cabin with 150 and 340 litres.

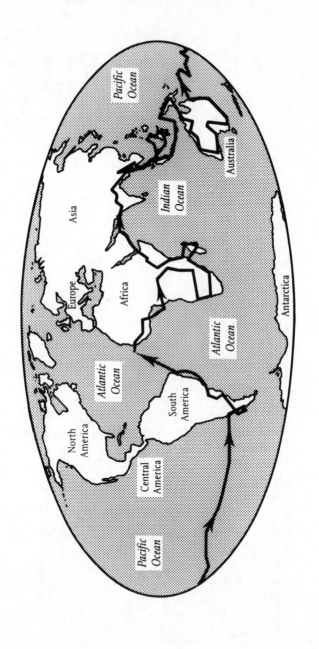

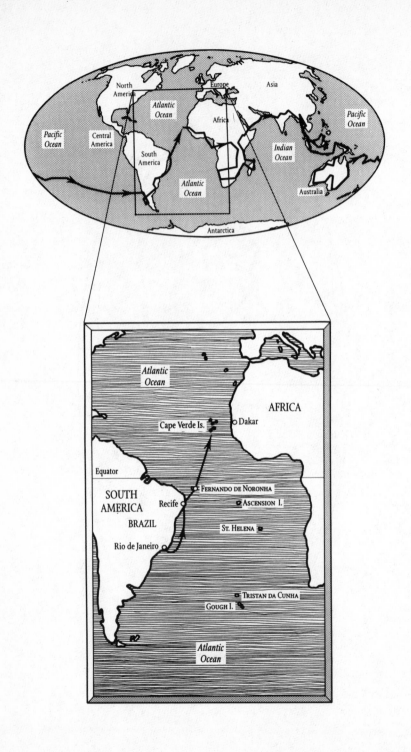

1 'You've married a madman'

Outside, pitch darkness. Above, below, all around. Inside, just the greenish state-of-the-art glow of the instrument panel. It felt as though we were buckled into the Voyager headed for outer space, being propelled towards an unknown destination with scant probability of return.

'What's the matter?'

'Nothing.'

A minute passed. The engine whirred normally. Or so it seemed. Each time I moved my head, it seemed to change pitch. My heart pounded anxiously, a painful thumping which felt like a heart attack. Gérard was hunched down, gazing obsessively at one of the gauges.

'There is something wrong, isn't there?' I asked, hating the question, dreading the response.

'It's ooo-kaaay.'

'So why do you keep staring at the instruments like that?'

'Well, it's just strange. The oil temperature's rather high. Never been this high before. Perhaps I left a rag by the oil cooler when I was checking the engine.'

I leant over to his side of the cockpit. The needle was almost on the red line. I felt I'd been kicked in the stomach. Why now, on this of all flights? We were still climbing, painfully slowly, foot by miserable foot. Behind us, the merry lights of Fernando de Noronha, surely one of the world's most beautiful islands, had snuggled back into the night's embrace, leaving us utterly alone over a black sea in a black sky of lustreless stars.

'Please let's turn round,' I thought, sweaty fists clenched. 'Oh God, please make him turn round. I never wanted to make this damn trip. I hate it. I wanna go hoooome.'

But there was no room for hysterics. After all, Gérard, who understood better than I the seriousness of the problem, was perfectly calm. He did not need a frantic woman on his hands.

I sat there, craving the solid earth of Fernando de Noronha, wishing we were still there. Life had seemed so eternal, so indestructible as we walked to the airfield after dining at the island's only hotel, a former American army barracks. The road had unravelled ahead of us, like a grey ribbon lit by a tangible oval moon. A hundred frogs had serenaded us in a raucous chorus from a swamp. Arm in arm, caressed by the sea breeze, we drew deep breaths of warm air filled with the scent of wild grasses. We lived those moments intensely, one by one, like a Space Shuttle countdown. The scenario was electrically romantic. But the apprehensions of what we were about to do – fly off in a small plane across 1,356 nautical miles of Atlantic Ocean – quashed any inspiration for a long, passionate kiss which might resemble a desperate farewell . . . It was no time for goodbyes: we were embarking on the trip of a lifetime, to far exotic lands.

As long as we made it to the other side . . .

Fernando de Noronha, the Emerald of the Atlantic, lies off the bulge of Brazil, 300 nautical miles north-east of Recife. It first appears on a nautical chart dated 1500. In 1503, it was awarded to the Portuguese nobleman Fernan de Loronha, in recognition of his financial support of exploratory expeditions to the New World. He never showed the slightest interest in his prize, but his name lives on in corrupted form. Over the centuries, the island passed through Dutch, British and French hands until the Portuguese finally ousted the latter in 1737. In the 1920s and 1930s, it was used by the pioneer aviators opening up air routes across the South Atlantic from Africa and Europe. In 1922, two Portuguese pilots, Gago Coutinho and Sacadura Cabral, made the first flight from Europe in a Fairey IIID flying boat, landing in the bay after various mishaps. The current airport was built by the Americans, who stationed 5,000 men on the island during World War II.

For us, it was a convenient stepping-stone shortening the long haul over the Atlantic by two and a half hours. Since no fuel was available, we had made a ferry flight to deliver our own supply of Avgas (aviation gasoline), 100–130 octane low-lead fuel required by piston-engine aircraft. We had siphoned it into two barrels and left them in the care of Sr Paz, the local Petrobrás man. He duly locked them away in his depot because of a tendency for fuel to evaporate into the islanders' vehicles. Before final departure from Recife on 21 June 1989, we sent a message asking for it to be transported back to the airport.

When we landed just before dusk, there was no sign of Sr Paz, or the fuel. The depot was several kilometres away and there were no buses or taxis on the island. We were already tense in anticipation of crossing the ocean that night and the missing fuel did not augur well. Antônio, an airport employee, led Gérard by torchlight across the fields to Paz's house, a converted cattle stable, where he was engrossed in a football match on TV. The barrels were duly fetched in a decrepit Kombi, loaded onto a fork-lift and suspended in turn high above each wing until the tanks were full.

'We're only at 5,000 feet, but I'm going to level off to improve the air flow,' Gérard announced, jerking me out of my reverie. 'Maybe that'll bring down the oil temperature.'

14

'Shouldn't we turn back before it's too late?' I couldn't contain myself. It was a hateful concept. Turning back, giving up already. We had only just begun. What a pathetic failure it would be.

'Let's see what happens in the next five minutes. We're very heavy.' His engineer's mind was clicking over. There had to be a logical explanation for the problem.

PT-RXE, nicknamed *Romeo*, is a Sertanejo, a six-seater 300 hp low-wing single-engine built in Brazil by Neiva, a subsidiary of Embraer, under licence from Piper. It has a standard autonomy of eight hours, a range of 1,000 nautical miles. To cross the South Atlantic, Gérard had designed two additional aluminium fuel tanks and installed them in place of the middle seats, over the aircraft's centre of gravity so as not to offset the balance. These extra 330 litres of fuel increased our autonomy to fifteen hours, almost doubling our range. 715 litres of fuel are extremely heavy. *Romeo* had been some 100 kilos over maximum take-off weight.

But the oil temperature in the red – that was *Bad News*. Did it mean we were losing oil? Without lubrication, the engine would not last fifteen minutes. Noronha was already an hour away. I glanced hatefully at our miserable two-man life-raft.

The commonest cause of engine failure is sloppy maintenance – unsecured twist-on oil filters, loose magneto mountings or power linkages. Gérard had carried out a detailed check of the engine before departure, retightening nuts, bolts, hose-clamps, injectors, and spark plugs. He had inspected all cables and safety wires, and topped up the oil to full capacity.

After levelling off, the oil temperature did indeed stabilise, but it remained higher than usual. There were still over 1,000 miles to go. Why not turn back while still relatively close to Brazil, instead of pressing on and ending up floating in the mid-Atlantic?

But Gérard wasn't chicken, like me. The engine had worked perfectly on the flight from Recife. So on we went while he cursed continually, loud and strong in French, which comes more naturally to him, blaming himself for some omission. All this nervous tension and fear clasped at my bladder. No amount of crossing my legs and trying to think of other things helped. We had no toilet, and the solution was a custom-built urine bottle bought in an aviation shop in the USA. I had not yet tried it out, putting off the experience until bursting. First, it was necessary to squeeze through the eight-inch gap between the two inside tanks, and then squat foolishly over the wretched bottle beside the back door. It was a tricky question of aim which Gérard was better equipped to handle.

'Wind 110 at eight knots. PAPA-TANGO-ROMEO-XRAY-ECHO cleared to Ilha do Sal, Flight Level 090. Cleared for take-off.'

Cleared for take-off . . . cleared for take-off . . . the controller's words had reverberated through the cramped cockpit. They meant, 'This is it, folks. You wanted to do it. Off you go! What are you waiting for? Ciao!' As Gérard revved the engine on the threshold, the runway lights twinkled tantalisingly, joining at a point in infinity in the darkness ahead. On our left, the dramatic 1,000-foot Morro do Pico, silhouetted against moonlit clouds, flashed a warning to ships in the night. To me, it said, 'Don't go. Stick around here, where you're safe.' That had been at 02:35, or 04:35 GMT. Greenwich Mean Time, on which all aviation clocks throughout the world are standardised, takes the confusion out of flying through different time zones.

We were established on radial 045 from Noronha VOR, an air navigation aid coupled to the DME (Distance Measuring Equipment) which we had lost twenty-five nautical miles out. With relatively light winds, Gérard had deemed five degrees correction to be sufficient to maintain course. Since very few unpressurised aircraft cross the South Atlantic, Winds Aloft charts are only prepared for flight levels of 18,000 feet and over. The winds at our meagre range of 5,000–10,000 feet were anybody's guess.

And there we were, two hours later, chugging above the invisible Atlantic, racked with mechanical worries. We had estimated eleven hours' flying time to Ilha do Sal, Cape Verde Islands. Two days after full moon, the spectacle had initially been magnificent: a black velvety carpet smeared with a shiny yellow stain and splodges of fluffy grey cloud. But the moon had set, leaving us in the dark. To avoid inundating Gérard with my fears, I took solace from our mascot, Monte, a teddy bear kitted out in flying jacket and goggles sent by Lesley, a dear friend in Scotland. He was blissfully ignorant of our predicament. I had named him after my first flying instructor, Marco Montenegro.

Six months previously, once it had been decided that the vehicle of our travels was to be an aircraft, it became pertinent that I learn to fly. Gérard had been a private pilot for seven years, but mastery of the common car is challenge enough to me. The thought of driving an aeroplane was terrifying, but I agreed to some experimental hours with Montenegro.

Peering into the impenetrable darkness that night reminded me of an incident with Montenegro caused by excessive light. We had headed west from Santos Dumont to practise turns and stalls off Barra da Tijuca. The evening sun reflected blindingly off the sea below. I was concentrating on manoeuvres at 2,000 feet, when I noticed Montenegro squinting ahead with intense concern. Over the radio, he had heard that an Electra (how we miss the Electras on the Rio–São Paulo shuttle) was approaching at 3,000 feet. I spotted it immediately. It was heading straight for us. My survival instincts gridlocked; I only managed to point. 'There!'

Montenegro had forgotten his glasses. He wrinkled his eyes and strained to see. 'Where?'

'There!'

'Where?'

'There!'

I pointed and Montenegro peered, and the Electra bore down on us. When he focused at last, he grabbed the yoke and plunged us downwards.

'They're supposed to be at 3,000 feet!' he gasped weakly.

This alarming near-miss disinclined me to continue flying. As a way out, I enrolled for the theory exams. If I failed these, which seemed most likely, I would have an excuse to give up flying. All five exam subjects – Air Regulations, Theory of Flight, Meteorology, Navigation and Mechanics – were Greek to me. It was necessary to pass all five before taking the Private Pilot's Licence and I would have only one chance before we were due to depart. For two months, I crammed my despairing brain with intangible concepts such as aerodynamics and the vocabulary of the intimate parts of piston engines.

On the day of the theory exam, a bundle of nerves, I sat in a vast hall with some two hundred would-be pilots. They were all young and male. I felt out of place: old, female and foolish. I imagined them snickering to themselves about what the hell I was doing there. When, weeks later, the results finally came out, I was sure I had failed. But, miraculously, I passed.

So I had to resume flying. Montenegro had been struck down by meningitis. Heitor, my next instructor, looked eighteen but assured me he had been flying for over ten years. During our second lesson, he read the newspaper all the way to Saquarema while I fumed at his lack of interest. After several touch-and-goes, he told me to pull up at the end of the runway. Thinking we were stopping, according to Brazilian ritual, for a *cafezinho,* I was horrified when he jumped out and told me to take off on my own and make a circuit. I soloed. It was a nerve-wracking and exhilarating experience.

But now there was much nerve-wracking and nothing exhilarating about this night flight over the ocean. It was lonely, terrifying and quite mad. From time to time, the curt voice of the Recife controller gave us comfort. It made us believe that someone cared. He did not: he was just doing his job.

With the oil temperature still stable, we climbed to 7,000 feet. We had lost the Noronha VOR after an hour and ten minutes. Navigation was left to the compass and the Magnavox Satellite Navigator (SatNav), an instrument designed for boats and adapted for light aircraft, a primitive ancestor of the now commonplace GPS – Global Positioning System. In theory, the SatNav would give us fixes pinpointing our geographical co-ordinates every couple of hours. It had done so on the test flights. Provided with an accurate position update, we would correct our course to remedy any deviation caused by the unknown wind factor.

However, the machine rejected the first fix. This was a serious blow, since we had bought the SatNav specifically to ensure a safe crossing and had, foolishly in retrospect, not brought along a sextant. This first fix was vital to establish our position early on, so that corrections could be made before we moved too far off course. A tiny three-degree error at the beginning of the flight would lead us disastrously far off target after twelve hours. Way out over the vast, empty ocean, we had no means of determining our position, or of knowing which heading to adopt. The next fix was announced for 11:49, by which time two thirds of the journey would be over. We felt betrayed.

When, after three hours, twinges of pink defined the horizon, daylight was welcome and falsely reassuring, for the only difference it made was that the ocean became visible. In the sunlight, the cramped cockpit even began to feel cosy. Speeding along in a flying box, high above an empty sea, dawn seemed a good time to partake of biscuits and water, the only sustenance we had brought along.

One hundred and fifty litres of fuel lighter, we climbed at last to the assigned level of 9,000 feet. A growing population of stratocumulus spread below us. The oil temperature was back to normal and the engine, at 55% power, purred delightfully: manifold pressure – twenty inches; RPMs – 2,300. Gérard relaxed.

At 09:00 GMT, we had a rendezvous with Andre, an amateur radio operator on Noronha who had agreed to chaperon us across the water. It was a heartening contact with a far-away world. Gérard told him our estimated position, based on dead reckoning, and warned him that Hugo would phone for news. Hugo, Gérard's brother, was the only family member aware of our exploit that night. We had deliberately avoided telling our respective mothers which day we planned to make the crossing, to preserve them from a sleepless night. From some obscure geographical co-ordinate above the South Atlantic, the world where they all breathed seemed unreal to us. I gazed at the cotton-wool clouds below, nebulous shapes constantly changing, as hypnotic as fire. Then, scouring the gaps between them for potential life-saving ships, of which there were none, I wondered how I had agreed to this craziness.

For some time, Gérard had been compelled by an urgent inner voice, a call of the wild. Life has more to offer than pin-striped suits and office timetables; a big, fascinating world lay waiting ... Would it still be there when we were old? Wasn't it better to explore while we were (moderately) young and healthy in our mid-thirties? If we had to pay for such liberty by working hard at fifty, well, too bad! Gérard is a healthy, energetic guy inspired by challenge. His youth was spent racing Formula Ford on European circuits, when not skiing barefoot on the chilly waters of Geneva's Lac Leman. He had lived for a year on a yacht in San Diego, and sailed across the Pacific to Hawaii and back. Life on the ocean waves, he tried to convince me, was one of carefree bliss.

I'm not so brave. In fact, I'm scared of boats, planes and automobiles. Worst of all, I'm afraid of the sea and various suffocating nightmares convince me I will go by drowning. Terror of the sea apart, though, my concept of yachting is an endless succession of storms, pirates and killer whales. The thought of frying eggs in the cramped galley of a pitching boat fills me with nausea. His claim that yachting is a good way to see the world seemed, to me, an absurdity: yachties spend their time in port repairing generators, varnishing decks and scraping off barnacles. They venture ashore on a quick recce and then cocoon themselves into their mobile homes. How many yachties see the Taj Mahal or climb Kilimanjaro, I would ask him. I had grown up in Nairobi, Kenya, firmly on the ground and far from the sea. As a child, the muddy, battered Land Rovers of overland travellers had enchanted me. I suggested to him that four wheels were a good alternative to a hull. But deep down, there was another apprehension: a fear of casting aside a comfortable urban existence achieved through hard work and perspiration, just for a whimsical desire to travel. Curiosity about foreign climes had brought us, separately, to Brazil. Separately, we had fallen in love with the friendly, carefree people, learned Portuguese and decided to settle in Rio. Kindred spirits, we only met, much later, one Christmas Day in Búzios. It wasn't long before we moved in together. I was working as a sales executive for British Airways, and we made full use of the travel benefits: theatre weekends in New York or London, Carnival in Peking, Easter in the Galapagos.

'Why don't we take the plane?' Gérard had counter-offered one day. I thought he meant a round-the-world ticket on a jumbo jet. He didn't. At that time, he had a four-seater Corisco (Piper Arrow) in which we would fly to Búzios at weekends. We had even been to the Caribbean in it. But around the world? I played along with his new caprice, yes-dearing his enthusiasm while praying it would fizzle out. Maps of the world began to cover the sitting-room floor, and he would spend hours plotting courses and measuring mileages. In mid-1988, when I wasn't looking, he changed the Corisco for a bigger model with 100 hours on the clock and I realised there was no way out. *Romeo* became part of the family.

Of course, we could have avoided so much ocean and taken the usual light aircraft route: USA, Canada, Greenland, Iceland, Europe. But the sanitary efficiency of North America and Europe did not inspire us; rather, the wild untamed spaces of Africa and her tribes beckoned. We wanted to see native peoples still wearing their traditional costumes rather than T-shirts, watch animals in their own environment before their world shrinks to three-metre cages, and marvel at trees growing collectively in forests before chainsaws make more space for cows, cabbages and concrete. So, long hours were spent on fuel consumption and weight calculations. Having steered Gérard away from the notion of yachts, I was faced with a worse prospect: crossing the Atlantic in a single-engined aircraft.

The shortest route from Brazil to Africa is not easterly, as one might imagine, but north-north-east to the Cape Verde Islands. I initially offered to alleviate the weight limitations by taking a commercial flight to Dakar, but with time, his estimate of eleven hours' flying to reach Ilha do Sal sounded less unreasonable. I overcame the cowardice of leaving him to cross the ocean alone and warily accepted to go along on the Atlantic leg, even if it was his hare-brained idea. So there I was, months later, anxiously scanning the waves ahead for any vessel specifically designed for the high seas. I even longed to see a much-berated yacht. There were none.

Altostratus layers cut out the sunlight, announcing the approach of the ITCZ, the Inter-Tropical Confluence Zone, renowned for its tempestuous weather. In due course, menacing cumulonimbus, like vultures round a dying horse, joined forces around us, spiking the sea with forks of lightning. Feeling trapped and unfairly persecuted, we chose a path through the mildest build-ups. Rain lashed the screen while violent turbulence malevolently tossed our fragile craft. It was like my nightmares of a storm at sea. Again, I wanted to scream, to get away from that claustrophobic aluminium shell in which we were imprisoned, side by side, at the mercy of the elements.

'How far does this damned ITCZ spread?' I asked tremulously.

''Bout five degrees latitude,' he answered, sickeningly cool.

I tried to absorb this information. One degree is sixty nautical miles. That meant 300 miles. At 130 knots, that made two hours and twenty minutes. Of unadulterated hell. Oh my God! There was only one thing to do: tighten the seat belts and try to keep my stomach contents where they belonged.

The wind intensity had increased. We needed to alter the correction factor. But by how much? If the SatNav had been working, we would have known exactly. It was down to guesswork. How about increasing from five to ten degrees east? It was hit or miss. We battled on. There was no choice.

At 10:30 GMT, fiddling with the SatNav, I discovered that an unexpected fix had been recorded at 08:49: Lat. N. 3 degrees 45', Long. W. 28 degrees 02'. It placed us forty-five miles south-east of our ideal course. So initial crosswinds had been weaker than estimated. Gérard reduced the ten-degree correction back to five as ample compensation.

After six hours twenty minutes, the inside tanks were empty. Fuel consumption was our only yardstick of progress. We were, we thought contentedly, well over halfway to Sal. Starting afresh on the wing tanks theoretically gave us eight more hours' autonomy. Estimating four hours to touchdown, our spirits rose, despite the harrowing weather.

'Ha, ha! We'll show 'em!' I thought smugly of the many friends who had made derisive comments when they heard of our plans. Their remarks had initially exacerbated my apprehensions, but to save face I had defended our project so ardently that I convinced even myself. Once, dining in the Cheval Blanc in Búzios, a long finger had beckoned me from another table.

'I need to speak to you,' Charles Reade had said.

'Charles, mind your own business,' his wife, Dymmy, scolded.

'I must warn you,' he continued, undaunted. 'You've married a madman.'

'Charles!' Dymmy exclaimed.

'Now just listen to me. One simply doesn't cross the Atlantic in a single-engine. I'm a professional, I know.' Charles, a veteran Second World War RAF pilot, was being deadly earnest.

But I knew Gérard was no irresponsible lunatic. Impetuous, perhaps, but Swiss enough to be meticulous to the extreme. The fuel tanks had been installed and a thorough service of the engine carried out at an excellent aviation workshop in Goiânia. He had accompanied every move, precisely so that he could thereafter maintain the aircraft himself. Our lives would depend upon that engine.

While the plane was serviced, I resumed flying lessons at Goiânia's secondary airfield, an uncontrolled strip on a slight hill where landings are often effected in the opposite direction to take-offs. It was a rough world of *garimpeiros* (gold prospectors) and bush pilots who had no radios and did not bother with maintenance. Overloaded with supplies and manpower, the aircraft, in varying stages of decomposition, are flown into rudimentary jungle strips and return laden with gold and gemstones. Many crash. We thought they were crazy to fly like that, breaking every aviation rule in the book, but politely said nothing. They thought we were completely nuts to fly across the Atlantic and told us so in no uncertain terms.

When the breathlessly-awaited 11:49 satellite fix failed, I began to believe them all. Bitter disappointment and frustration compounded my fears that we would eventually crash in the ocean. We had relied on a modern gadget, and it had failed us. We were lost. Might our current course lead us to Cape Verde, or would we miss the islands and fly right past into a watery grave?

Once clear of the ITCZ, sunlight poured in, temporarily assuaging my misgivings. Gérard was quietly confident. The outside temperature gauge read 12°C. Not bad for 9,000 feet. At least the warm South Atlantic was a preferable place for an engine failure than icy northern waters. Vertical visibility was fine: calm, blue seas glimmered below. Despite the cloudless sky, however, forward visibility was impaired by a puzzling thick yellow haze. Could smoke from the ruthless burning of the Amazon waft so far out to sea? Of course not, the winds came from the east. Was Africa also on fire?

Two later fixes, at 13:35 and 13:44, came up Error. After nine hours in the air, we had no idea where the winds had blown us and no means of ascertaining our position. By our estimates, we were two hours short of landing. Yet we could not raise Sal Control, nor had we received any beacon signals from Cape Verde. When, much later, the pointer of Sal's NDB beacon showed signs of life, it brought mild relief. But the signal was so erratic, flipping from side to side, that it was impossible to judge if the island lay to the left or right. The VOR was ominously silent.

At last, we made out Sal Control, through frustrating crackles, and snatched frantically for the elusive world we had so glibly abandoned and now craved. Joy overwhelmed us and we naively expected reciprocal joviality from the controller, but he indifferently posed the statutory questions on position and estimates as if we were the fifteenth single-engine to arrive from Brazil that day. Gérard gave our position as one hour from landing, maintaining Flight Level 090 (9,000 feet).

However, if we really were one hour out, we should have been overflying Santiago Island. Perhaps we hadn't noticed it in the dense haze? *Romeo* was the epicentre of a small circle of ocean which moved along with us, a constantly changing platform of swells, white crests and foam.

Nothing solid. No land. No ships.

The first hint that we were not as close as we presumed was when the NDB at Praia, on Santiago Island, came in strongly ahead of us. But it should have been behind us already. After twenty minutes, the needle dipped to the right. Why the right? Praia should be on the left! Sal's NDB signal suddenly became so weak as to be useless.What was going on? Where the hell were we?

2   'Quoi? Vous êtes venus du Brésil . . . avec ça?'

We had been using a nautical chart which encompassed both sides of the Atlantic. I dug out the more detailed ONC aeronautical chart.

'Jeeeees! There's a volcano somewhere out here at 9,281 feet. Fogo Island. That's 300 feet higher than us!'

'Whaaaaaat? Let me see.' He snatched away the map. 'Where? Oh, that. Calm down! It's fifty miles away.' Gérard was more concerned about the mysteriously erratic beacons than some distant peak.

'Fifty miles away? What d'you mean? We have no idea where the hell we are!' I huffed. 'We're lost and can't see a damned thing!'. Perched on the edge of the seat, I peered obsessively into the impenetrable haze to monitor the sea at the rim of our forward vision, maybe half a mile ahead. 'There's a bloody mountain out there higher than us,' I muttered periodically. My conviction, moments earlier, that we would die by drowning now changed to instant death on the side of a volcano.

'Forget the effing mountain,' he exploded.

Exhaustion was getting the better of us. We sulked, one on each side of the cockpit. Gérard hunched over the calculator and I stayed glued to the windshield, searching for the mountain. On we chugged for half an hour.

'Look, look, look! Waves breaking on rocks! Land at last!' I yelled and laughed, spirits soaring. Directly ahead, the sea crashed against a dim jagged coastline. We forgot our sulks and hugged each other.

'Thank God! Must be Santiago,' Gérard raved. It was impossible to make out the shape of the island but it didn't matter: we knew, from that moment, that we had made it. In fact, since the Praia beacon had veered off to the right, it could not be Santiago Island at all, but I was too relieved to argue. We maintained course directly towards the rising slopes. Arid black slopes that scrambled higher and ever higher.

'C'moff it! This has to be Fogo! It's way higher than us.'

At last he veered. Aghast, through the haze we made out the perfect cone of a volcano just three hundred feet away, soaring up past the cockpit window to a shrouded summit. Of all the disastrous endings we had envisaged for this ocean crossing, a head-on collision with a volcano had not been one of them. The exhilaration of at last finding land was tempered by the stark realisation that we had almost hit it.

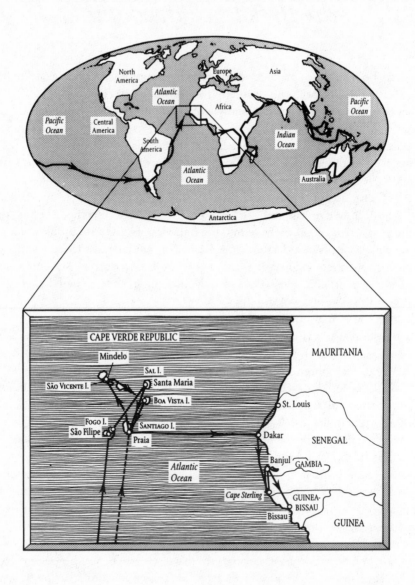

At least this near-miss pinpointed our position exactly. Strong winds during the latter part of the journey had blown us sixty miles off course. Presumably the bulk of the volcano had distorted the beacon signals. Sal was still an hour away. Technically, we were on an IFR flight – under Instrument Flight Rules – whereby the trajectory of the aircraft must comply with published procedures and instructions from Control. In general, we flew VFR – under Visual Flight Rules – whereby the pilot is responsible for maintaining separation from other aircraft and clear visual reference with terrain. However, VFR flights are not permitted more than ten miles from the coast. We had filed instrument on Airway UA32 at FL090. Sal Control had been aware of our approach, but had no radar. Earlier, we had confidently given our position as sixty miles east of Fogo, so they had no reason to alter our flight level. In the hands of Control on an IFR flight in bad visibility, we had been foolishly complacent; hitting terrain had been the very least of our worries. The vastness of the ocean had made a molehill out of a mountain, the only one of any significant height between the Atlas Mountains and Mount Roraima.

'PAPA-TANGO-ROMEO-XRAY-ECHO, on the ground at 16:34,' the Sal controller announced matter-of-factly, oblivious to the twelve hours of nervous tension we had suffered just to be able to make that twenty-knot crosswind landing at Amilcar Cabral International. To him, it was just another plane.

To us, it meant everything, particularly LIFE – yes, in capital letters. In spite of everything and everyone, we made it! In the dark, we had left behind a lush green island dominated by a dramatic granite peak. In dazzling haze, we landed on a flat yellow-white desert island, with not a tree in sight. Was this Cabo Verde – Cape *Green*? What the hell, it looked like heaven to us.

Gérard's fuel calculations had worked well, leaving us with three hours' reserves as we pulled in behind a monstrous Lockheed Galaxy, the world's second largest aircraft. It was an acute reminder of our smallness. The throbbing of the engine, which had reverberated comfortingly in our ears for twelve hours, was abruptly replaced with steamy silence. The feeling was more one of tremendous relief than excitement. We opened the door and crawled out into the smudgy sunshine on shaky legs that refused to work. Tottering like new-born pups, we stared at the plane in stupefaction. It had changed colour! A fine yellow powder was stuck to the shiny-white original. The dense haze in the mid-Atlantic had not been air pollution: it was the Sahara's finest sand, carried hundreds of miles out over the ocean by the Harmattan winds.

At Flight Operations, we were received with polite smiles and surprisingly little bureaucracy: not even Gen Decs (General Declarations, standardised forms presented by an aircraft on each international entry and departure) were required. But the utter lack of interest in our arrival from Brazil in a single-engine came as a surprise. Somewhat astounded by our own feat, we had expected fanfares and hearty handshakes, or at least a mite of reciprocal excitement. Nope, we were treated with the same nonchalance as any old jet.

Ilha do Sal's runway had been paid for by 'an international organisation', in those days a euphemism for South Africa. During the boycott of South Africa, most mainland African countries would not allow South African Airways to land. They required a refuelling point for their European and US-bound flights, and Cape Verde needed the money. Ironically, it was the South African regime's arch enemies – Russia, Cuba and Angola – who most benefited from it. Together, they provided Cape Verde with its second largest source of revenue – landing fees.

A dented black taxi sped us across the Godforsaken treeless moonscape to the derelict village of Santa Maria. Many houses, all the same dull colour as the terrain, had no roofs, considered superfluous since rain is extremely rare. Scraggy goats, pigs and donkeys meandered through the bleakness like the dazed survivors of a nuclear holocaust. There was nothing for them to eat but dust and stones. On the beachfront outskirts of Santa Maria, two hotels had been custom-built for transiting aircrew. The luxury of a swimming pool and well-stocked bar grated against the dry, abject misery of the village. But we were too tired to care. The jet of shower water washed away the nervous tension of the last twenty-four hours and, overcome by exhaustion, we collapsed between cool clean sheets and slept.

Flight Operations had warned us that special permission would be required if we wished to travel in our own plane to the other islands. This, they said, had to be obtained from the Foreign Affairs Ministry in the capital, Praia. Foreign Affairs referred us to the Ministry of Transport and Commerce, who put us on to the Ministry of Tourism, who tried to sell us air tickets. It was eventually suggested that we contact the Civil Aviation Department. In retrospect, this was patently obvious, but we were new at this game. It was a lesson well learned. For the rest of the journey round the world, we dealt exclusively with aviation authorities.

Although we were sure Hugo would have found out from Recife Control that we had reached Sal safely, we needed to make a reassuring call. In fact, he had tracked our progress by phoning Andre in Noronha. He was bursting with enthusiasm, exactly the reaction we had expected on arrival and not received.

'When I told Montenegro that you'd crossed the Atlantic safely,' Hugo said, 'he just muttered: "Your brother is the craziest man I know."'

We all laughed, but Montenegro did have a point.

As the bleak mountains of Santiago Island loomed out of the yellow haze, I thought back to the clerk in Sal who had described it as *muito verde mesmo*. Small groves of spartan trees grew in the gullies, but only a convicted desert dweller could classify it as 'really very green'.

Praia, or Beach, was a droll name for a capital city. After the lushness of Brazil, its aridity startled us. Platô, the picturesque old town, stands appropriately on a small plateau overlooking shanty-like suburbs, immeasurably more depressing than Rio's *favelas*. The average annual rainfall is just 250 mm. The rain falls between July and October, the taxi-driver informed us, turning everything 'a bit greener'. This 'green' business was niggling.

'Why is the country called Cabo Verde?' I asked him.

'Because the Portuguese arrived in the rainy season,' he chortled. 'They should have called it Cabo Seco!'

In fact, this archipelago, comprising ten islands and a handful of islets is thus named because it lies 650 kilometres off Cap-Vert du Sénégal, a peninsula which juts out into the Atlantic at Dakar, forming the easternmost point of Africa. The Islands used to be marginally greener, but the climate has become Sahelian. Dust-laden Harmattan winds scourge them from October to June and droughts have long plagued them. The earliest records dating from 1773 show a third of the population died in two years. As late as 1946, a two-year drought again killed one in three.

Ribeira Grande, founded in 1462 as the first settlement on Cape Verde, is a twenty-minute bus ride from Praia through a boulder-stricken landscape. A dramatic medieval fort, more appropriate to Castille, is perched on a crag above it. The town's five-hundred-year-old history was disintegrating with the ruins of three more forts constructed to safeguard the Portuguese claim. Beside them, the appendages of Catholicism – convents, chapels and a cathedral which had elevated the town to city status in 1533 – crumbled and returned to dust. Ribeira Grande, now referred to simply as Cidade Velha, flourished during the slave trade as a post for baptising and evaluating slaves captured on the mainland, before their arduous journey to the New World. It prospered and grew as a victualling station for European sailing ships plying the route to India. Despite its fortifications, it became a target for pirates and was finally abandoned in 1772.

At the end of the empty, dusty main street, a few trees lent a superficial sedateness to what was once the shameful *pelourinho*, where slaves were tied and exposed for sale. Three old men played dominoes quietly in the chiaroscuro of a doorway. Silent, brooding faces stared from open windows as we passed by in the breathless afternoon. The atmosphere felt resentful. We fled to the beach where the black, volcanic sand emphasised the turquoise uplift of the breaking waves. A row of identical black-and-red canoes were beached beside a colourful carpet of laundry spread on the sand to dry. Some cheeky children, who had initially amused themselves by throwing pebbles at us, decided it would be more lucrative to ask for money. Not feeling in the least endeared to them, we ignored their begging, so they resorted to chanting 'You've got AIDS, you've got AIDS', as if we would feel gravely insulted. We were simply glad they knew what AIDS was. Three muscular youths emerged stealthily from a nearby house and marched threateningly towards us, scowling. We watched them approach with trepidation. As they bore down on us, Gérard fumbled for the can of mace tucked inside the camera bag. We had debated whether to take a weapon with us on the trip for self-defence and had opted for mace, less offensive and easier to hide than a gun. Yet here we were, in our very first country, already putting it to use . . . But the lads strode right past us without a glance, and shouted angrily at the kids, chastising them for mistreating foreigners.

Since the journey to Tarrafal, at the northern tip of Santiago, involved a precipitous climb to a mountain pass at Assomada, the driver of our fifteen-seat minibus, or *lotaçao*, restricted the head count to twenty adults, two babies and a squealing black pig whose nose protruded from an orange bag.

The mountain scenery is a spectacular sequence of parched brown peaks and crags. Beside occasional hamlets built with black volcanic stones, small oases of cultivation enliven the grey scree of dry riverbeds. Terraced hillsides and valley floors are cultivated with well-water. Bare hillsides have been planted with American acacia to combat erosion, but their heat-resistant shrivelled leaves give no impression of greenery.

At Assomada, hopeful onward passengers pushed their way into the *lotaçao* before anyone had the chance to alight. It was pandemonium. One climbed in through the window. From then on, the road was downhill, so the load was increased to twenty-four adults and six children. The large bottoms of the female passengers did nothing to help the seating arrangements.

Tarrafal, a tidy town of half a dozen dirt streets leading off a main square, is popular for its white beach and sheltered bay. We rented a bungalow under some token palm trees and fiery flamboyants and, with a plump kingfisher for company, listened to the crickets shrieking. The worries and tensions of the last months, the foreboding image of the Atlantic that had plagued our sleep, were definitively washed away by the gentle swish of its waves. We vegetated in that calm corner for several days.

'There's no real poverty here,' Senhor Pantaleão, the bungalow administrator, surprised us by saying. 'Look around, everyone wears shoes. If they wear shoes, it's because their bellies are full.' He went on to give us some historical background.

As Portugal's favoured African colony, geographically close to the homeland, more schools had been built in Cape Verde than other colonies and the literacy rate in 1985 was estimated at 89%, one of the highest in Africa. It does not suffer from the tribal conflicts that beset other African countries because its population, descended from detribalised slaves, is essentially of mixed blood. Interbreeding was widespread between the Portuguese traders and African slave-girls and the language of the islands, Cape Verde Creole, is a blend of West African languages with Portuguese. The country achieved independence in 1974 when the fall of Salazar gave the *coup de grâce* to the Portuguese empire. Cape Verde formed a union with its neighbour, Guinea-Bissau, which had fought a fierce fifteen-year struggle against the Portuguese. A guerrilla force of 10,000 men, under the command of Amilcar Cabral (born in Guinea-Bissau of a Cape Verdean father) successfully fought 35,000 Portuguese and African troops. After Amilcar was assassinated in 1973, his half-brother, Luís Cabral, took up the fight and eventually became the first president of the joint republic. He was ousted in 1980 and the two countries then went separate ways, Cape Verde opting for a more liberal style of government than its Marxist partner.

The population of the islands is approximately 400,000 but a million Cape Verdeans work abroad (chiefly in the USA), sending money home to their families and providing the country with its main source of revenue. Despite their comparative well-being abroad, they ardently miss their arid homeland. This concept of homesickness and longing is epitomised in Portuguese in a single poetic word, *saudade*, which is the main theme of the *morna*, the wistful song of Cape Verde.

In the evening, we strolled up to the square to taste the national dish, *cachoupa* ('catchupa' in crioulo, unrelated to tomato sauce), a tasty concoction of maize, beans, pumpkin, beef, pork, *salsicha*, and salted dried fish. We washed it down with fiery *grogue*, a home-brew rum which, besides making us groggy as the name suggests, induces violent headaches.

Back in Praia, we met up with Rino, a good-looking blue-eyed Italian (one of the four tourists we saw in all Cape Verde) who had done the islands by ferry-boat, a nightmare of pitching and rolling in violent seas. He had not disembarked at Fogo Island, where waves had destroyed the jetty and passengers were shuttled ashore in small heaving boats, and he laughed at our rabid desire to visit the volcano ('It's just another Vesuvius!' he muttered). But the truth was, it acted like a magnet on us. The Director of Civil Aviation had staunchly refused us permission to fly ourselves there, since even the local airline, TACV, complained about the dangerous runway. If only he knew how close we had already been to crashing into the mountain!

We booked seats on TACV's Twin Otter, and soon saw their point about the runway at Mosteiros. A hefty crosswind blew across the short dirt clifftop strip. The volcano soared into haze on one side, and Atlantic rollers smashed on the rocks on the other.

The main town, São Felipe, was a two-hour bus ride along a windy road with precipitous drops to the boiling ocean. Its shady squares and neat Portuguese houses dip sharply down to jet-black beaches. Behind rises omnipotent Fogo. After patient cajoling from Gérard, a certain Senhor Nené at Restaurante Vulcão agreed to rent us his pick-up to visit the crater with his sullen nephew, Zé, driving it. We squashed three abreast into the cabin and set off sedately along the cobbled streets. No sooner had we left the town than we had to clutch frantically for handholds. Zé hunched over the wheel with a malicious grin and, horn blaring, aimed the truck at goats, chickens, dogs and children in the scattered villages. Fortunately, habitation soon ceased and the steep incline forced him to slow down.

Fogo, the youngest island of the archipelago, rises abruptly from the sea floor to 9,281 feet. We entered the crater over the eroded southern escarpment, descending to the floor at 5,500 feet to meet petrified rivers of contorted lava and lakes of fine black ash punctured with red volcanic blisters. To the east, the growing central cone towers 3,800 feet above the massive caldera, eight kilometres in diameter. Planted on the dusty crater floor is the village of Portela, where three hundred people live in black houses built with lava rocks, trapped between an immense sea of twisted lava and the sheer escarpment wall rising 3,000 feet in a dramatic semi-circle. Frayed pockets of manioc and beans grow on patches of soil that have escaped recent coatings of lava. It is a remarkably desolate setting for habitation.

In São Felipe, we had sampled a surprisingly good bottle of 1985 Vinho do Fogo produced inside the crater. Vines had first been planted by the Portuguese in the 1500s. Today, a concrete wine-making co-operative, built with German aid money, produces a dozen barrels annually. It was difficult to imagine how grapes could grow in that bleak crater but the vines, together with peach and grevillea trees, flourish by the escarpment walls, producing a dubious hue of green. Dona Matilda, a skeletal lady with a dozen children, took care of the co-operative. She explained that the soil retained sufficient moisture from the 'rain' brought by the South Atlantic trade winds in July to last all year. Only young plants had to be watered. Inside the co-op, a pile of 1985 neck labels lay on the floor.

'Did you finish the labels from later years?' I asked.

'No, no,' she replied. 'Too many were printed in 1985. We've got to use them all up before we make any more.'

It was 1989.

The Jeppesen Manual, a sort of aviator's bible to airports of the world, did not list Praia as an Airport of Entry. However, it operated as such and we were granted permission to depart from there for Sénégal. No officials showed up to clear us. In fact, no one was remotely interested where we were going. It was clear that if we had an emergency over the 360 nautical miles that separated us from the African continent, we were on our own.

Fortunately, it was an uneventful two and a half hours later that the instruments indicated we were closing in on Dakar-Yoff airport. The customary sandy haze acted like a bathroom window, so we only found the airport once it was directly beneath us. No commercial flights were expected at that hour. Most airport employees in the terminal were sleeping soundly, heads plopped on desks. Limp bodies lay spreadeagled on the conveyor belt, others curled up on the floor. It was as if someone had injected the building with poisonous gas. The immigration officer had to be shaken awake. With eyes half-closed, he stamped us in and sunk back into his afternoon zizz.

Romeo was squeezed into a space on the crowded light aircraft patio beside the Aero Club. On the clubhouse terrace, several Frenchmen tucked into afternoon beer.

'*Alors, vous êtes en panne?* So you've had a breakdown, eh?' one smart alec chimed whilst his cronies snickered. Taken aback by this gratuitous aggression, Gérard nevertheless explained we had arrived from Cape Verde, after crossing the Atlantic from Brazil.

'*Quoi? Vous êtes venus du Brésil aux Iles Cap Vert avec ça? Sans vous arrêter?* You came all the way from Brazil to Cape Verde in that thing, without stopping?' A deprecating finger was jabbed in the direction of our valiant *Romeo*.

'Yes, without stopping. If you're privy to some island in the middle of the ocean, do tell us all. As far as I know, there aren't any,' Gérard retorted, hurt. He had expected interest and curiosity from fellow pilots, whom he had thought to consult on local conditions and airports.

It was a bad start for us in Dakar. Things did not improve. After negotiating an assortment of stenches and depressing scenes of filth and squalor, a taxi dropped us at the Marinas on Hann Plage, once Dakar's most beautiful beach. It had been recommended as a quiet place to stay. We were not exactly captivated by its location on a litter-strewn beach next to a putrid slum, although the men who emerged from the lugubrious shanty dens magically wore immaculate flowing pastel *boubous*. After the puritanical dress of Cape

31

Verde, the mélange of vibrant African textiles worn by Sénégalese women was captivating. The *pagne*, traditionally a colourful piece of cloth wrapped around the body, had been tailored into a long, distinctly African two-piece with matching head-dress.

Vast fishermen's *pirogues* had pulled into shore, after several days on the high seas, and there was a frenzy as the fish were sorted and divided up for sale. The women set to work gutting them amid swarms of chattering onlookers and impatient flies. Discarded fish heads joined plastic bottles, rusty tins and yesterday's vegetables at the water's edge. Although the scene was intriguing – it was the reality of Dakar – we preferred to seek less odorous accommodation. But the taxi had gone and we were stranded down a dirt track far from town. We hailed a passing car, thankfully falling upon a Frenchman with a generous heart, who drove us to Chez Georges. He sought to reassure us by advising that this was where *'tous les Européens vont à la plage'*. Beside the bar, two glum monkeys paced neurotically inside cages. The beach was clean, but it was washed by a mushy ashen sea. Across a bay dotted with ferruginous container ships and a drilling platform rose the jagged skyline of Dakar's industrial area, oil refinery and peanut oil factory. It was the ugliest beachscape we had ever seen. *Tous les Européens* were welcome to it.

After a couple of days, we decided they could keep dirty Dakar too. It was impossible to walk the city streets in peace. We were harassed mercilessly by an epidemic of arrogant vendors, pushing everything from cheap 'n' nasty sunglasses and cigarettes to mass-produced wood carvings or peanuts. They refused to take no as an answer, bellowing curses after us as we walked on.

Gérard removed the larger of the internal fuel tanks, creating welcome space in the cabin and still leaving us with an extra margin of 150 litres in the smaller tank for long distances with no fuel supplies. Passing over Lac Rose, startlingly pink in colour due to the concentration of certain micro-organisms in the water, we joined the coast at Plage d'Almadies, a beach of soft, treacherous sand that is the finishing stretch for the Paris–Dakar rally. It stretches unbroken to Saint-Louis 100 nautical miles away and, periodically, we spotted ocean-going *pirogues* beached above the high tide mark at the rare fishing settlements. Inland, military rows of windbent trees were evidence of reforestation projects, seemingly futile attempts to block the relentless advance of the Sahara.

Saint-Louis, France's first settlement on the African continent, was founded on an island in the mouth of the Sénégal River in 1638. Sénégal's first capital, and a trading centre for slaves, gold and ivory, it inspired our curiosity due to its prominent role in pioneer aviation routes across the Atlantic to South America. At Hôtel de la Poste, we were allocated the Mermoz room. Vivid African textiles now decorate the walls, but otherwise it was the very room used by Jean Mermoz, the dashing French pilot who carried the first sacks of mail – 130 kilos of it – to South America. He and his crew took off from Saint-Louis on 12 May 1930 in a single-engine Laté 28 on floats. They landed in Natal, north-eastern Brazil, twenty-one hours later. Now, that was courage! We kicked off our shoes and lay on his bed, imbibing the spirit of the illustrious aviator who had often slept there before his epic flights. Our total crossing time of seventeen hours, broken at Noronha and Cape Verde, paled into pathos. Mermoz flew the route many times before being lost at sea in the *Croix du Sud*, a Laté 300, in 1936.

In the crumbling core of the old town on Saint-Louis Island, former colonial government buildings with spacious reception halls where chandeliers once hung had been taken over by squatter families, who scraped a space to sleep between the debris of cracking walls and their own refuse. The streets were crammed with kids whose French was limited to three phrases: *'Donne-moi cadeau'*, *'Donne-moi bonbon'* and *'Donne-moi cent francs'*.

The torrid afternoon brought on a raging thirst. In the hotel bar, the heads of erstwhile noble beasts – buffalo, waterbuck, and Derby eland – spewed mouldy straw stuffing through the lethargic leather of their skins. The head of a bald lioness grinned tragicomically, the stitching of her mouth split open. In faded photographs beneath each trophy, a proud assassin grinned beside his defenceless victim. Beers in hand, we fled to the shady terrace where, overlooking the bustle of *taxis brousse*, ox-drawn carts and pedestrians in flowing robes crossing the Faidherbe bridge, we drank to the memory of Mermoz.

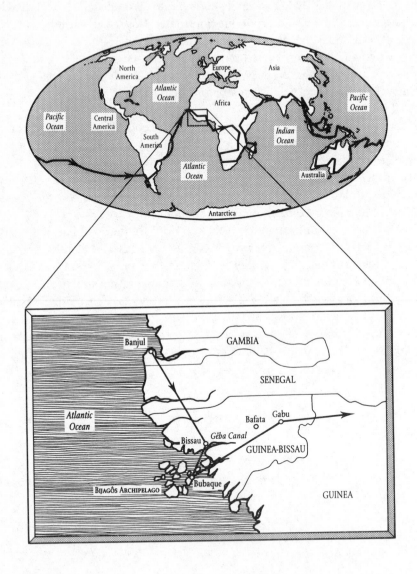

3 'T.G.I.S!'

Guinea-Bissau, a small impoverished country on the west coast of Africa, was a place we had been strongly advised to avoid. After independence in 1974, it became a shaky Marxist state with scant respect for human rights. But a French pilot we met in Sénégal had compared its Bijagós Archipelago to Tahiti. Paradise sounded too good to miss.

We expected Osvaldo Vieira international airport serving the capital, Bissau, to be heavily guarded. It was deserted but for two immigration officers who strolled over to where our shoes stuck like chewing gum to the melting tarmac. Their sole interest was the chance of finding jobs in Brazil, regarded as an eldorado by the Portuguese-speaking nations of Africa. We had to disenchant them.

An ominous mass of slate-coloured cloud dragging an iron-grey curtain towards Bissau spurred us over the Canal do Géba to the myriad islands of the Bijagós Archipelago where the sea, a patchwork of blues and greens, swished at golden sandbanks. Only Bubaque Island exhibited firm signs of habitation, its handful of whitewashed buildings gleaming against the dark green jungle which stepped aside, just briefly, to allow a yellowing grass airstrip to beckon us down.

At the village port, where the weekly ferry from Bissau had just arrived, returning villagers were joyously embraced as they unloaded their luggage, consisting primarily of crates of beer. The fishermen treated us with hostility, presuming we were Russian. At the mention of Brazil, however, there were plenty of volunteers to take us to visit the islands. We made a deal for the next morning with two muscular young fishermen, Alberto and Pedrinho. But first, Alberto announced, a contract had to be drawn up in the *Capitania dos Portos*. This seemed like overkill for a beach outing, but he was adamant – it was the law. The port captain's office was located in a disused palm-oil factory. He dourly interrogated us as to the precise terms of the agreement, and demanded identification papers. Since signing legal contracts was furthest from our minds when we had strolled down to the port, we had none with us.

'In that case, I can't draw up the contract,' the captain announced, tucking his pen into crispy hair behind his ear.

'But, *Senhor Capitão*, I can spell out my name and give you the passport number,' Gérard suggested.

'Ah ha! But you might give me a false name!'

'Why would I bother to do that?' Such suspicion smacked of a police state. A Russian tome lay before him on the desk.

'How can I know if you are telling the truth, if you have no documents?' he contended, eyes creased with suspicion.

'So you speak Russian?' Gérard asked, changing tactics.

The captain's face gleamed with pride. 'I do indeed. I studied there for six months.'

'But I bet you hated the cold, *né*?'

Snap! The ice was broken by a mutual dislike of sub-zero temperatures. He reminisced of weeks spent huddled in a cheerless room, craving his tropical homeland, unable to face glacial Muscovite streets. The Russians, he admitted, had been unfriendly. This idle chit-chat seemed to convince him we were *bona fide*. Without further ado, he wrote the contract.

The next morning, we allowed Alberto to select an island for diving and duly ventured out over tranquil waters which changed colour like a chameleon, from grey to blue to green. In a mid-channel *trompe-l'oeil*, flocks of pelicans seemed to walk on water as they paced the submerged sandbanks. Instead of a crown of lush forest, like many islands we passed, Alberto's choice isle had been torched. Blackened fronds of charred palms drooped against the skyline. A group of naked pot-bellied children played beside three round huts squatted under thatched roofs reaching almost to the ground. They stared at us distrustfully. Alberto strode towards the scorched hillock, beckoning us to follow into the scene of desolation. Immense tree trunks straddled the bare earth beside piles of charcoal. The Bijagós women were planting maize and some kind of hillside rice. They smiled, but spoke no Portuguese. Alberto made a poor translator. He pointed to a lush island nearby, the permanent home of this group. They had come here for the rainy season to cultivate their crops, after which they would return home. Peculiarly for an island people, the Bijagós live hidden in the interior of their islands. They do not fish and only venture into a canoe out of necessity. Their villages are invisible from the sea, and it is assumed they took refuge in the jungles in the days of roaming slave-ships.

Three bare-breasted women pounded heavy wooden pestles into a single mortar, squelching palm nuts to extract a lurid orange oil. With perfect timing and amazing alacrity, each brought her pestle thumping down into the mortar, the effort not interrupting the rhythm of their banter. They laughed heartily when I had a go, clumsily banging against the other pestles. Although the men had donned ragged shorts cast off by Western civilisation, the women wore traditional grass skirts. These consisted of candlewick-like tassels about eight inches long, made of crude home-spun thread and dyed natural ochre, graphite or crimson. Those endowed with generous behinds, impossible to obscure with just one fringe, simply wore two in layers. One young girl challenged me to don such a skirt. To general amusement but Gérard's embarrassment, I substituted

36

my shorts with the minuscule frill. Although I was wearing a bikini considered prudish by Brazilian standards, the virtually naked women were amazed at the sight of so much white flesh. Willing hands helped to tie the skirt. Their excited chattering built up to a puzzling crescendo, until another frill was produced to hide my bottom peeping shamelessly below the hemline of the first.

The headman, a wizened gentleman with few teeth and grisly grey hair, led us to a sacred hut built of palm fronds, completely enclosed on all sides like a chicken coop. Chanting ceremoniously, he smeared greasy black paste between the big toes of our right feet. Alberto explained this was a blessing for *muita comida* – plenty of food. Coming from a people whose lives centred on the struggle to provide sufficient food, a wish that we would never go hungry was equivalent to a blessing for great riches.

An officious message awaited us on return. We were to report to Sr Justinho, the immigration officer. The *Comité do Governo* occupied a decaying clifftop mansion, once the *Residência do Administrador Português*. The paint was peeling; substitute doors of old crating hung haphazardly where solid wood once swung. Swallows darted skilfully through broken window panes into the gloomy rooms to build their mud nests in the penumbra above the listless civil servants, whose desks were splattered with dusty papers and bird droppings.

There was no electricity. The town's generator had long ceased to function. In the half-light that slunk through the doorway, we sat on rickety chairs before Sr Justinho, a tidy bespectacled man who looked like an accountant. We elaborated on our intention to stop in Gabu, in the interior of Guinea-Bissau, where we had been told of a wonderful wildlife reserve. Justinho was adamantly against this, maintaining that Gabu airport was not operational in the rainy season. He conceded that we could only land there if Control approved. Bissau Control duly accepted our flight plan to Gabu without query, merely suggesting we overfly the runway before landing to check for holes. The chart actually showed a major airport. Guinea-Bissau was better endowed with airfields than any other country in the region. They had been built by the Portuguese during the independence struggle.

Tracking east over Ilha das Galinhas to the mainland, we headed over steamy mangrove swamps to the twining tributaries of the Rio Gêba and Rio Grande, lined with luxuriant forest. After some navigational difficulties, due to a low layer of cloud which obscured sight of land, we found a small town nestled beside a vast red expanse resembling a runway. It was overgrown on all sides and devoid of any airport buildings. Unsure if this was Gabu, we buzzed the field as instructed. Immaculate tarmac, 3,000 metres long. Why such discrepancy about its condition? We quickly coaxed *Romeo* into a corner of the deserted patio as a hundred bellowing children raced over and formed a dense circle a foot away, jostling and chattering excitedly. The indignant tinkling of a bell announced the arrival of a bicycle, and the crowd parted like the Red Sea waters. A clean-faced young man in a beige uniform and safari hat dismounted.

'I'm Oliveira, *Comandante da Artilheria Anti-aéreo,*' he announced. 'What is the purpose of your visit?' The words 'Anti-aircraft Artillery Commander' flashed warning lights for us.

'*Bom dia*, Oliveira. Is this Gabu?'

'Indeed it is,' he replied, taken aback. '*É uma pista militar*. Follow me to the barracks to explain yourselves.'

Pista militar! Gérard and I exchanged glances of consternation, but tried to look cool. It meant BIG trouble. Why had Control not mentioned this?

With the children already wiggling rudder and ailerons, *Romeo* could not be left unattended. We debated together which of us should go with Oliveira. Of course, Gérard was best at handling both situations. Since the problem at the barracks was probably just a little bureaucracy – after all, Control had cleared us – and since Gérard was more severe and effective than I at fending off the kids, we decided I should go.

Wheeling his bicycle, Oliveira led me along a mud path through peanut fields, explaining that such a small plane had never landed at Gabu before, so the kids thought it was a toy. At last we arrived at a large courtyard surrounded by yellowing Portuguese buildings. Desultory soldiers lolled in the shade playing cards, their guns propped against the trees. I was interrogated by an acrimonious officer who punctuated every phrase of my drawn-out explanation that Bissau Control had authorised us to land with an accusatory 'We were not informed'. With a flourish, I produced the original flight clearance to enter Guinea-Bissau, although Gabu was not specified. Since it was in English, I knew he could not understand it, but it impressed him. A chair was set for me in the courtyard and I was told to wait. Much yelling into the telephone ensued.

An age passed. As the temperature of the torrid afternoon rose, I knew Gérard would be getting impatient out there on the hot tarmac, keeping the children at bay, while I sat at the barracks, infected by the lethargy of the soldiers. Each time I asked what was going on, I was curtly instructed to wait.

A blue Volvo suddenly screeched into the courtyard and skidded to a halt in a cloud of dust on the far side. The soldiers scrambled to their feet, muttering '*O Comandante! O Comandante!*', and raced to stand to attention. When the dust had settled and there was a semblance of order from the soldiers, the rear door opened and a very black portly gentleman in a bright white naval uniform emerged. Without a glance in my direction, he disappeared through a dark doorway.

The atmosphere turned distinctly hostile. I was escorted by armed soldiers across the yard to the antechamber. Oliveira and the other officer proceeded into the Commandante's office. Their humble murmurs were brutalised by harsh tones of indignation. Four soldiers stood guard over me, clutching their AK47s and staring dully into the middle distance. I initially felt quite calm, confident in our sanctioned right to be there. But, as the minutes clunked by, the dire warnings of those who had advised us against venturing into Marxist Guinea-Bissau reverberated through that room full of soldiers. The solemn face of Amilcar Cabral surveyed us, unsmiling, from a large photograph. Why had Control not mentioned that Gabu was a military airfield? It looked completely abandoned, but no doubt what we had done was tantamount to Martin Rust's landing a Cessna in Red Square. I wondered, as if it was a joke, whether a prison in Guinea-Bissau was worse than Siberia. Come off it! We hadn't done anything. I looked through the open door into the courtyard, where the merciless midday sun had shrivelled the shadows of the scrawny trees into sticks, and hoped Gérard had remembered to put on a hat.

At last, I was summoned before Comandante Marciano. Exuding fury, he sat portentously behind a large desk. Trying to be cheerful, I apologised for causing him to come to the office on a Sunday. He was not to be cajoled.

'*O problema é muito, muito sério.* We were not informed that you were coming.'

I explained several times that Bissau Control Tower had cleared us to land, but he disbelieved me.

'You must go to Bissau,' he concluded. 'I need written proof that you were cleared to land at Gabu.'

'I'm afraid we don't have enough fuel to go to Bissau, return here and continue to Bamako,' I fretted. It was true.

'The aircraft stays here. You will go by bus.'

'How long does the bus take?'

'It is very slow. They are few. You will have to wait.'

I knew if Gérard was in my shoes, he would probably have already resolved the situation by now. He'd done military service in Switzerland. He would have sorted it out, man to man. I felt despairingly useless. To my surprise, Oliveira suddenly backed me up, boosting my morale.

'She has a telex, Comandante. Show him, senhora,' Oliveira chirped encouragingly. I slipped it across the table.

The Commandante glowered. 'I don't understand a word of it,' he said crossly, pushing it aside. It dawned on me that this was a case of hurt pride. We had dropped out of the heavens onto his airfield without his consent.

'Senhor Comandante,' I ventured, 'couldn't we just phone Control in Bissau? They'll confirm my story.'

'Telephone? You telephone them! Go right ahead – phone them!' He waved an imperious arm towards the apparatus. '*À vontade!*' he challenged.

My heart sank. Either the telephone did not work, or he knew I would never get through. Feeling foolish, I asked for the number. Of course, no one knew. Oliveira had a brainwave and rang a buddy in Bissau, asking him to persuade Air Traffic Control to call Comandante Marciano. We all sat down to wait.

The relief generated by this major step forward gradually dissipated in the silence. Tension mounted. Inside, all eyes scrutinised the floor. We waited . . . and waited. Vociferous bands of yellow weaver birds were decorating a palm tree beyond the window with neat hanging baskets. Their merry house-building chatter came from a world I had lost. What if the man never phoned?

'*Seu marido deve estar com a cabeça quente.*' Comandante Marciano's remark emerged like an Exocet. 'Your husband's head must be hot.'

'It sure is hot,' I agreed. 'But don't worry. He has a hat.'

'You misunderstand me,' he smiled wryly. 'His head will be hot because he is wondering what has happened to his little wife, all alone for such a long time, in the military barracks.'

My heart jolted. It had never occurred to me that there was any danger. They had treated me with respect. But suddenly I became a white woman, all alone, an impudent trespasser, at the mercy of a bunch of bored soldiers. I no longer dared look at their sardonic smiles and struggled to breathe. Neither of our families knew we were in Guinea-Bissau. Minutes earlier, the Commandante had despatched some soldiers to the airfield, supposedly to guard the plane. Perhaps he had instructed them to dispose of Gérard? Gérard was also cornered, an unarmed white man arrogantly shooing inquisitive black children away from his precious aeroplane. What better symbol of a hated white capitalist? They could easily wipe him out, steal everything from the plane and push it into the bush. No one would ever find it – or us. And what would Gérard think when the soldiers approached and there was still no sign of me? Perhaps the Commandante was right. Perhaps he was already tormenting himself with visions of his wife being raped in the army barracks.

A shrill ring slashed the air. We all jumped. The Commandante snatched up the phone, and yelled into it for three minutes, defending his supreme authority over Gabu airstrip. This was clearly disputed by Control, which claimed the right to clear an aircraft anywhere and confirmed the veracity of my tale. Initially piqued, he soon thawed.

'Let's go and relieve your husband's hot head,' he said with a grin as he escorted me to the Volvo like a princess.

As we drove onto the airport tarmac, the kids fled in all directions. Gérard, looking as cool as the Camel man, was chatting to the soldiers. He tactfully greeted the Commandante with respectful bowing and scraping.

'You are very lucky that today is Sunday!' Marciano declared, making sure that we, at least, appreciated who was the boss. 'If it hadn't been Sunday, and if I had been at the barracks instead of at home, and if I had been advised that a strange aircraft was flying around, I would have ordered them to shoot you down!'

Gérard thanked him profusely for his tolerance, agreeing how naughty it was of us to have arrived unannounced. He blamed the incompetence of Control, and winked at me when Marciano was not looking. 'TGIS!' he muttered. Thank God It's Sunday!

Comandante Marciano gave the guards strict instructions to look after the aircraft of the esteemed visitors. He dismissed his driver with an imperial wave and drove us himself to a hotel, a collection of thatched bungalows which he inspected personally before grilling the receptionist about the price – US$8.

The whole purpose of the stopover in Gabu had been to visit the nearby game reserve. We duly set off down the only tarmac street, the main road to Bafatá and Bissau. There was certainly no sign of any buses. It was lined with hawkers' stalls selling cigarettes, tinned milk, torch batteries and Chinese toothpaste. We sought out Senhor Agouba, the contact we had been given to go to the reserve, and found him standing forlornly beside a wrecked jeep which two mechanics attacked with spanners.

'All the vehicles are broken down,' he said, kicking angrily at a wheel. 'Anyway, during the rainy season, the roads are impassable. The animals scatter and are impossible to find. You can't go.' That was that! The matter closed, he stomped off.

We were speechless with frustration. The traumatic landing in Gabu had been in vain! No one was to blame. It was just a typical case of WAWA – West Africa Wins Again.

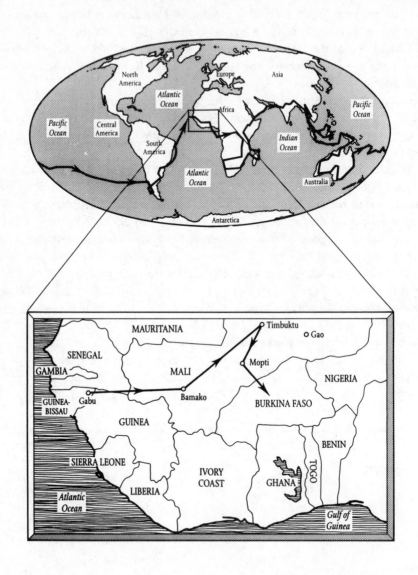

4 'Le Gouverneur est très malade'

Since leaving Dakar, we had flown 820 nautical miles and made six take-offs and landings without refuelling. We reached Bamako, capital of Mali, with just thirty-five minutes of reserves, well below the legal minimum of sufficient fuel to reach an alternative airport, plus forty-five minutes. As we refuelled, a thunderbolt drew our attention to the sudden approach of a colossal storm, proving the point about fuel reserves. We were lucky to be on the ground.

As the downpour began, the met officer, anxious to augment his monthly earnings, offered to drive us to town in his car. We raced through the deluge to his Peugeot 304, flinging the luggage onto the back seat and squashing three abreast in front, only to discover that none of the windows closed, and neither windscreen wipers nor lights worked. Raindrops like pebbles thumped the screen, reducing visibility to a metre beyond the bonnet. Unperturbed, he set himself a course on the centre line of the waterlogged highway. The first sound we heard unrelated to weather was the enraged hooting of an oncoming vehicle as it swerved to avoid us.

'*Vous voyez quelque chose, par hasard?*' Gérard asked with irony.

'*Wé wé,*' came the nonchalant reply. '*Je suis très habitué.*'

At full speed, we discovered there were no brake pads.

'I removed them,' he explained, 'because they make a noise.'

So, no windows, no windscreen wipers, no lights, no brakes and no shock absorbers. Interesting! Halfway to town, the rain stopped. The drive became more terrifying with visibility than without it. When other dilapidated bangers pulled out in front of us, our valiant driver kept his foot firmly to the floor, yelling 'It's my right of way!' and hooting furiously as he strained to overtake. At least the horn worked.

We crossed an unappetising stretch of the Niger River, and wound into Bamako's army of mobilettes and decrepit taxis where a melting pot of tribal peoples wearing traditional desert garb looked ill at ease in a city centre. Desperate hawkers dogged us, their arms full of Taiwanese watches, shiny sunglasses and imitation Lacoste underwear.

'*Il faut l'acheter, M'sieur. Aujourd'hui, c'est moins cher,*' they pleaded. They were not aggressive like their Sénégalese colleagues. They were ragged men, battling to support families on the unlikely sale of goods nobody wanted. We felt desperately sorry for them, but how could we help such an army?

At Les Hirondelles Hotel, where decades of dust lay thickly in the corridors, the lift had long ceased to operate. There was no light bulb in the windowless bathroom of the room we were allocated. 'Sorry, no light bulbs,' said the lad who had escorted us there. We persuaded him to let us change rooms. He grudgingly led us down the corridor and flung open the door of another room, as if showing us into the Ritz. Fast asleep on the bed, a picture of cherubic innocence, air-conditioner full blast, was one of the male cleaners. All three of us gaped in amazement. Too nonplussed to say anything, the clerk shooed us on to yet another room, this one with soiled orange bedspreads, and the sweepings pushed into a heap under the desk. It did have a light bulb – which showed all too clearly that when the toilet was flushed, the water welled alarmingly up to the rim of the bowl where, thankfully, it changed its mind and descended to the basement. A handwritten sign taped to the wall read: *Prière de ne pas laver les pieds dans le lavabo.* 'You are kindly requested not to wash your feet in the basin' was an exhortation only likely to be found in a Muslim country.

As a child, I had thought Timbuktu to be an invention, a sort of Wonderland or Shangri-la. Once I understood it was for real, it remained a place aloof, never to be visited, like Ulan Bator or Prudhoe Bay. But here we were, off to Timbuktu! We made the flight plan and received the latest weather: CAVOK – Ceiling and Visibility OK: all clear. Once airborne, we followed the Niger for a short distance before heading out over the desert. Fifteen minutes after take-off, Bamako Control suddenly advised that the visibility in Timbuktu was zero, and that the airport had closed. CAVOK to zero visibility was rather drastic. We were puzzled but altered the flight plan to Mopti, two hours away, and rejoined the course of the Niger.

An hour later the lower horizon ahead had turned ominous grey, although, in the sunlight, the white cumulus above looked quite friendly. They trailed a strange brown cloak which, instead of falling down like rain, bulged outwards like a steam-roller. Like a defective traffic light, the stormscope flashed red, yellow and green, frantic warnings of dangerous electrical discharges over the whole 140-degree arc ahead. This was no isolated thunderstorm: the way ahead appeared to be blocked. We tried to raise Mopti Control, to no avail. It was lunchtime. What finally came into focus was a billowing brown wall that barrelled menacingly towards us over the plains like a rogue breaker headed for the beach. It was a massive sandstorm. Perhaps another like this had blotted out Timbuktu. We tried to skirt it, veering onto a northerly course for twenty miles, but it continued, unbroken, out of sight.

The closest airport, Kara, on the banks of the Niger, looked abandoned and would offer no protection against the storm. Mopti was tantalisingly close – merely thirty miles – and we desperately tried to make radio contact. The response was high-pitched crackles. Indecisive, we circled, marvelling at the startling phenomenon, reluctant to fly back, afraid to continue.

At last, through the static, we distinguished a voice: 'XRAY-ECHO, Mopti Mopti Mopti. Do you read? Mopti calling XRAY ECHO.'

'Mopti, XRAY-ECHO. We read you. Please advise local weather.'

'It is raining at this time but you come, I wait you. Visibility two kilometres. You come.' If it was only raining in Mopti, then the storm that separated us was not wide.

'Mopti, what are your winds? And the winds in the storm?'

'You come Mopti. I wait you,' the controller lured, beckoning like a siren's song, ignoring our pleas for details. We approached the wall of sand for a closer look. It was an awesome sight: the dark brown mass swirling relentlessly forwards, like a giant combine harvester rolling across a wheatfield.

'XRAY-ECHO, why not you come Mopti?' There it came again, the cajoling, tempting. 'I wait you. You come Mopti.'

Such storms, we conjectured, were common in Mali. We knew absolutely nothing about flying into sandstorms. It sounded a completely daft thing to do, but if there was any danger, surely he would not insist that we proceed? The chart indicated no terrain higher than 1,800 feet. Should we dive through the sand wall or through the cumulus? In either case, we were in for ferocious turbulence in zero visibility.

The sanitary whiteness of the cumulus above was somehow more inviting. We climbed to 9,000 feet. With seatbelts firmly tightened, stomachs in a knot and teeth clenched, we flew at the swirling clammy whiteness. It was strangely silent. For a moment. Then *Romeo* was catapulted skywards by an updraught, leaving our stomachs behind. Rate of climb 2,000 feet per minute. The stall warning started shrieking. Moments later, we were falling in a down-draught, falling, falling – and our stomachs hit the back of our throats. I clutched the panel as we soared and plunged, again and again.

'Let's get the hell out of here,' Gérard yelled, fighting to keep the plane more or less level and upright, eyes glued to the instruments: artificial horizon, altimeter, airspeed indicator, heading indicator. It was an unfair contest against Nature's immeasurable forces. She could flip us over like a coin.

The engine noise changed, revving high. The nose was dropping. Gérard pulled the throttle back, but the sensation of speed increased. He was grimly silent, concentrating hard. I glanced over. The artificial horizon looked strange: the blue upper section of the dial was underneath, and bobbing wildly. We were upside down and falling at 2,000 feet per minute!

'This is it,' I thought, heart racing but strangely calm, resigned. 'What a stupid end this will make.' I could imagine the headlines: SMALL PLANE DESTROYED IN SANDSTORM. TWO DEAD.

Long seconds later, Gérard seemed to be back in control. Having thrust the yoke forward, he was slowly drawing it back. I couldn't move my arms. Was this what they meant by 'paralysed with fear'? I had never been under such G forces before. Never again, God willing.

Aeons passed, and then the pounding stopped and we broke free to behold the desert, a welcome carpet that Mother Earth unrolled beneath us. An immense gratitude welled up inside me, and I looked over at Gérard. Beads of sweat glistened on his forehead. He looked as though a train had hit him.

'Jesus, how the hell did you do that? You were fantastic. Fantastic. I thought we were gonners. I can't believe you got us out of there. Well done, chéri.' We looked back, with respectful awe, at the monster storm behind us.

'Never been upside down before? It's quite something, eh?' He brushed off the praise, but was secretly chuffed he had mastered the engine and the elements. 'We must have hit severe windshear on one side. The wing stalled. With all that turbulence and insufficient air flow, we flipped over in a split second. It's so fast you don't notice until the controls don't respond any more.' The explanation did nothing to appease me.

'Horrible, horrible, horrible. For God's sake, don't let's ever go into one of those things again. Promise?'

'Promise. Didn't like it much myself. To hell with Mopti!'

Back in Bamako, Gérard grilled the met officer on duty as to why we had been told the weather was CAVOK at Timbuktu, and then ten minutes after take-off, the visibility was zero.

'Because, at the moment when you asked for the weather, it was CAVOK. *Après, la tempête est arrivée.*'

'But didn't you know there was a sandstorm system brewing?'

'*Monsieur,* did you ask for the forecast? No, you didn't. When you asked what the weather was like, it was CAVOK. You should have asked for the forecast,' he scolded.

There was an Irish flavour to this conversation which made arguing impossible. The noon weather report from Mopti was on the clipboard: surface winds at forty knots. Had we tried to pass underneath, *Romeo* would have been sandblasted.

At six a.m. the next morning, Gérard pointedly asked for the forecast. CAVOK again. Off for another try. The desert displayed the complete gamut of brown, a great emptiness of golden sand, dirty sand, beige, ochre, reddish and dark brown: The rains had filled hollows with *café au lait* ponds. We were carrying two bottles of emergency water, a foolishly paltry amount for a desert flight.

The truth was, after the Atlantic we felt smugly safe flying over land, any land. Realising our mistake, I made a mental note of where the puddles lay in case the whir of the engine stopped.

The scarcity of landmarks on the arid terrain made it hard to keep track of our position. After exceeding our estimated flight time, we scoured the horizon anxiously and met up again with the Niger. Surely Timbuktu would be easy to spot? In the fifteenth century, it had 100,000 inhabitants, having grown from a humble wintering camp for Tuareg nomads beside a well (Tin Bouctu – Well of Bouctu) into a powerful city and revered seat of Islamic learning. In the thirteenth and fourteenth centuries, Mali was a powerful kingdom and centre of the world's gold trade. The local Mandinke, Soninke, and Songhai peoples adopted Islam, the religion of their Arab clients to the north, for commercial reasons. Timbuktu controlled the trans-Saharan trade routes, levying taxes on the transport of gold and ivory from West to North Africa, providing this patch of desert with a healthy income. Gold was traded against salt, considered almost on a par.

So where was this legendary city? In the middle of nowhere, we discovered a tarmac airstrip stretched out like a fireman's blanket on the sand beneath us. Beyond lay a dark brown smudge, like a dried-up lake. The shell of Timbuktu! We descended from the cool heights of 7,000 feet into a turbulent approach over the hot desert, zooming over the nervous heads of an astounded camel train and a sobering plane wreck. It was my first attempt at landing *Romeo*, and my heart was pounding. I am not a flying fanatic, and really only learned to fly in case Gérard had a sudden attack of food poisoning. Being heavier than the Cherokee in which I trained, *Romeo* sank like a stone. Thank God for dual controls.

A scalding breeze swept over the scrub and dunes. At that time, there were no commercial flights to Timbuktu, so the tower personnel were maintained for overflying traffic and emergencies. They showed us the results of the sandstorm: a fine red powder had blasted its way through every crevice, smothering furniture and sensitive electronic equipment alike.

Hotel Bouktu, commonly referred to as the *Campement*, had been the barracks of a garrison of the French Army. It was a square sand-coloured building dotted with arabesque arches and parapets, and spacious rooms facing onto a central courtyard. We retired for a siesta. It was all anyone could do in the crushing midday heat. No sooner had we dozed off than Gérard was summoned to reception where *le représentant du Gouverneur* wanted to see him. Two elderly blue-robed gentlemen waited discreetly in the bar. After introductions, there was an exchange of trivialities. It seemed to be a social visit. Then the tone changed.

'*Le Gouverneur est très malade*. Can you take him to Bamako?'

We were startled. Was this an emergency airlift? And was it a request or an order? From the moment we arrived, numerous people had asked us for a lift, alleging an array of maladies or deaths in the family. We had decided to take whoever was at the airport when we left.

'We are going to Mopti, not Bamako,' Gérard said warily. 'What's the matter with him?'

'*Ouf! Une petite maladie* . . . Mopti's fine. He'll carry on to Bamako by car.'

'But what illness does he have?' I insisted, envisaging a frail sage with a heart condition. The question was ignored. What if the old Governor had a heart attack in the plane? We would be blamed for killing him! The more I pressed to find out what was wrong, the more evasive they became.

'Don't worry, Madame. His bodyguard will care for him.'

'Bodyguard? What bodyguard?' Gérard exclaimed. 'We have a single-engine, not a jumbo jet! We can't fit in a bodyguard as well!' The aides shuffled awkwardly, but beamed because they had achieved their mission. We had agreed to take the Governor to Mopti in the morning.

Today, Timbuktu is slowly withering away. Tourism is its best chance of earning income, but the number of visitors prepared to make the long haul into the desert to get there is minimal. Alexander Gordon Laing was the first European to do so, reaching the forbidden city in 1826. He was murdered by Tuareg bandits on departure. Two years later, the French explorer Réné Caillié, spent some time in the bustling city disguised as an Arab merchant. He was the first white man to return alive.

At three, when it should have been cooler, we set off to explore, mooching through the hot deserted alleys trying unsuccessfully to conjure up the magic of the city's heyday. The houses were built of *banco*, a mixture of earth and water which hardens in the sun. Through open doorways, we glimpsed families reclining on cloths stretched over the soft sand floor, drinking eternal cups of tea. Two handsome young lads, Assim (a tiny Tuareg in bright blue *boubou*) and Omar (a typically tall, thin Peul), tagged along, chattering cheerfully, pointing out landmarks such as the Djinguereber, a surrealist *banco* mosque of windowless walls and turrets, originally built in 1325. It prickles with protruding wooden stakes used to facilitate mud patching.

As the huge red ball of the sun dipped into the hazy horizon, we contemplated the city from a large dune on the outskirts. It was a magical moment. Tuareg woven mat tents complemented the rounded dunes. Below, a hunchbacked old man plodded home behind his weary donkey laden with gnarled firewood. At that moment, we captured a shiver of the excitement the first white men approaching the city must have felt. A string of camels was being loaded with blocks of salt, like quarried stone, as in the days of the *azalai* or salt caravans. As dusk fell, they set off into the desert, where they would navigate by the stars and rest by day. Gone were the days when this was an everyday occurrence. It was a fifty-two-day trek to Tangiers. The boys spoke longingly of when they would have camels of their own.

Sitting on the warm sand, we watched and listened to the day wind down. Gentle hues of candlelight or the glow of hurricane lamps framed scenes of domestic life in flickering doorways. The town generator had been out of service for months for lack of *gasol*, supplies of which had to be trucked in. In the wet season, it is a three-day drive from Bamako.

Twelve-year-old Assim confessed with pride that Tuaregs were nomadic warriors prone to violence, who picked fights with glee, especially against the Songhai, creating serious tribal problems in Timbuktu. Sometimes, the government led violent incursions against them, trying to urbanise them by force. He already knew his wife-to-be, chosen by his parents, and explained that Tuaregs could have several wives, *'mais ça donne des problèmes'*. Women became unreasonably jealous, he said, and would even resort to poisoning each other. But never mind, the boys agreed solemnly, Allah put women on this earth exclusively to make men happy.

We chatted for hours. Above, zillions of stars invisible to the world's city freaks, glimmered like sequins on black velvet.

'There's a star up there for each of us,' Omar whispered. 'When we die, that star falls.'

We meandered back to the *Campement*, longing for a bath. The hotel's water pump and generator were only switched on at night. From the courtyard, we could hear the welcome tinkle of water dripping onto the shower floor. I peeped round the door, screeched with horror and propelled myself into Gérard's arms. Herds of huge cockroaches scrambled over each other to get at the moisture. Their thirst quenched, they waltzed into the bedroom and preened themselves on the reed mats. Gérard tried vaporising them with the spray provided while I cowered on the bed. He only succeeding in making the room smell like an old lavatory, which lured in yet more roaches. If I wanted a shower, there was no option but to squelch over them. Squirming with revulsion (snakes or rats are fine by me, but cockroaches – ugh!) I stood under the cascade of water as they crawled up the walls, antennae twitching. Blessedly, the beds had mosquito nets. I dived into my cocoon and lay there, listening to their scuttling, until overtaken by sleep. By morning, there was no trace of them. I thought it had been a bad dream, but the odd squashed carapace told otherwise.

The Governor's black sedan arrived for us at 7:15. At the airport, we prepared the plane while the car went to collect him. On returning, it drove straight out onto the tarmac. From the back seat emerged Commandant Lamine Diabira. Not a shrivelled invalid with a long white beard and a cane, but a tall ox of a man in his thirties wearing a beaming smile and an ochre *boubou* with exquisite white embroidery. He looked like one of the Dream Team. I enquired gingerly after his health. He was sick all right – sick of Timbuktu!

Having told his emissaries there was no room for a bodyguard, we had omitted to mention baggage, presuming it would proceed in the Governor's car which had been sent ahead. But no, an outsize red Samsonite and bulging black canvas bag emerged. Undiplomatically, we expressed reservations as to how these items would fit inside. The Governor promptly opened the case and began sorting through his collection of *boubous* as his minions crowded round to stare. Embarrassed, Gérard stopped him. After rearranging all our luggage so that the heavy case could be placed as far forward as possible so as not to upset the centre of gravity, I squeezed into the backseat and Commandant Diabira was accommodated in the co-pilot's seat. He immediately recognised the SatNav, since the Landcruiser in which he would patrol his 500,000-square-kilometre domain was equipped with the same model.

'When we get lost in the desert,' he said, 'we take it out of its bag, plug it into the cigarette lighter, and wait for a satellite. Sometimes we wait ten minutes, sometimes several hours.'

He showed great interest in aviation, asking numerous pertinent questions on air traffic control and air regulations. Gérard was so engrossed in conversation that we overshot Mopti and had to turn back. The flight had taken less than an hour. The Governor's car, obliged to travel up to Gao to cross the Niger, would take thirty-six hours. Another official car had been sent to collect him. He offered to drop us at an hotel but was so horrified when we suggested a hostel, that he insisted we use his room at the smart Sofitel. He would use a government *pied-à-terre*. After the previous night's roach-ridden hell, we graciously accepted the press-button luxury of air-conditioning, water and electricity.

We invited him to join us for dinner. Vivacious and well read, he was poignantly aware of the injustices of the colonial system and vehement to improve the lot of his people, 'not by giving them TVs and crockery they don't need, nor by teaching them to read French, but by schooling them in their own languages on how to use the land to its best advantage, teaching them the value of trees and of protecting their environment'. Mali's poor, he pointed out, had communicated happily in their own languages for thousands of years. They had no need of French. His baby was *éducation sélective*, a theory whereby only the brightest children were given further education, and others just the basics they need. From a peasant family himself, he had been top of his class and the winner of a scholarship to Canada. However, the less bright son of an influential member of the government had been sent in his place, abandoning the course within a year. Such wasted opportunity irritated him greatly.

Discussing Timbuktu's energy problems, we mentioned how impressed we had been by the use made of wind power in Cape Verde. He sat bolt upright, enthralled. Timbuktu is always windy. It was the obvious energy source and would eliminate the problem of transporting expensive diesel oil over bad roads. Gérard offered to obtain information on the latest windmill technology and send it to him. Unfortunately, we never did. Now it is too late.

In 1990, we received a New Year card from him. But the *Daily Telegraph*, dated 16/7/91, reported: 'A coup attempt led by Mali's Minister of Territorial Administration, Col. Lamine Diabira, was thwarted yesterday . . . The acting head of state, Lt. Col. Amadou Touré . . . said all the ringleaders had been rounded up.' He could have made an excellent president. Not surprisingly, there has been no response to our letters. Is he languishing in jail, or has a worse fate befallen him?

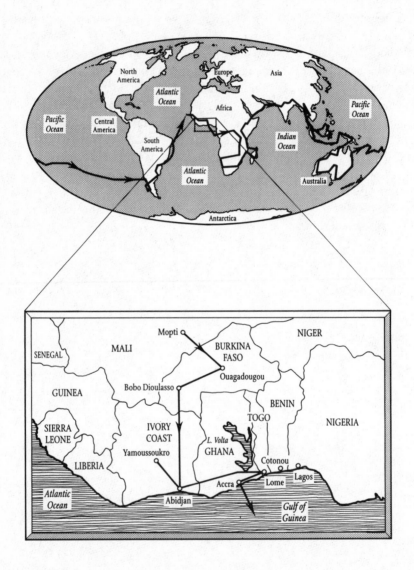

5   'Vous avez trop de médicaments'

'Right, all set for Bobo Dioulasso!' Gérard announced with childish excitement, after completing the regulation fifty-hour engine service in the Aero Club hangar in Ouagadougou, capital of Burkina Faso. Poring over maps of Africa, this name had drawn him like a magnet.

When we landed on Bobo Dioulasso's humpbacked runway, the surprisingly young controller, Sinaré Moumouni, shyly invited us to stay. Touched by his spontaneity, we imagined he would take us to a moderate house overflowing with family. Instead, he led us fifty metres to where he lived alone in a large yellowing mansion used to lodge airport personnel. He showed us to a huge room with two dormitory beds.

Bobo Dioulasso is the economic capital of one of the poorest, least fertile and most densely populated countries on earth where life expectancy is thirty-three years. Things are so bleak that two million Burkinabé work in the Ivory Coast and their remittances provide the country with its largest source of revenue. Mango trees lined the pot-holed streets and shadowed the terraces of run-down hotels. In the crowded market, where hundreds of tiny stalls were crammed along muddy alleys, wooden trays exposed the local delicacy: fat black-and-green worms. The yardstick of poverty was the fact that salt, sugar and washing powder were sold in 100-gram portions. Survival is a day-to-day achievement.

Thomas Sankara, the charismatic former president, was responsible for renaming Upper Volta as Burkina Faso. Burkina, in Moré, the language of the Mossi tribe, means 'man of integrity' and Faso, in Dioula, another local language, means 'native land'. Sankara, the creator of the Land of Men of Integrity, was ruthlessly assassinated by his best friend, Blaise Campaore, who assumed the presidency.

We invited Sinaré to dinner, suggesting he choose the restaurant and presuming he would take advantage of being treated to a free meal to frequent an establishment beyond his means. Not so: he was a true Burkinabé, a man of integrity. He led us into the back room of a wooden hut where a large mama swaddled in shiny purple stirred a cauldron. The multi-coloured plastic of the tablecloths had also been used as wallpaper, producing an hallucinatory effect under the strip lighting. There were no other customers.

'*C'est mon restaurant préféré,*' he said coyly. 'It's only simple. I hope you don't mind. But the food is good.'

It was true that, for fear of catching hepatitis, we generally ate in slightly more upmarket establishments. So we were happy to be in a true African restaurant, reassured of the quality. I chose *poulet avec légumes*, while Sinaré and Gérard preferred the *poulet couscous* from the massive cauldron. It was all quite delicious.

At seven next morning, pounding on the door was followed by an announcement that breakfast was ready. Sinaré had been to buy a fresh baguette, and had made a huge pot of coffee. The bread was coated with thick lashings of margarine from a half-kilo tin, specifically designed for fridgeless tropical temperatures. I made the excuse that I never ate at breakfast and just drank mugs of coffee. Gérard, ravenous as usual, ate his share of the bread and most of mine.

The Ivory Coast was a sharp contrast to impoverished Burkina Faso. In Abidjan, a multi-lane highway sped past an unexpected array of skyscrapers overlooking numerous waterways. The taxi pulled up at the plush five-star Hotel Ivoire and we plucked up the courage to walk inside. Such hotels were neither compatible with our pocket nor our general preference, but Gérard's cousin, Jean-Louis Butticaz, was the sales manager and had invited us to stay. We followed him on tip-toe down a long silent corridor to an elegant bedroom overlooking lush gardens and a squiggly pool dotted with little jungle islands. Beyond, across Baie de Cocody, was the proud city skyline.

We were unaccustomed to such luxury, but the timing was perfect. As we waded excitedly through the fat pile of letters that awaited us, Gérard felt feverish. Since most men with a cold are convinced they are dying, I sceptically chivvied him along to our sundowner rendezvous with Jean-Louis and Carmen, cheerfully suggesting that he probably had malaria so that he could feel justifiably sorry for himself. Some sympathetic wife! It soon became clear that he was seriously unwell. His teeth chattered uncontrollably. We all decided he did have *la palu*, fed him six Nivaquine, and put him to bed under two thick blankets. As the night progressed, the shivering intensified to jelly-in-an-earthquake proportions. He clamoured for more blankets. Diarrhoea struck. Gently at first and then with increasing intensity, accompanied by acute abdominal pains. When Jean-Louis phoned for news, I begged him for medical help. Some time later, a nurse telephoned on the instructions of the French doctor contracted to care for the hotel's clients, and who had decided this was just another case of malaria. She paid no heed to the new symptoms I described, and recommended a glass of hot milk as if he was a child with insomnia. Hot milk was sent for, and reluctantly drunk. Within moments, it was churning in the toilet bowl. And so the night inched on, punctuated with severe shivering, copious sweating, acute pains, chronic diarrhoea and violent vomiting. I felt utterly helpless, and furious that the doctor had not bothered to attend. Our own comprehensive first-aid kit was in the plane. By three a.m., Gérard was hallucinating and groaning in such pain that, without telling him, I resolved to go and fetch it.

The hotel receptionist allocated me a reliable taxi-driver by the name of Sharif. As we sped along the deserted highways, I doubted whether the airport security guards would actually let me in. Avoiding the main terminal, I directed Sharif to the cargo entrance beyond which lay the Aero Club. The gates were wide open and unguarded! Unchallenged, we continued to the club where all was darkness and eerie silence. Surely there must be a guard of sorts? I called out, nervously at first and then in full voice, in an attempt to awake any dozing nightwatchman. Nobody came. An iron gate cut off access to the unlit aircraft patio. As I walked towards it, a voice boomed in my brain. It was that of the nightwatchman at Bamako who had told us he had shot at a pilot who returned one night to collect something from his plane. Feeling horribly conspicuous and vulnerable, expecting a volley of angry shots, I climbed over the gate and walked, with a pounding heart, to where *Romeo*'s lovely white form gleamed enticingly. My trembling fingers struggled clumsily with the knots securing the outer canvas. I immediately located the medical kit, and since there was an empty taxi at my disposal, grabbed two other bags. Although my confidence grew as each moment passed, I still felt like a thief. Clutching the booty, I tried not to run back across the patio.

The backseat of the taxi felt like a long lost friend as I sank back into its cushioned warmth, scarcely able to believe it had been so easy. Knowing our actions would be difficult to explain to a trigger-happy nightwatchman, Sharif had been as nervous as I. We both *oufed* with relief. So much for security!

The euphoria was short-lived.

On the highway, a gang of five armed soldiers flagged us down. Sharif seemed afraid but I arrogantly assumed that once they saw the passenger was a lone white woman, we would be waved on. A horrid face, a scar on one cheek and hooded malevolent eyes, peered through the window.

'*Descendez!*' he ordered.

It seemed imprudent to refuse. An interrogation followed.

'*Qu'est-ce que vous faites? Où est-ce que vous allez? Qu'est-ce que vous avez là dedans?*' No attention was paid to my replies. The same questions were barked out several times. They muttered amongst themselves, wasting precious time. Gérard was agonising and here I was, stuck on that damned highway. Were they plotting something? The hard glint of their guns made me nervous. I looked to Sharif for reassurance, but he was staring straight ahead, uninvolved.

'*Ecoutez, mon mari est très malade . . .*' I pleaded. 'Please may I go, I'm in a hurry-'

'What's in those bags? Open them!' the churlish leader snapped. He examined the first-aid kit. '*Vous avez trop de médicaments*,' he accused. A fat hand extracted a fistful of pill packets which were held up individually for inspection. 'Too many medicines,' he repeated.

I envisaged him helping himself to them all, leaving nothing for Gérard, and wanted to grab back the kit. His colleagues were rummaging through the other bags.

'Aaa-haaa! And what is this?' a voice boomed.

'It's a spray,' I replied noncommittally, sure they would have no idea what mace was.

'I can see that. I'm not stupid,' the leader retorted. 'What's it for? Killing people, isn't it?'

Drat! Now there'd be trouble. He thought it was a deadly weapon. His scarred cheek twitched as he showed the can to his colleagues, graphically describing the use of mace as he understood it. They all looked askance at the tiny yellow and red can on which a black diagram showed a lady spraying an armed aggressor. I decided the best form of defence was attack.

'Look, you have pistols, don't you? I'm only a feeble woman. This is all I have to defend myself.'

'*Mais ça, c'est pour tuer les noirs*,' he accused, pointing at the black figures in the stylised diagram.

It had become a racial issue. I felt panic surge up inside me. They wanted trouble all right, and would not let Sharif stand in their way. He would probably be treated more brutally than I. They would want no witnesses. The empty highway unrolled to either side, as collaborative as the gleaming metal of their weapons. Gérard didn't know I had gone out. Even when he found I was missing, he was too sick to do anything about it. When two bodies were found in the bush beside the highway, they would say I asked for it, going out in the middle of the night like that. The fight in me faded. My knees went weak at the thought of impending violence.

'All women in Europe carry these sprays against muggers,' interceded Sharif, suddenly standing there, beside me. His neck was also on the line, but his unexpected support gave me courage.

'*C'est vrai*. This doesn't kill people,' I stammered.

'But it makes them blind!' Smart-arse Scarface had an answer for everything.

'No, it doesn't. It makes the eyes sting a little, that's all.' I watched in dread as the soldiers manhandled the spray can. If they set it off, they'd get really mad.

'It's true what *madame* says,' Sharif intervened again. 'This really is an emergency. Her husband is very, very ill. Monsieur le Directeur Général of the hotel personally asked me to bring her to the airport. He is waiting for us.'

'Keep the spray, but please let me take the medicines,' I added, impressed with Sharif's story.

'I don't want it. *Montez dans la voiture*,' Scarface muttered, throwing it at me like a hand grenade with the pin out.

I hesitated. Was the ordeal over? They had taken nothing.

'*Montez!*' he yelled.

Grabbing up the bags, I obeyed. As Sharif pulled away, we both snorted with relief for the second time that night.

'They wanted to arrest you, but they didn't because you're white,' Sharif declared, explaining that the government was trying to eradicate a busy trade in medicine smuggling!

Back at the hotel, Gérard was still groaning, completely unaware of my absence. I fed him anti-nausea and anti-diarrhoea pills, but he continued to inspect the plumbing with unabated enthusiasm. In the morning, Jean-Louis sent for the same arrogant doctor again. When malaria had been suspected, he had deemed it a waste of his precious time to examine Gérard. Now this was clearly not the case, he still refused to come, claiming he would be unable to make a diagnosis without laboratory tests. Carmen and I loaded a haggard Gérard, shivering in a long-sleeved woollen shirt despite thirty-degree temperatures, into her car. At a spotless Canadian-built clinic nearby, a charming Ivorian doctor in Emergency instantly diagnosed gastroenteritis without resorting to any tests. Completely dehydrated, Gérard was immediately put on a drip and the fever raged on.

Still physically weak, he was nevertheless pig-headed enough to discharge himself from the clinic the next day. Since he hadn't been carrying any extra ounces of fat, the loss of five kilos in thirty-six hours gave him a Biafran look. He launched into a course of Strongenol, ampules of revolting brown liquid supposed to cure emaciation. The laboratory verdict was bacillary dysentery, or shigella. Something in magnetic Bobo Dioulasso had been to blame: either the *poulet couscous* or Sinaré's rancid margarine.

Until 1950, Yamoussoukro was a normal African village of adobe huts with a population of 500 inhabitants, surrounded by dense forest. Home village of the late President Félix Houphouet-Boigny, it is now the Ivory Coast's political capital, boasting the *crème de la crème* of modern buildings. The lavish geometric arrangements of concrete and glass of various palaces and *écoles supérieures* are planted in splendid isolation on a grid of empty avenues.

But it is the awesome dome of the basilica of Notre Dame de la Paix, the largest Catholic church in the world, which dominates the skyline. Utterly incongruous with its African hinterland setting and higher than St Peter's, its classical dome soars 500 feet into the tropical heavens. No expenses spared. When doubts were expressed as to the justification of spending an estimated US$200 million on such a building in a country where only twelve per cent of the population is Catholic, Boigny claimed to have financed its construction from his own pocket. This was self-condemnatory – how did a career politician find so much money in his bank account? To extricate himself from the embarrassment of having to explain his wealth, he resolved to pass the hot potato to the Vatican. Unimpressed with the magnanimity of such a gift, the Vatican demanded Boigny cough up for the annual maintenance. He did, for his greatest fear was that when he died, this monumental folly would rot in the jungle. Perhaps it will yet, but now acclaimed as one of Africa's greatest statesmen, Boigny lies there in state.

A new game park was under construction twenty-five kilometres from Yamoussoukro, as visiting heads of state expect to see wild animals in Africa. The park was not open, so we circumnavigated its shiny, new fence which defiantly pressed back cultivated fields. Not a four-legged beast in sight. The Ivory Coast's wildlife had been hunted out, so animals to populate the park were being purchased from other countries. A sorry situation for a country named after its abundance of elephants. Newly independent countries often change their names. The Ivory Coast certainly should have done so. Instead, it passed a decree that it be called Côte d'Ivoire, in all languages. The misnomer lives on.

For all the grandeur of their basilica, sixty-five per cent of Ivorians practise animism. But it was in Lomé, the capital of Togo, that we visited the *Marché des Féticheurs*. It is not a market for kinks, as the name might suggest, but where items such as parrot beaks, chameleon legs or dog skulls are purchased for voodoo ceremonies. Black magic (voodoo, *fétiches*) is part of life's rich pattern in Africa and still a force to be contended with. Transported to and internationalised in the Caribbean by the slaves, voodoo is a Fon word from Benin.

There is nothing African about witchcraft, and modern-day horror stories of covens leak out regularly in the USA. Brazil is perfectly at home with witchcraft. In 1992, the white wife and daughter of a mayor perpetrated the mutilation and death of a blond blue-eyed boy of seven in order to guarantee themselves long happy lives. In West Africa, there is no prudery about black magic. Those requiring a remedy for physical, domestic or social ills can consult a *féticheur* at this market. In the large square surrounded on three sides by low thatched huts, the dried or putrefying corpses of mammals, birds, reptiles and amphibians lay neatly on trestle tables or in rows on the ground. In the case of larger animals (chimps, gorillas, dogs, cats, lions, horses, cows, jackals, crocodiles), only the severed heads lay on display alongside the bodies of monkeys, rats, snakes, chameleons, frogs, owls, cormorants and even sparrows and swallows. Various ingredients are ground up to solve a particular problem. Freshly ground parrot, for example, is supposed to improve intelligence. The 'produce', we were told, came from neighbouring Benin.

Our Beninois taxi-driver persuaded us to chat to his *féticheur* friend, Docteur Paul, a perfectly normal, clean-shaven young Beninois. We suspected a money-spinning con, but he insisted there was no fee. The dark interior of the thatched hut was a mock-up of an *ainou* (I have written the names as he spelled them), the forest grove in which voodoo ceremonies are carried out. The 'altar' was decorated with animal horns, monkey skulls, cowrie shells, figurines, skins, hooves, odd bits of bark and roots. It was dedicated to Kouhossou, a god responsible for happiness and chasing away evil spirits, who was personified in a wide, square-faced wooden statue adorned with two cow horns under tresses of wiry horse hair.

Dr Paul began by demanding 500 CFA francs to pay for *sodabi*, a kind of palm alcohol without which the ceremony could not proceed. He chanted while ringing a small bell with one hand and spraying the liquid on the altar with the other. The remnants had to be drunk. It smelled like cleaning alcohol. We each took a sip. He downed the rest and then introduced us to some common fetish charms. *Soudeme*, a little wooden figure with a wide-open mouth and huge stopper, is a sort of St Christopher. Holding it in the left hand, a traveller whispers to *Soudeme* where he intends to go, places the stopper in its mouth and tucks the charm into his pocket. Painless, permanent travel insurance! *Botemi*, an elongated wooden box, is a love *fétiche*. To become effective, it is sprinkled with perfume and rubbed on the hands. When the pretender shakes hands with the one desired, the latter will fall instantly in love. The wonderful thing, Paul added, is that you can use the charm on as many people as you like. The pebble-like seed of the ebony tree works wonders on memory and intelligence. Sprinkle it with three drops of fresh water, make the sign of the cross on your forehead, and pop it under the bed. Not only do you sleep profoundly, but you wake up more intelligent. Better than sleeping pills!

Dr Paul insisted we should each choose two charms as souvenirs. Being modest, we selected one each. He began to wind up the ceremony by chucking cowries on the beaten earth floor, chanting hypnotically to Kouhossou. According to the shells, he said, Kouhossou sent a message to say how much he liked us, so much so that he had decided to make a special price of only 10,000 CFA francs (US$30) for each charm. We had expected this ploy and grunted with indignation. Paul raised a hand for silence and consulted Kouhossou again. This time, the cowries said, 'I'll give you a good price: two for 10,000 francs!' Gérard wryly suggested Paul was miscounting the zeros.

Why didn't we hand back the charms and walk out? That creepy, dark hut, pervaded by the stench of rotting animals, trapped us on the brink of a mysterious world of black magic, a macabre spiritual realm which held our jet-age cynicism in a primeval stranglehold. Paul's hypnotic chants closed off the exit. He instructed us to remain seated in a voice that did not allow for disobedience. I kept expecting Gérard to get up, send him to Hell, and stride manfully out into the sunshine with me trotting behind. The truth was, the Underworld kept us inexplicably shackled to that gloomy bench. Our legs were no longer our own. It was like a horror movie. We did not even dare to whisper to each other.

The chucking of cowries and chanting droned on. Of course, we could have paid the US$30 ransom, but we were still sufficiently aware of the real world not to fall for that. In a final consultation, Kouhossou agreed to 1,000 francs. It seemed that the gods, when not fixing marriages, enjoyed a good bargaining session.

6 *'Il est interdit de survoler la mer dans un monomoteur'*

Libreville, as the name suggests, was established as a settlement for freed slaves in 1849 by the French naval lieutenant, Bouet-Willaumetz. It remained a small provincial town, capital of a densely forested, scantily populated country, for over a century until rich oil reserves propelled Gabon to the dizzy heights in the late 1970s of having the largest income per capita of sub-Saharan Africa. That was before the slump.

We arrived after a five-hour crossing of the Gulf of Guinea, a watery route we chose specifically to avoid Nigeria where even commercial airlines have a tough time with bureaucracy and corruption. The dinghy and life jackets had been brought back from redundancy and were poised cautiously by the rear door. Upon landing, we had been surprised at the number of light aircraft. This was a good sign, as we needed advice on the best route to take to Nairobi. At the Aero Club, an obese Frenchman, sweating heavily in a lurid green T-shirt, attended to paperwork. We introduced ourselves cheerfully, asking for tips on where to fly locally.

'*Quel avion avez-vous?*' he barked.

'It's an Embraer 721. Like a Saratoga.'

'Well, you can go to Port Gentil. Single-engines are not allowed to fly to Franceville.'

'Why's that?'

'Because the forest is considered a *région inhospitalière.*'

'But we've crossed the Amazon before now, and we are IFR-equipped,' Gérard reasoned.

'That's beside the point. A single-engine cannot fly in *régions inhospitalières.*'

The door opened and a tall, grey-haired Frenchman came in. He looked up and down our scruffy attire. 'There are too many non-members around here,' he spat, and departed.

The *région inhospitalière* was clearly not the forest, but the Aero Club. Thick-skinned, we persisted. We were keen to visit São Tomé & Príncipe, a former Portuguese island-colony 170 miles offshore.

'Could you just tell us if it's difficult to get clearances for São Tomé?'

'You may not fly to São Tomé. *Il est interdit de survoler la mer dans un monomoteur.* It is prohibited to fly over the sea in a single-engine.'

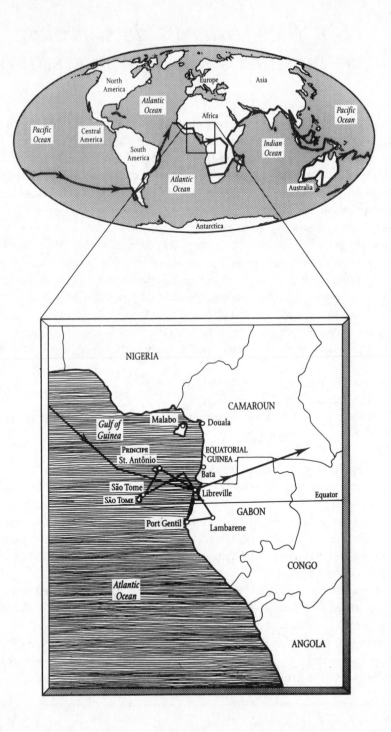

'But we just flew in from Accra across the Gulf of Guinea. Before that, we crossed the Atlantic from Brazil to Dakar.'

'Je m'en fous. The rules here do not allow it. *Point final,'* he muttered crossly. 'Excuse me, I'm busy.' We were dismissed.

The next day, as Gérard was trying to solve a problem we had with the DME, a kinder French pilot, Pepe, came over to chat. He knew Central Africa well and strongly recommended avoiding Zaïre. The best option to reach Kenya, he suggested, was to track up to Bangui, in the Central African Republic, and proceed to a dot on the map called Obo. From there, we could cut across the empty north-eastern corner of Zaïre (without bothering to get a clearance) to Uganda. This route had the added advantage of avoiding the notoriously bad weather around the Virunga volcanoes and the wall of the Ruwenzori mountains, some as high as 17,000 feet. It was sound advice.

Despite the Gabonese regulations prohibiting us from flying out to sea, we were determined to visit São Tomé. Since our flight plan had to have a credible destination on it, Gérard requested a clearance to Bata, in neighbouring Equatorial Guinea, the only Spanish-speaking country in Black Africa. Senhor Menezes, the São Tomé Consul in Libreville, was delighted to hear that we would fly there in our own plane, as we could give his aunt a lift. Remembering the embarrassing suitcase situation with the Governor of Timbuktu, we explained there was a shortage of space.

'She's not large, is she?' I joked.

'She's eighty-five,' Menezes replied.

'Eighty-five! Surely a lady of her age will be terrified in a small plane?'

'No, no,' he laughed. 'She is eighty-five kilos, not eighty-five years old!'

Eighty-five kilos was clearly not an unreasonable weight for a well-to-do lady from São Tomé. Let's just say Maria Aparecida was a very buxom woman. The luggage allowance of one small bag was interpreted to encompass a ghetto-blaster, a green plastic basket bulging with vegetables and a heavy brown bag. We sat her in the back seat, arranged all her belongings around her, and set a northerly course towards Bata.

After fifteen minutes, having signed off from Libreville Control, we simply advised Bata of the change of destination and headed west out across the Gulf of Guinea towards São Tomé, invisible under a monotonous layer of cloud stretching *ad infinitum.* At last, a proud mauve-blue mountainous outline cracked the horizon ahead, soft white clouds parting to reveal its 6,000-foot peaks. The substantial size of the runway surprised us, especially compared to the tiny parking patio, jammed with a TAP Tristar and a locally registered Gulfstream jet. We were advised to tuck *Romeo* into a corner, out of the way of an arriving Angolan Hercules. São Tomé airport was unaccustomed to light aircraft. The clerk wanted to charge us landing fees for a DC4, because it was the smallest category of aircraft on his list. Gérard tried logic and reasoning, anger and whingeing. All in vain: the clerk stubbornly referred to his list. We had to pay up.

'*Desculpe, senhor,*' the clerk added, 'but I must also charge you US$45 for the use of Equatorial Airlines' stairs.'

'That's not necessary. We didn't use them.'

'But my instructions are to charge all aircraft.'

'That may be, because all the other aircraft that come here are big. They use the stairs. Look outside. Our plane's very small. We don't need stairs!'

'But I have to charge ALL aircraft, *senhor.*'

There was no sign in São Tomé of the Russian presence we had expected. The People's Palace had been built by the Chinese. The then president, Dr Manuel Pinto da Costa, had persuaded the omnipotent Partido to become receptive to the West, for the Russians had left them with nothing. Doors were gradually creeping open, and visitors were allowed in. In fact, all the *pensões* in town were full, forcing us to stay at the only hotel, the Yugoslav-built Miramar. Despite the torrid equatorial heat, the town had the peaceful air of a Portuguese village on a Sunday. Cars were a rarity in the shady avenues, ankle-deep in red and golden leaves from the *amendoeiras*. Many of the multi-coloured houses, abandoned upon the exodus of the Portuguese in 1974, had fallen into ruin: teenage trees sprouted through the roofs; chickens and pigs romped in dusty quadrangles where green lawns once lay.

At the end of the leafy promenade stands the stolid Fortaleza de São Sebastião, constructed in 1566 by the Portuguese (who had been on the island since 1470) to defend São Tomé from French pirates. Inhabited till independence by the hated Portuguese troops, it has been made into a national museum rather than razed, as Eastern Europeans might have done. Silver chalices, fine china and other vestiges of colonial wealth were displayed amongst bronze busts and oil paintings of Portuguese kings and governors. The Portuguese *colonos* (mostly *degregados*, the Luso equivalent of Australian convicts) maltreated their slaves, who continually revolted despite bloody reprisals by the authorities. One room in the museum is dedicated to the worst episode of São Tomé's history: the Batepá Massacre in 1953. In the space of a week, Portuguese troops, under the orders of Governor-General Gorgulho, gunned down over 1,000 islanders under the pretext that they were trying to start a resistance movement.

'What year did slavery end in São Tomé?' I asked the young girl who had shown me round, chanting out the names of the individuals in the portraits and their misdemeanours.

'1974,' she replied. The year of independence!

Cottars Camp, Kenya. Before landing, we had to buzz the airstrip to drive the zebras and gazelles off, and preparing for take-off, they just meander slowly out of the way.

The island of Ibo, in Mozambique.

Fog along the Skeleton Coast, Namibia. Its rocky shores are a cemetery for fifteenth-century caravels and modern ships alike.

Loiyangalani, Kenya.

Loiyangalani, meaning Place of Trees, is an oasis in the hostile desert landscape near Lake Turkana, Kenya.

Gérard pointing to the altimeter, which reads 500 feet below sea level, while overflying the turbulent Lake Assal depression in Djibouti.

50-hour service in Kathmandu.

Gear maintenance in Kathmandu.

We feel dwarfed in the line-up for take-off from Bangkok International.

At the last minute, the clouds parted and we found the national park airstrip at Taman Negara, Malaysia.

Having a picnic in the spectacular Bada Valley.

Having discovered Bada airstrip was too short for us to take-off with the load we had, Gérard starts off-loading avgas which was joyfully received for the local motorbikes.

The crowd gathered at the terminal hut at Bada.

Willing hands help push *Romeo* back.

At last we spot the outline of Flores Island, Indonesia.

We explored the island by Mini-Moke, bouncing over the pitted roads unmaintained since the Portuguese left. Steep hillsides were planted with cocoa trees and merry piles of crimson, bright orange and yellow cocoa pods awaited collection by the roadside. The smell of chocolate from a cottage factory mingled with the sweet spring scent of a thousand white blossoms from overgrown coffee plantations. Sporadic gaps in the greenery revealed breath taking views of inaccessible beaches and mysterious mountain peaks. At Santana, several huts were tucked beneath the coconut palms which lined the exquisite beach. In the shade of a large kapok, the fishermen gathered round a draughts game, guffawing and egging on the players. They were blissfully unaware that the complex of luxury bungalows under construction on the nearby clifftop was about to destroy their peaceful lifestyle. The French project engineer told us that the fishermen were to be relocated. After all, he said, they did not appreciate the loveliness of the beach. Any old place was good enough for them.

Two young Brazilian missionaries, Baldassar and Gustavo, were awaiting us at the hotel on our return. They had spotted the Brazilian flag painted on *Romeo's* fuselage and had hunted us down. They were thrilled we really had flown from Brazil and offered to show us two wrecked Constellations lying in the bush beside the runway. We set off through the waist-high grass beside the entrance to an Angolan army camp. São Tomé had neither the means nor men to build its own army. Fears (not unfounded) of an outside invasion in the late seventies had led the government to borrow 1,000 Angolan soldiers for national security. The islanders resented the dour, gun-toting Angolans who, thoroughly bored with island life, became trigger-happy. After recent encounters with soldiers elsewhere, we were sceptical about their proximity, but Baldassar assured us that he took this path every day to reach Gamboa village where he worked. The derelict Canadian-registered Constellations raised majestic noses above circles of trampled grass. Gérard scrambled inside. They had been picked clean. Baldassar said they had been used to drop emergency supplies to the famished during the Biafran War. I walked back several yards to fit the planes in the viewfinder, climbing up an anthill for a better view. Out of the corner of my eye, I noticed the Angolan soldiers slouched in the shade nearby, but they ignored me. I took my pictures and rejoined the others by the aircraft.

Moments later, shouts rang out and three soldiers, AK47s at the ready, approached in single file through the long grass.

'*O que estão fazendo aqui?*' a sullen soldier with droopy eyelids demanded, positioning himself to one side, as if to prevent us from fleeing. 'You not allowed take photos. Give me film!' he ordered threateningly.

It seemed I'd learned nothing that night in Abidjan. I put the camera behind my back. Another soldier raised his gun and gesticulated that I should pass it to him. God knows what possessed me, but I obstinately tucked the camera into my bag and hugged it defensively.

'I only took photos of the planes.'

'Open camera. Then I will see what photos you took.'

How was I going to get out of that? If that was what he believed, he would think the black film was a trick.

Gérard looked daggers at me. 'C'mon Margi. Pass it over.'

'We're only looking at the aircraft,' Baldassar intervened, in his gentle manner. 'You know very well that we pass by here every day.'

They muttered between themselves. We made out the words *espiões americanos*. All the time I hugged that bag, scarcely believing what I was doing. In Brazil, I would never hesitate to hand over my watch or purse to an armed man, let alone a soldier with a machine-gun. Such stubbornness could have tragic consequences. All for a silly film!

'How come you speak Portuguese?'

Speaking Portuguese made us suspect! CIA language training probably.

'We speak Portuguese because we are from Brazil,' Baldassar wooed. 'What's the problem?'

'You are not permitted to be in this area. Hand over the film immediately, or the Commandant will be summoned.'

'So, let's talk to the Commandant,' Baldassar agreed.

We were marched single-file towards their camp under the ominous glare of their gun barrels. Baldassar, with calm patience and hope eternal, continued to reason with them. Feeling comically unlike spies in our beach attire, we waited in the scorching sun beside the collaborative anthill, surrounded by soldiers pointing weapons at us. Twenty minutes later, a jeep screeched to a dusty halt before us. A good-looking, surprisingly young Commandant emerged, still fastening his uniform buttons.

'Why did you take photographs of my soldiers?' he blasted.

'*Senhor Comandante*, we took no photos of the soldiers. Only of the aircraft, *Senhor Comandante*,' Baldassar continued his role of meek mediator.

The Commandant glanced perfunctorily over his shoulder at the aluminium carcasses in the bush, cast a look of exasperated vexation at his men and dismissed us with a run-along motion. No doubt it was as much of an anti-climax for him, hastily summoned to deal with American spies, as it was for us to be let off so lightly. We were fortunate that he, unlike his soldiers, was not looking for an excuse for action.

A forty-five-minute flight brought us to the unexpectedly dramatic island of

Príncipe, its volcanic plugs disappearing into the clouds like Jack's beanstalk. Cliffs soared above black volcanic beaches in some places, and golden sands in others, and then sloped off to form lush green hillsides.

The noise of our landing on the plateau airstrip above the only town, Santo Antônio, attracted the attention of Nando, a young *mestizo* who drove a blue Toyota pick-up, the only vehicle on the island with any gasoline. Santo Antônio nestles in an inlet beside the mouth of the Rio Papagaio. It humbly consists of a triangle criss-crossed by six paved streets in which it was rare to see another person at any time of day. There was no electricity: oil for the generator had run out. The air of neglect was generalised. Príncipe relied on São Tomé's goodwill for vital supplies. It was ignored. The island had consisted primarily of cocoa farms or *roças*, with large *fazenda* mansions. Since independence, these had either been nationalised into co-operatives or abandoned.

The white ramparts of the belvedere at Belo Monte hung over a golden beach lapped by turquoise water a hundred feet below. We decided it would be a wonderful place to camp, the perfect paradise island beach. Nando descended the cliffs with us, sliding down on a vague footpath between overgrown cocoa trees. A flock of egrets scavenging for frogs and lizards gleamed startlingly white against so much greenery. Above the din of noisy long-tailed blue-black starlings which inhabited the canopy, we occasionally heard the screech of African Grey parrots. There used to be many on the islands, but they are being driven ever higher into the mountains. While admitting that their capture and sale was illegal, Nando immediately offered to obtain one for us.

A numerous family was clambering up the cliff after a fishing expedition. A ray and a sand-shark, duly quartered to facilitate transport on the head, dripped blood down the face of each child. Nando stopped to chat. This was his godfather's family. A young girl brought up the rear with a live turtle balanced on her head. My soft spot for turtles was spiked into action. I asked if I could buy it, intending to set it free. Wily Nando explained that the shell alone would fetch 3,000 dobras (US$15). We paid up, explaining we would release, not eat, it. Merry peals of laughter rang out as we proceeded down the hill with the heavy turtle, turned the right way up, furiously flapping her flippers. Eventually, she sank into a hopeless depression, head and flippers dangling as she resigned herself to a fate in the cooking-pot. Even when Gérard held her in the sea, she hung limply, not wanting to believe in freedom. At last, after a few tentative strokes, she began to paddle vigorously and was gone. Nando had told us of a *crioulo* saying that if a turtle escaped from a lax fisherman, it would never be caught again. We hoped it was true.

Left alone, we gathered coconut husks discarded from copra pickings and, as dusk fell, made a fire to cook our standard camping meal, spaghetti. A brilliant moon rose. It illuminated the whole beach, our beach, and invited us into the warm phosphorescent water. It was indescribably romantic. We lay at the water's edge and, caressed by gentle waves, made love under the astounded gaze of the zillions of white crabs which shimmered on the sand beside us.

Next morning, we climbed back up the cliff to meet Nando. He announced that his godfather, Sr Neco, had been so impressed with our turtle antics that he wished to invite us to lunch. His simple wooden house stood in a yard of broken-down vehicles, awaiting spare parts and petrol. His wife and two grown-up daughters fussed around the table. It was set for four – Sr Neco, Nando, Gérard and myself. A dozen children of all sizes lined the walls to watch us munch on roast chicken and fried manioc. We took tiny portions.

'*Comam mais!*' Sr Neco insisted indignantly, leaving us in a quandary: should we eat in front of the hungry children, or offend his sense of hospitality?

Then, bursting into a grin, he asked about the turtle. We expounded incomprehensible theories about extinction. They listened with startled bemusement.

'Do you know why we were all laughing when you took the turtle away?' Nando asked. 'Well, we thought you wanted to play with it in the water before eating it. We knew you'd never be able to catch it again and thought it very funny that you'd thrown away 3,000 dobras!'

That we might have made such a mistake was an acceptable laughing matter. But it was inconceivable that we would pay good money for a turtle and deliberately set it free. They must be musing about that to this day.

7 'Si tu es pilote, où est ton uniforme?'

The hot tropical sun beamed down, vaporising the moisture into steam which wafted up from the rainforest in fine misty plumes which amalgamated into clouds. Cooled down, the moisture condensed and fell back onto the trees in bursts of life-giving rain. This impressive primeval natural cycle unrolled before our eyes as we droned along above northern Gabon and Cameroun, like a pesky fly, towards the Central African Republic. French pilots describe such forest as *champs de persil,* parsley fields, a perfect depiction of the colour and apparent texture of the forest below. We reflected sadly on an appalling statistic given to us by a forester in Gabon: eighty per cent of the trees cut are wasted, either not collected where they fall, left to rot in port, or washed out to sea where they become a shipping hazard. Such negligence is unforgivable.

We spotted the tiny village, a cosy conglomeration of small huts tucked against a hillside, before discovering that the same hillside flattened off into an elongated grass clearing. A precipice at each threshold gave the impression of an aircraft carrier. OBO was spelled out in bold white stones. As we touched down, Gérard braked vigorously to prevent plunging off the end into the bush below. The strip was much shorter than we had supposed and despite being well-maintained, fly-in visitors were extremely rare in this remote corner of the Central African Republic. We were soon surrounded by curious villagers and children. A number of soldiers appeared: they were on R&R from duty at Bambouti, 100 kilometres away on the Sudanese border. It was closed because of bad feeling between the two countries, so not even motor vehicles passed by. A gendarme led me off to deal with the formalities, while Gérard stood guard. Obo Poste village was delightful, its red earth streets spotlessly clean. In the dilapidated hut which served as the gendarmerie, I completed the immigration forms to the furious squeaking of tiny bats hanging from the ceiling. In due course, the police commissioner was summoned from a funeral, and our passports were inscribed: *Vu de passage à l'aéroport d'Obo pour Kenia.*

Back at the airstrip, Gérard was chatting to Jean, the met officer, who operated a battery-fed radio on which he sent weather reports to Bangui. So Obo was not totally cut off from the rest of the world! He had armed himself with a

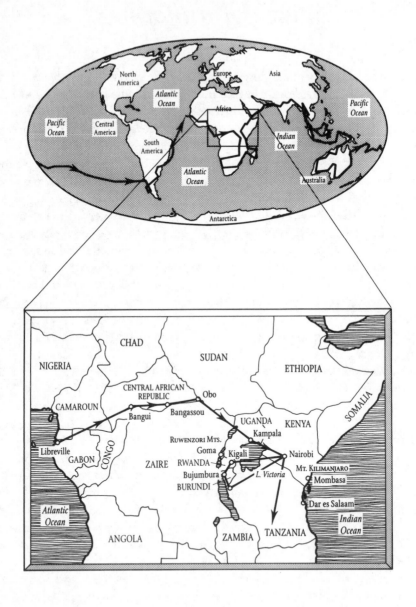

big stick and would periodically hurl himself, with a great roar, at the throng of children. They would take to their heels screaming with delight and inevitably creep back for more. This daredevil game continued until the witching hour. The equatorial dusk is sudden. One minute they were all there, staring and giggling. The next, when instant darkness fell, they were gone.

'You aren't going to sleep out here, are you?' Jean asked, suddenly nervous, visibly horrified as he saw us preparing camp.

'*Bien sûr!* Why not?'

'Aren't you afraid?'

'Afraid of what?'

'*Les mauvais esprits,*' he whispered, eyes lowered. Evil spirits had been furthest from our minds. We said no.

'*Eh bien, les hyènes?*'

No, we weren't afraid of hyenas either. If anything, we were afraid of the take-off next morning. Gérard had paced the field, confirming his worst fears: loaded with sufficient fuel for the 1,270 nautical mile leg to Nairobi, it was going to be tight, even at dawn temperatures. One advantage of the hilltop airstrip was that we would be projected into space over the precipice.

We settled down to make supper: *pot-au-volaille* packet soup, followed by spaghetti with tomato purée and a fine bottle of Macon, the last of a caseful bought in Accra. The night was jet black, darker than it had been even in Timbuktu. The stars reigned supreme, unchallenged by man-made light. Not the glow of a candle emanated from the village. Only shrill wailing wafted on the wind, accompanied by the thump of distant funeral drums. Gérard stretched out his sleeping bag on top of the left wing. I slumped on the back seat as uncomfortably as slumming it in an overcrowded 747, and waited for the hyena. The smell of spaghetti did not inspire them.

By 04.30, a pre-sunrise limbo-light chased off the darkness. We made tea as soft golden sunshine illuminated the treetops, casting gentle shadows on the grass. Veils of thin mist floated ethereally across the empty plains beneath the plateau. Leaving three lines like fat snail tracks on the dewy grass, we taxied to the last possible inch of runway, and warmed up the engine. On full power, *Romeo* strained against the brakes like a nervous racehorse in the starting box. Upon release, the wet grass glued us down, so that we proceeded in terrifying slow motion as we waved regally to the handful of early risers assembled on the sidelines. By the time we reached the precipice, still winding up to only sixty knots (normal take-off speed is eighty knots), our heaving hearts had sunk well below waist level. Gérard yanked on twenty-five degrees of flaps, as the runway literally fell away from beneath the wheels and we dipped over the edge, stall warning screaming. The treetops braced to catch us as *Romeo*

71

plummeted, gaining the precious speed which enabled the air flow to keep us airborne. It was a close shave.

After a mere twenty-five miles, we crossed illegally into Zaïre. The bush stretched lazily to the horizon, on either side, just as God had sown it. Occasionally, a tiny village of mud huts floated by. And so it continued, until three hours later we guiltily skirted the sizeable Zaïrean town of Bunia and rushed on to the green hills of Uganda beyond glassy Lake Albert. Just forty miles to the west towered the dramatic blue Ruwenzori mountains, the fabled Mountains of the Moon.

Uganda lay like a huge, ruffled patchwork quilt, millions of tiny farmed plots and villages moulded onto hilly contours, interspersed with papyrus-choked lakes and linked by tight webs of dirt roads. Entebbe Control, unperturbed by our sudden appearance on their network without a flight plan or clearance, offered in clipped African-English to radio our ETA to Nairobi. It took thirty minutes merely to cut just a corner of the crocodile-infested waters of Lake Victoria, the world's second largest freshwater lake, to reach Kenya. Later, the escarpment of the dry, volcano-dotted Rift Valley merged into the Ngong Hills, beyond which a proliferation of corrugated iron huts and maize plots gave way to the herbaceous borders, swimming pools and red-roofed mansions of the Nairobi suburb of Karen, where Karen Blixen's farm once lay.

Wilson Airport, for light aviation, lies at 5,500 feet bordering Nairobi National Park. It was Gérard's first landing at altitude. Being noon, air density was low, provoking a frighteningly fast descent bringing us down like a stone short of the runway. Increasing to full power, he kept vaguely airborne until we thumped, with relief, onto the threshold. A hard landing! The place was buzzing with light aircraft and action, quite unlike anything we had seen so far, even in the wealthier West African countries. Suddenly, for the first time since we left Brazil, a customs officer wanted to inspect our luggage, asking us to lay the items on the tarmac. None of the twelve countries we had visited until then had shown the slightest interest in the aeroplane or its contents and we had become blasé. After our camping spree in Obo, the cabin was stashed with unwashed pans, dirty clothes, rumpled sleeping bags and pee bottles. Embarrassed, I visualised the horrified glances we would receive from the parade of tourists in brand new safari suits striding out to Air Kenya's DC 3s. I tried to deter the officer, warning him that the plane was a terrible mess. This convinced him I had something to hide. He strode towards it with gleeful determination. When I reluctantly opened the rear door, he almost turned white.

'Whaaat a meeeess!' he exclaimed.

I flashed a told-you-so smile.

'How can I possibly inspect this?' he asked incredulously.

'Well, you don't have to bother. It's only personal effects,' Gérard intervened. 'We've been camping,' he added, as if we had just been away for the weekend.

'Ummmmmm,' the officer articulated, unsure how he could profit from the unappealing disarray. Most aircraft were tidily packed and it was easy to home in on the odd bottle of whisky. He stared at Gérard. 'That's a nice shirt you're wearing,' he finally resolved.

It seemed an easy way out. 'Would you like it?'

'Not this one. I want a clean one. You can bring it to the office,' he said. He turned to walk away. 'And bring one for my assistant too,' he added.

So there we were, in Nairobi, my birthplace. A warm feeling of contentment swept over me. It had looked impossibly far on the maps spread on the floor in Rio de Janeiro. Unattainable, in fact. Unlike Gérard, an optimist to whom everything is possible, I had doubted we could survive those thousands of miles. Yet, why not? Luckily, he had not let my something-might-go-wrong fears hold us back.

Kenya became our base for four months. It is a country of astounding natural beauty. We travelled far and wide, resuscitating childhood memories in Nakuru, Maasai Mara, Amboseli and Tsavo. It is impossible to tire of the spectacular horizons: yellowing savannahs teeming with wildlife; snow-capped mountains and àwe-inspiring volcanoes; lakes shimmering pink with flamingos. In close-up, the kaleidoscope necklaces of the Maasai; the toothy yawn of a lioness; the tip-toed elegance of the gerenuk; the gaudiness of the Superb starling; the silhouette of a thorn tree against the setting sun.

The first engine service in Ouagadougou had involved little more than changing the oil, basic checks, and fixing a leaking oil seal on the left gear. But every hundred hours, the service is more complete. Although we carried a good supply of tools and spares, it was important to have access to a proper workshop. CMC at Wilson Airport came to our help, especially to fix a bent aileron. How did we bend an aileron? A hefty male baboon had jumped onto it at Tsavo!

One day, we set off overland to Tanzania in an old VW Kombi Camper we had bought for general transport. The road to Namanga passes through unspoilt scenery, thick with thorn trees and sudden rocky outcrops where the Maasai graze their cattle in harmony with herds of zebra, impala, Thompson's gazelles and giraffe, all visible from the roadside. As a child, we never went anywhere beyond Nairobi without seeing wildlife roaming free by the roadside. My sisters and I would compete to see who spotted which animals first. I was pleased to see that, though to a lesser extent, this was still possible in modern Kenya. At lunchtime, we drove off into the *bundu* near a quiet spot beside a herd of Grant's gazelles, with a direct view across the plains to Kilimanjaro. The magical peace of the bush was broken only by the grunt of zebra, until a young Maasai *moran* (warrior) materialised from nowhere. Bunches of earrings hung from the elongated lobes of his ears, and his decoratively plaited reddened hair dangled down his back. He wore the customary red cloth, tied over one shoulder.

'*Gari mgonjwa?* Is the car sick?' he asked, peering disconcertingly, for he was completely cross-eyed. I assured him the car was well and offered him water. '*Nataka maji kunua?*' He nodded, his cross-eyes bulging with amazement as Gérard filled a glass of pristine water from the electric tap at the sink. He tasted it hesitantly – a car that could be milked of water? – and then drank it down. We invited him to eat with us. From the water boiling on the camp stove, he gathered we were making food of some sort, but the dried-up yellow sticks that we put in it were new to him. He announced that he had to keep an eye on his goats and departed at a gallop.

Moments later, from the same direction, an older man approached. Cross-Eyes must have advised him of the wonders of the *wazungu* car. Unabashed, he marched straight up to the open door and peered inside, making *eeeeeh* noises, until Cross-Eyes returned. We had only one bottle of beer. Gérard offered them each a glass. Cross-Eyes refused, perhaps in deference to his elder, who took both glasses, whooshed them straight down, belched loudly and sat back, the picture of contentment. When the spaghetti was ready, we dished it onto four plates. The old man shook his head vigorously. Cross-Eyes accepted out of curiosity. The dry sticks we had put into the water had been transformed into long white worms that wriggled on the plate. He watched carefully as we toyed at the worms with forks and, with great sucking noises, transported them into our mouths. With admirable deftness, he imitated us.

'Yuuuuukkkk (or the Maasai equivalent thereof)!' A mouthful of spaghetti splattered on the red earth as he pushed the dish away with contempt. Smirking contentedly, the old man shot him told-you-so glances. We had to hide our amusement. Cross-Eyes was disgusted by our food, and that was that. We would feel the same if presented with the Maasai standard fare of fresh blood collected from the jugular of a living cow, and mixed with milk. But would we have the courage to spit it out in front of him?

Such was their fascination with us that they had momentarily forgotten their goats. We showed them how, with the binoculars, they could keep an eye on their animals from afar. The old man was enthralled with this magic and passed them to Cross-Eyes, jabbering excitedly. But poor Cross-Eyes, he looked and looked, with one eye and then the other, but clearly could not focus on anything and handed the contraption back with disdain.

We offered them a lift back to the main road, the direction in which the goats were heading. After manipulating their walking sticks and long, exceedingly sharp spears into the back, the old man climbed in front with Gérard and I sat behind with Cross-Eyes, who had evidently never been in a car before. As the Kombi lurched off over the rough terrain, he began to rock back and forth, bellowing: 'Uh-huh, uh-huh, uh-huh!' With a grin, he elbowed me so that I would imitate him. To humour him, I did so. It was a mistake. If for a moment I ceased rocking madly and grunting uh-huh uh-huh, he would dig me sharply in the ribs, and say 'Mama, Mama, uh-huh, uh-huh.' The old man, who had been in a car before and was above such tomfoolery, stared stonily ahead, forcing Gérard to maintain a sense of decorum. But I knew Gérard was watching these antics in the rear view mirror with ill-concealed hilarity. Peeved, but not allowed to stop, I lurched about bawling uh-huh uh-huh. At the main road, after warm handshakes, they ambled off to gather their goats.

'You can't imagine how daft you looked! Uh-huh, uh-huh!' Gérard immediately burst out laughing. 'Uh-huh, uh-huh!'

'Oh shut up!' I sulked. 'He wouldn't let me stop.'

'Uh-huh, uh-huh!' he roared on. And on. And on.

Grrrrr!

The profusion of banana trees in Rwanda was glowing bright green in November 1990 when we visited it, in the days before Hutus and Tutsis tragically inserted themselves into everyday newspaper vocabulary. Before its latest ethnic war, Rwanda gained fame from *Gorillas in the Mist*, the film which brought worldwide attention to Dian Fossey's fight to save the mountain gorilla. Only an estimated 400 mountain gorillas remained in the world, including those which, despite their innocence, are kept behind bars for mankind's pleasure. Although posters of the film abounded, the Rwandan government was unhappy that it had shown too much of the gorillas and not enough of Rwanda. Worse still, it inferred that Dian Fossey was murdered by a Rwandan, but an American was the prime suspect. Wayne McGuire was a PhD student studying gorillas at Karisoke Research Centre; Dian's camp up at 10,000 feet on the saddle between the Karisimbi and Visoke volcanoes, when her skull was hacked open on Boxing Day night in 1985. Tipped off by the American Embassy before a Rwandan court could try him, McGuire fled the country. *In absentia,* he was charged together with Rwelekana, one of her faithful members of staff (later found dead in his prison cell), and found guilty of her murder. There is no doubt that both were scapegoats. Dian's aggressive defence of the gorillas and her intransigence had rankled many, from the poachers to their bosses and unscrupulous Western zoo collectors whose ignominious trade she tried so hard to disrupt.

Rwanda had realised its gorillas were enormous dollar-earning potential. That visitors were prepared to pay US$175 to scramble about in a muddy forest for a peek at them was worth capitalising on. Visits to wild gorilla groups are restricted to eight tourists per day for one hour and bookings have to be made well in advance. Our guidebook advised that the entrance fees for the Parc National des Virungas, across the border in Zaïre, were only US$60 per head. It seemed worthwhile saving US$200.

Leaving the plane in Kigali (locally pronounced Shigali), we took a bus to Gisenyi along an immaculate highway which curved graciously between highly cultivated, verdant terraces. Once richly forested, there was not an indigenous tree to be seen, only bananas, pines, grevilleas, and infernal eucalyptus. Gisenyi, Rwanda's equivalent of Montreux, was where the Belgian colonial elite had built mansions beside Lake Kivu, tucked in an alpine setting of blue mountains. Thousands of bodies were thrown into its translucent waters during the 1994 genocide. Lunching at the run-down Hotel Edelweiss on the only dish available – *steak, pommes frites* (another legacy of the Belgians to whom Rwanda had been mandated in 1916) – we tried to remember we were in Africa.

Thunder clouds loomed over the mountains, and we were thankful not to be flying. Although Goma has an airport, we had no clearance for Zaïre. Instead, we walked briskly to the border post two kilometres away, where immigration officials on both sides were too sleepy to bother us. Goma town centre, a pitted avenue named after President Mobuto, was lined with empty stores looking onto a shaded cement broadwalk. Violent Nyiragongo volcano looms threateningly behind the town, providing ubiquitous volcanic dust which enhances the general atmosphere of dirt and neglect.

At the Institut Zaïrois de Conservation de la Nature, we discovered that Zaïre had understandably joined the lucrative gorilla bandwagon. Entrance fees had risen to US$100. We didn't mind. It would still be a privilege to see the gorillas. However, the park was not of easy access. We had to reach Djomba, a small village seventy kilometres away, but the daily bus to Rutshuru had left. The only option was to hitch. We waited despondently at the roadside as the skies blackened and Nyiragongo disappeared into a fast-approaching storm. Providence sent an empty minibus under the command of an army sergeant who wanted to practise his English. We leapt in thankfully as the deluge struck.

It was dark when we reached Rutshuru, where we settled into a spotless room at the Polish mission. At midnight, we were woken by a brass band. Or so it seemed. In fact, it was torrential rain beating on the tin roof. It played for four hours.

Church bells roused us at six. It was pleasantly cool as we strolled back to the Djomba turn-off. Then our hearts sank. The day before, where a small stream had gurgled under the bridge, muddy water twenty metres wide swirled across the road. The bridge had disappeared. There was nothing for it but to wade. The cold muddy water was a minor inconvenience. The biggest blow was that no vehicles would be able to cross. Hence, no lift. It was twenty-six kilometres to Djomba, and another seven to the park. Our appointment with the gorillas was at dawn next morning. It was the only booking we could get. We had to make it.

The sun was shining, the air crisp and clean after the tempest. It would be a long walk, but we had no choice. We shrugged and set off light-heartedly. By midday, footsteps, hearts and backpacks were considerably heavier. No vehicle had passed in either direction and the road began to climb. All around the land was intensely cultivated and inhabited. The fertile black-brown soil produced maize, beans, manioc and cabbages. Surprisingly, there were few goats, and even fewer cattle. The compounds contained round huts and little grain houses of woven reeds, resembling huge baskets, set on piles of stones crossed with planks. As we passed, children would rush out, waving and shouting 'Go'mning' and 'Ow ah you'. We were surprised they should address us in English rather than French, but these were the only two phrases they knew. Six kilometres short of Djomba, we were rescued by a truck headed for Uganda. It dropped us at the park turn-off, where a sign merrily announced seven kilometres to the gate. We had already walked for five hours but were greatly cheered by the sign and resumed the slog in good spirits. At six kilometres, the road climbed sharply, but no gorilla-bearing forests appeared. After an hour, the local people were still telling us *'Encore six kilomètres'*. Perhaps it was their little joke, but it had a crushing effect. We were exhausted.

When, much, much later, a sign announced *'1 km au Parc National'*, Sylvestre, a waiter on his way to work at the hotel, admitted this lie was *'pour ne pas décourager les touristes'*, because the truth was closer to three. Gérard struggled valiantly, his spindly legs protruding beneath the weighty rucksack to bury themselves in burr-covered socks and muddy boots. The track ended suddenly against a hillside. Sylvestre pointed heavenwards. Roofs and tree-tops perched another kilometre atop the steep grassy incline. I just wanted to lie down. Gérard forbade me to do so, not even for a moment, as another thunderstorm was fast approaching.

The final ascent was excruciating. Swirling mists descended, obliterating the valley below. We staggered up to the fog-bound hotel verandah, utterly exhausted. It had taken three hours to walk the 'seven' kilometres. We had barely sat down when the storm exploded. Sylvestre chose that moment to announce that our *gîte* was another 500 metres uphill. Through lashing rain, we discerned the vague outline of a rooftop near the forest. It was a never-ending nightmare. We extracted the orange plastic raincoats, purchased with great foresight in Goma, and struck out for the hut, slipping on the sodden grass and falling over several times. When we reached it, completely drenched and miserable, the dark smoky *gîte* offered no relief. The wood for the stove was wet. Gérard tried in vain to light it, making the interesting discovery that *Time* magazine is indestructible – it will not burn! We felt cold and wretched. Our legs ached horribly.

Just after nightfall, two young Belgians arrived out of the dripping darkness. They were accompanied by the *gardien du gîte* who magically lit the fire, spending a practised age blowing at unwilling embers, thick smoke blasting into his eyes. The flames cheered us up. We pooled our rations and over a bottle of Carioca rum they had brought, exchanged travellers' tales. Bart and Hilda had spent ten months travelling in Zaïre's Heart of Darkness and were unaware that the Berlin wall had come tumbling down. They were incredulous, but no less so to learn we had walked to the park from Rutshuru. Bart immediately offered us a lift back to Goma the next day in the van they had hired. This excellent news worked like a sedative. We slept like babes.

A crystal-clear morning greeted us, but the barrel of water outside the hut for washing had a film of ice over it. Two guides, one armed with an ancient rifle, the other with a *panga*, led us into the dripping forest. We climbed gently at first, with frequent pauses to listen for clues.

'We don't always find gorillas,' one guide announced suddenly.

I felt crushed. It had never occurred to me that all those painful kilometres could possibly be in vain. But moments later, we came upon the spot where the gorillas had spent the night in huge nests they built on the ground, curving back the foliage. Fresh spoor, like strings of large round sausages, lay on the ground. Having chanced upon their last campsite, it was easy to follow the trail of crushed foliage through the undergrowth – too easy. That was how poachers tracked them too.

Crashing sounds ahead warned we were near. Then, unexpectedly, we almost stepped on a female and a juvenile. We stopped short, breathless, but they shot us a cursory glance and continued foraging within touching distance. The female's interest was taken by a *siafu* nest in a rotten tree trunk. She repeatedly thrust a hairy arm into the hole and extracted it covered with vicious soldier ants which she nibbled off her thick fur one by one, with a gourmet's expression of delight. After repeating this procedure several times, she shot up with biting ants in her pants and took off, the juvenile in hot pursuit.

All around, the bushes were busy with gorillas. Their eyes, whether pale watery-brown or black, were bright and full of expression. Their thick glossy fur was immaculately clean despite the wet, muddy surroundings. A strange, not unpleasant, smell pervaded the air and wafted up the slope behind them. The family group numbered twenty-four, and was led by a silverback, a dominant male whose back-hair, with maturity, takes on a sophisticated silvery-grey. He was well aware of our approach long before we saw him. Before habituation to humans, he would have risen on his legs and beaten his chest in warning. Instead, he shot us withering glances as if to say 'what a clumsy bunch you are', and continued chewing leaves. His sense of superiority was overpowering: he literally looked us up and down and understandably disapproved of what he saw. There was no doubt that we, and the rest of our bloodthirsty race, merited his scorn but he tolerated our presence. Gorillas are gentle giants and he had learned these daily visitors from humanoids meant no harm.

Without the reassuring presence of the guides, we would have been cowering behind trees a good distance away. Yet, we were close enough to stretch out and touch him. His coat was magnificent: thick, healthy, brilliant-black and well groomed. His shiny black eyes said it all, epitomising the humanity so evident in his facial expressions, in his hands. He shinned up a small tree to survey the terrain. Crack! Silverback and branches came crashing to the floor, narrowly missing our astonished upturned faces! Embarrassed by this undignified descent, he ambled off. For two hours, we accompanied them. The young ones would sometimes make a playful dash between our legs, as if daring us to play tag and see what Papa would have to say.

We left them on the hilltop, in dense forest. Within a few yards, we had crossed the park boundary and found ourselves in millet fields where not a tree remained, for miles around. Unrelenting human pressure will be the gorilla's demise.

Back at Kigali airport, we could never have been mistaken for first-class passengers. Gérard staggered along under the dirty rucksack, and I was no picture of elegance with a scruffy supermarket bag and muddy boots. As we made our way to the gate, a guard challenged us.

'Where are your boarding cards?'
'We don't have any, because—'
'*Bah alors*, show me your tickets!'
'We don't have tickets because —'
'Where are you going?'
'We're going to a small plane.'
'What plane?'
'It's at the Aero Club.'
'*Alors, où est le pilote?*' he asked with gleeful disbelief. Surely two such lamentable tramps could not be travelling by private plane.

'*Le pilote, c'est moi,*' Gérard replied.

The guard then knew for certain that this must be a lie.

'*Huh! Si tu es pilote, où est ton uniforme?* If you're a pilot, where's your uniform?'

He gave us a great idea. Back in Nairobi, we bought ourselves pilots' shirts. They opened airport doors for us everywhere.

8   'If you land, you will be arrested'

We had taken off from Nairobi at dawn, and were fifty minutes short of the Malawi border when Gérard called Lilongwe Control on the HF. What was our clearance number? The trouble was, we didn't have one. Despite various telexes and phone calls over the previous ten days, Malawi had not replied to our request. Our Kenyan visas finally expired and we were obliged to move on. Twenty anxious minutes followed, as Gérard yelled into the crackly HF, explaining that we had made the official request within the stipulated six-day time-span. We continued our approach as the controller investigated with the authorities. No such request had ever been received, he said. We were forbidden to land.

Our destination, Karonga, lay on the northern banks of Lake Malawi. Gérard offered to alter our destination to Lilongwe, so that we could show our telexes to the authorities, proving our sincerity. The answer was a consistent no. No to Karonga. No to Lilongwe. No to anywhere in Malawi.

'If you land, you will be arrested,' the controller warned. There was a pause. 'But your request is duly noted,' he added, 'and we will advise you if it is approved in six days' time.'

'Please, sir,' Gérard appealed, 'can't you explain to the authorities that we have negative landing permission for Tanzania, and negative clearance for Kenya. We are unable to remain airborne for six days!'

Lilongwe was unmoved. 'I must warn you again: if you land, we will arrest you.'

It was Friday. A weekend in jail in one of Africa's poorest countries was not an exciting prospect. We had ample fuel. Perhaps we could continue to Harare, even though we had no clearance for Zimbabwe? We put this idea to the controller.

'You have no clearance for overflight. If you overfly Malawi, we will arrest you.'

How exactly they planned to do that was a mystery. We flew in decision-making circles over magnificent green thorn-bush plains from which sudden outcrops of bare rock protruded. Signs of human settlement were scant. What if we overflew Malawi, regardless of the threats, and then encountered similar problems in Zimbabwe? We only had overflying and not landing permission for Tanzania, and although we knew their authorities to be sticky, we had to come down somewhere. It would be a predicament wherever it was. Mbeya

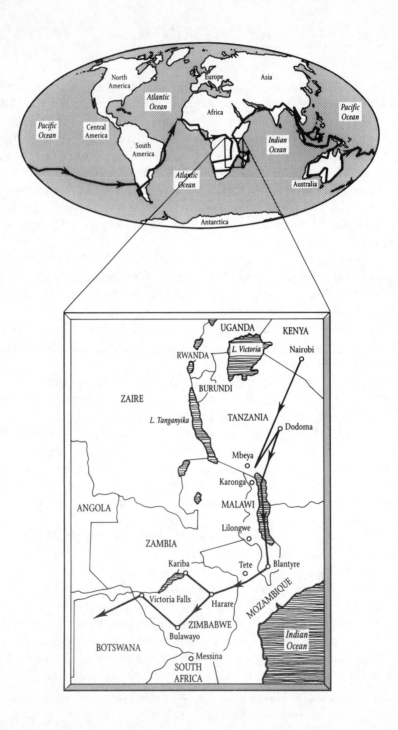

lay only forty nautical miles away, but was unlikely to have the telecommunications we would need to resolve our problem. Dodoma, destined one day to become the capital of Tanzania, seemed a better option although it was ninety miles back.

'Report on downwind leg,' was all the controller asked when we announced our unexpected intention to land.

This boded well. From the air, Dodoma had none of the trappings of a capital-city-to-be, its network of dirt roads making it identical to any African village. We expected an unfriendly reception to our unauthorised landing. On the contrary, we were heartily welcomed by all manner of people – immigration police, airport personnel, and the fuel attendant who rushed over with his manual fuel trolley. The controller, a hefty cheerful fellow called John, was remarkably understanding and immediately offered to send a plea to Lilongwe by telex while Gérard tried to telephone. Calls had to be booked through Dar es Salaam. It was futile. Lines to Malawi were down. In due course, John received a firm negative from Lilongwe, repeating that we must wait six days. As a special favour, however, they conceded permission to overfly to Zimbabwe. We consulted the Jeppesen Manual: if Malawi's six days' prior notice was a problem, Zimbabwe was worse! Seven working days! In the scorching midday sun, we stood beside the plane trying to decide upon a course of action as the fuel, expanding in the heat, dripped out of the overflows and sizzled on the hot tarmac.

'I can help you contact Harare,' John offered. He was a godsend. Another telex went off, requesting a clearance at short notice under extenuating circumstances. Even if we received a positive reply from Harare, it was already too late in the day to start a 900-mile journey. John insisted on booking us into 'Dodoma's best hotel', the Jambo Ree, promising to call as soon as he had news.

The room was clean, but the walls were black with hungry mosquitoes which had procreated in the two large buckets of shower water provided. We lay down, hot and weary, and deliberated on our two options: fly to Zimbabwe without a clearance and accept the consequences, or fly to South Africa, which only required a flight plan. Both would entail overflying Malawi, Mozambique and Zimbabwe without permission. To complicate matters, in those pre-Mandela days, we could not lodge a flight plan from Tanzania to South Africa. We would have to flight-plan to Harare, even if permission was refused, and divert to Messina, the northernmost tip of South Africa.

There was a loud banging on the door. 'Telephone!'

Gérard rushed across the courtyard to reception. It was John. Harare had replied. Permission granted! Not having to spend a week in dreary Dodoma was worth celebrating. In the bar, we chanced upon a couple of American relief aid pilots. They warned us an aircraft had been shot down six months earlier when flying over Mozambique between Lilongwe and Harare. A longer, safer route was recommended from the southernmost corner of Malawi. They stressed we must reach Harare by midday. Zimbabwe is renowned for ferocious afternoon thunderstorms which result in more annual deaths by lightning than any other country. We would need to start at dawn.

It was still dark when we pushed through the unguarded airport gates. Not a soul appeared. In the main building, a bare light bulb shone down on the duty officer. Gérard attended to the flight plan while I prepared the plane. Apart from the whine of mosquitoes, all was silence.

'*Jambo!*' a voice shot out of the darkness. I jumped, and turned to find a Maasai warrior, clad in red robes, two spears glinting. He told me in Swahili that he was from Arusha, but worked as an *askari* guarding the missionary aircraft in a hangar further on. After a brief chat, he moved away and took up the customary one-legged stance beside the fire engine where he began to sing. Soft, sad chants filled the dawn air with homesickness. I listened, entranced, as the carmine glow grew to the east. Earthly objects emerged from the darkness to assume their own identity and I noticed stains on the tarmac under each wing. Fuel had leaked out the day before due to heat expansion, but this should have stopped at night. Gérard's footsteps crunched back over the gravel towards me.

'Look at these fuel stains!' I called out naively.

He guessed immediately what had happened.

'Somebody's been draining fuel.' He rushed over and opened the wing caps on both sides where fuel had brimmed the day before. 'Shiiitt! The baaastards! We're almost empty. They've taken at least two hundred litres.'

The Maasai joined us, peering at the floor for clues.

'*Mwizi.* Thieves,' I said.

'*Mwizi? Apana. Apana hapa!* Not here.' He seemed surprised, tut-tutted and shook his head.

If he had been guarding the missionary planes as he claimed, he must have seen who had done it. To empty the tanks through the drainers is a slow operation. Furthermore, 200 litres of gasoline is no light load to cart away without a vehicle. We suspected the culprits were the soldiers who guard the airport, of whom there was no sign that morning. Understandably, the lone Maasai was unlikely to challenge them, nor to tell on them for fear of reprisals. Recriminations would resolve nothing. The thieves were gone. It was a sobering thought that we might have taken off with two virtually empty wing tanks, in the firm belief that they were full and, once airborne, disbelieved the gauges. We had to refuel. Fortunately, the fuel attendant lived close by. He punctuated the refill flow with an endless stream of so-sorries.

Airborne at last. The sun's rays cast elongated tree shadows on the dry plains. The Great Ruaha River led us over unspoiled *nyika* to a mountain range, and over a huge swamp to the first signs of cultivation. Ten minutes from the border, Gérard called Lilongwe Control.

'XRAY-ECHO, you do not have permission to overfly Malawi.'

Oh God, not again!

'Lilongwe, there must be a misunderstanding. Yesterday you sent a telex to Dodoma authorising this flight.'

'Affirmative, XRAY-ECHO. But that was for yesterday. Today, you do not have clearance. You may not enter Malawian airspace. Acknowledge?'

Gérard drew deeply from dwindling reserves of patience. 'Lilongwe, your clearance arrived too late. Unable to make the flight to Zimbabwe yesterday in daylight hours. Requesting immediate clearance to proceed.'

By the time approval came through, we had already decided to continue regardless and had crossed the 9,000-foot Kipengere Range and the Livingstone Mountains that plunge into spectacular Lake Malawi. By the time we reached Blantyre, it was cowering under a tremendous storm. We skirted the worst of it and proceeded south through heavy rain until it was time to veer south-west. Our route took us forty miles south of the infamous Tete corridor, a major road linking Harare to Blantyre and favourite haunt of Renamo guerrillas.

Ninety nautical miles of war-torn territory lay ahead. We were grateful for the protective cover of rain, assuming the guerrillas would not waste ammunition on an invisible drone in the sky. As a precaution, we climbed to 12,500 feet, hopefully beyond their missile range. Suddenly the rain belt dissolved into clear blue skies, and we felt as vulnerable as a dog crossing Piccadilly in the rush hour. The mighty Zambezi stretched its lazy waters between sandbanks and islets across our path. A disused railtrack peeped from beneath overhanging trees as it weaved between low hills. We were rigid with tension, expecting a missile any moment, but the empty bush unfolded harmlessly. When at last we crossed into Zimbabwe, the land became alive with confident habitation and agriculture, so different from the rare huts and abandoned fields of the terrorised Mozambicans.

Conversations in Zimbabwe are disconcertingly punctuated with 'before the war' and 'after the war'. These are not references to the Second World War, but to the War of Independence, a bloody war between black Zimbabweans fighting for self-rule and Ian Smith's white-minority government. Independence finally came in 1980. Despite the horrors of that recent war, we found black

Zimbabweans remarkably lacking in bitterness towards whites, whereas the reverse was not always the case. We asked one old-timer about the mysterious ruined city of Great Zimbabwe, capital of a Shona empire dating from the thirteenth century.

'The Zimbabwe ruins?' he replied. 'Never been there. Don't need to go all that way to see Zimbabwe in ruins!'

We did. Roads in Zimbabwe are straight and smooth, quite unlike any we had travelled in the rest of Africa. But there was a chronic shortage of buses for public transport. Long queues waited at every bus-stop, so we frequently picked up passengers. Gibson, a store-keeper, talked of the ingratitude of the whites who were so quick to condemn President Mugabe as a Marxist, when they had him to thank that there had been no reprisals against them, no witch-hunting nor questions about what any individual, black or white, had done during the war. Atrocities had been committed by both sides, and black soldiers had fought alongside whites in Smith's government forces. Many whites had been justifiably wary after losing a war into which they had entered with schoolboy glee to take potshots at *kaffirs*, but they had been left in peace. Graham, a farmer in a crisp crimson shirt who spoke faultless English, worked on a resettlement scheme planting maize, cotton and soya. 'We have to be thankful to the white people,' he said. 'They taught us many things. They built these good roads. Our forefathers were not clever. They would never build roads like this one.' In his view, there was only one problem with Zimbabwe. 'We are too many,' he said. 'We must have less children.' This humble Zimbabwean farmer was more enlightened than the Pope on the impossible equation of too little land to till versus too many mouths to feed.

Zimba in Shona means huge house, and *bwe* stones. The outer wall of Great Zimbabwe's Great Enclosure rises a majestic nine metres of beautifully cut granite blocks laid without cement, a masterpiece of architecture. In places, the walls are five metres thick. The enigmatic conical tower inside the enclosure soars to over ten metres, but it is solid. What can its function have been? No one knows. It is not clear when the city was founded, but it thrived between the thirteenth and fifteenth centuries, and probably peaked at a total population of 20,000 before being abandoned, it is widely presumed, because the surroundings had become too degraded to support it. This settlement was no isolated city, but part of an empire stretching all over Zimbabwe. Differing views on the origin of the city and its builders add to the mystique.

We had befriended Pierre and Antoinette Jaunet, who operated a Catalina, the 'last African flying boat', along Imperial Airways' routes from Cairo to Victoria Falls. They lent us their Land Rover to explore Mana Pools, on the banks of the Zambezi. At the Wildlife Department Office, an obese American was rubbing his hands at the prospect of shooting a lion and an elephant. Our game-viewing entrance fees were a paltry US$2 each for four days. People pay more to go to the cinema for two hours. If the park increased these absurd prices, it could depend less on hunting to pay its way.

At Ndungu, our bush camp-site, there was not another human being in sight or earshot. We set our tent on a twenty-foot bank overlooking a potential ox-bow lake beside the meandering Zambezi. Our nearest companions were a hippo family which wallowed and bellowed in a pool twenty yards away. A pair of red-legged black-winged stilts strode the waters beneath our bank, yapping and pouncing on morsels in the shallows. On the sandbanks, African pied wagtails, rear ends swinging incessantly, chased insects amongst foraging Egyptian geese and a pair of hamerkops (whose name derives from the blunt crest which gives them a hammerhead). Along the riverbank, a colony of white-fronted bee-eaters nested in holes, their calls like the squeak of gym-shoes on a wooden floor. Their vivid arrangement of green back, red lower throat, beige belly, turquoise undertail, white throat, thick black smudge of eyeliner, and a long curved beak would rival the most exotic carnival costume.

By day, we contemplated the rugged hills that rose sharply on the Zambian riverside opposite. A few thatched huts were the only indication of human presence. It was wonderful to sit quietly on an unspoilt patch of Africa with only wild animals for company. At night, we slept fitfully on the hard ground as the nocturnal noises crescendoed around us. The hippo emerged to graze and the groaning of a lion drew so close that it seemed only metres from where our hearts pounded inside our fragile tent. The consumptive cough of male impalas warned the master of a nearby herd that there was eager competition about. It is said that a male impala can service sixty hinds in a single night! Later, elephants came to drink. Their black hulks silhouetted against the moonlit water as they splashed contentedly from sandbank to sandbank.

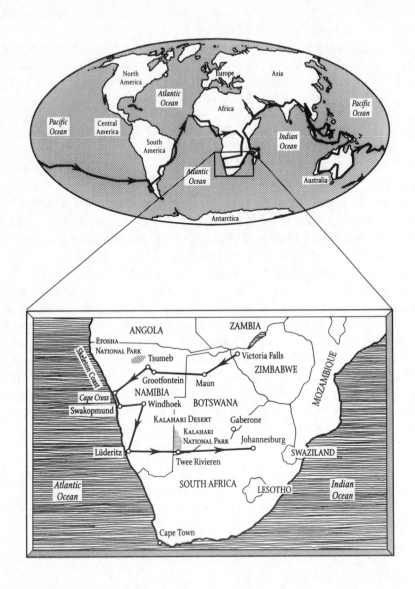

9 'My name is Englishman'

After nine months in each other's company twenty-four hours a day, we were happy to be joined in Bulawayo by two dear friends, Kees, a jovial easy-going Dutchman, and his French wife, Michèle, a kindred animal lover. Having left luggage and equipment in Nairobi for collection on our way back north, there was ample room. We felt honoured that they should entrust their lives to us over the empty skies of southern Africa and it was fun to share our travelling experiences.

After Victoria Falls, where the mighty Zambezi flings itself into a deep chasm forming the largest curtain of falling water in the world, we left the nourishing influence of the river. The vegetation thinned out, its arid flatness scratched by rare tracks which, according to the map, fizzled out in the Kalahari Desert to the south. Onto these parched plains pour the waters of the Kubango River, sidling down from the Angolan heights to form a veritable Garden of Eden, an intricate swampland called the Okavango Delta. In Botswana, a country composed primarily of desert, rain brings forth the richness of life. It is intimately associated with wealth, so the Setswana word for rain, *pula*, is also the name of the currency.

Maun, an overgrown village of mud huts and shabby concrete buildings, is the launching pad for visits to the Delta. Ignoring Michèle's warnings that she loathed camping, we outvoted her and chose to go to Oddball's Campsite – 'for people who do not want to be pampered but want the Okavango experience at first hand', rather than an expensive luxury lodge. In the store in Maun where we sought provisions, she scowled at the uncleanliness of the place. During the twenty-minute flight to the grass airfield at Delta Camp, she stared stonily ahead while apple-green swamps dotted with tree-covered islets whizzed below.

'My name is Englishman,' said the young Tswana who awaited us at the grass airfield. I thought I had misheard.

'Did you say Englishman?' I asked him.

'Yes. That is my name. Englishman,' he answered naturally. 'It's a half-hour bush walk to camp. We must hurry to reach it before sunset, as there are no lights there.'

This information did nothing to improve Michèle's mood. We set off down the airfield, chasing our elongated stick shadows under the bemused regard of a family of baboons seated on an anthill. The golden evening gleamed off the green grasses, enhanced by a backdrop of doum palms and dark rainclouds. Arriving at Oddballs, Englishman insisted we retrieve what we needed from the equipment shop so as to erect our tents before nightfall.

'You can take this damn sleeping-bag back, Kees,' Michèle pouted. 'I'm not sleeping in that. It's filthy.' (She was right, but there was no choice.)

There had been no tinned *soupe à l'oignon* or *coq au vin* in the store in Maun, so dinner consisted of tins of beef casserole heated on a gas burner. They contained lumps of dog meat complete with gristle, soggy carrots and flaccid potatoes.

'I'm not going to eat this. It's disgusting,' Michèle spat. She was absolutely right, again. We ate it anyway, drowning the taste with gin and tonics served under the glow of a hurricane lamp in the rustic bar. The cheerful barman's name was Botha, yet no name could be more symbolic of the hated neighbouring *apartheid* régime than Botha!

What might have been a peaceful night's sleep surrounded by nature was rudely disturbed by tirades of vomiting in the bushes behind our tent. Some raw young Englishman had misjudged his resistance to alcohol. The rowdy dawn chorus came as a relief. All around, the swamps were coming alive. A giant kingfisher, with russet breast and fine white-spotted black coat, vociferously evicted a pair of diminutive pied kingfishers each time they settled on a branch to contemplate the water.

Michèle, by her own confession, was a bad riser at the best of times. Gérard and I had learned to give her a wide berth in the early morning and fled to the deserted bar to contemplate the placid water lily-choked river. Two *mokoros*, regional dug-out canoes, rounded the bend and pulled ashore. These would be our means of transport into the swamps. I feared there would be further protest from Michèle, especially since one of the polers was a one-legged, middle-aged man. The other, an agile young Tarzan, helped his elder manipulate his crutches to shore. He hobbled over and introduced himself as Royal. Between Englishman, Botha and Royal, it was not surprising the camp was called Oddballs! The younger man at least had a local name, *Gabanne* pronounced Habani. Michèle put on a brave face as the *mokoros* were loaded, sinking alarmingly low under the weight of tents, food and saucepans. By the time we piled in, the freeboard was only three inches. Gabanne led the way with Kees and Michèle. Polers normally stand, but Royal had to tackle his job, which he did with dexterity, from a sitting position. We glided gingerly off into the swamps, holding our breath as we tried to accustom ourselves to the unnerving balance of the canoes. The thought that Royal may have once upon a time left his leg in the jaws of a crocodile encouraged us to concentrate. Capsize seemed a certainty.

Under an unblemished blue sky, we slid over transparent peaty water, weaving among water lilies where elegant jacanas, or lily-trotters, darted on elongated toes. We would round a bend and surprise hosts of blacksmith plovers, which would take to the air complaining bitterly. Fish eagles soared overhead, piercing the swamps with their haunting cry. Periodically, we would pull into the bank to bail out excess water. The heat throbbed intensely, so when, on one occasion, Royal ordered 'You swim here', it was an inviting prospect. The absence of his leg made us hesitate. Trying not to look at it, I asked about crocodiles. The point was not lost on him. With a merry laugh, he explained it had been amputated because of an infection thirty years before. So Kees, Gérard and I plunged joyfully into the transparent black water. It was so delicious, we drank gulps of it as we swam. Michèle stayed prudently on the bank, concerned about bilharzia, an endemic tropical disease caused by parasitic blood flukes carried by snails.

All day, we slid up-river, filled with a glorious sensation of utter calm. Gabanne and Royal poled along effortlessly at a speed that suited them. To our amazement, they talked non-stop as if recounting lengthy epics, drowning the delicious silence of the swamps. In the rare moments when they could think of nothing to say, the only sounds were the poles swishing through the water, the rustling of grasses as unseen creatures scuttled away, and unadulterated bird-song. Sausage trees, named after their enormous fat seed-pods which dangled on strings, formed island-copses on higher ground between the flood plains. A campsite was selected under one such tree where vociferous grey-and-green Meyer's parrots argued in the branches. We were impressed how respectfully Gabanne treated his disabled elder, despite having his own workload almost doubled. As we set up camp, there was a roll of thunder, and a solitary cumulus darkened the sky above us. Michèle refused to participate in the chores to make the point (in case we hadn't understood) that she never wanted to go camping. Rain fell with a vengeance. Michèle and I took refuge, each in our respective tents, whilst Kees and Gérard stripped off and enjoyed the refreshing shower, whooping like kids and jumping in puddles.

'I hate this. I want to leave.' Michèle grumbled from her leaking tent. A crisis was brewing, despite Kees' patient cajoling. Once the rain stopped, she refused to join the game-walk. 'I'm not going. It's stupid. There are no animals here.'

Royal looked crestfallen when he learned she would stay in camp. Because of his handicap, it was his duty to stay behind if one of the party did not go. He had been eager to accompany us on his crutches, and promised to find us buffalo. I fervently hoped there weren't any around. Gabanne led the way int the bush. The undergrowth dripped down our back and within moments we were drenched and muddy. It was lucky Michèle had not come along. As we ventured across patches of savannah, the lowering sun glinting off the grasses, nothing stirred. She was probably right; we would see nothing, but it didn't matter. It was a beautiful evening.

In fact, Gabanne soon spotted tsessebe, a darker version of hartebeest, grazing in taller grass. They raised their heads warily to monitor our progress, transmitting their apprehension to five giraffe and some zebra beyond them. A distant herd of lechwe, antelope with long hooves adapted for swampy grasslands, became jittery at our approach. It was exhilarating to face them on foot, on equal terms, rather than from the metallic cocoon of a motor vehicle.

As we returned to camp, the black silhouettes of doum palms, rocked by the breeze, were stroking a fiery-red horizon. Michèle's clothes were draped on twigs around the camp fire.

'*Ça suffit!* Tomorrow, I'm going back to Maun,' she declared. 'The bloody tent leaks. All my clothes are soaked.'

'You should've come with us,' Kees chirped bravely. 'We saw all sorts of animals, including baby giraffe.'

Dinner this time consisted of tinned chicken curry, tinned spaghetti, tinned vegetables and tinned peaches. No improvement on the night before. Michèle, of course, wanted none of it. We were ravenous and happy to eat her portion. Beaten, Kees assured her they would return to Maun in the morning. It meant explaining to Gabanne and Royal that one couple would return to Oddballs in the morning, the other would continue. They were distressed, convinced they had displeased us and some complaint would be lodged against them. They became glum. On the other hand, once Michèle knew she would sleep in a 'nice hotel' the next night, she reverted to her usual cheery self. The improvement was so dramatic, we opened the KWV Roodeberg, the sole bottle of wine we had brought, and chatted merrily beside the hypnotic flames of the camp fire. No lion's roar could be heard, but loud plopping noises came from the bubble fish, rising to snap up insects, and falling back with a smack into the river.

The Oddballs leaflet had warned that the polers would be more perplexed by our behaviour than we would be by theirs. Long after we retired to sleep, the murmur of their voices filled the night. It was mostly Royal who spoke, probably explaining how weird white men were, based on a lifetime of experience. Gabanne hummed in agreement and asked occasional questions.

A glorious morning dawned, and Gérard and I were delighted not to be returning to Maun. Michèle emerged in good spirits, and admitted the place was astoundingly beautiful. Kees snapped at the chance to persuade her to stay on. The previous day's tantrum forgotten, she readily agreed. Royal and Gabanne found the change of plans typically puzzling, but were enormously relieved.

Namibia became independent on 21 March 1990. When we landed at Grootfontein on 1 March, it still 'belonged' to South Africa, to whom it had been mandated by the League of Nations in 1920 after South African troops, on behalf of Great Britain, defeated the Germans at Otavi in 1915.

After clearing immigration, we proceeded immediately across the Otavi and Jakkalsberg ranges, and arrived at Tsumeb, the pot at the end of the rainbow. Its copper ore-body is so rich it contains over 180 minerals, ranging from gold and silver to beautiful azurite crystals and arsenic. Ten of its mineral substances are unique. Yet its mundane modern main street, lined with vacant parking meters, was conspicuously empty. The scarcity of living souls is a reality of life in Namibia, which has one of the lowest population densities in the world: 1.5 people per square kilometre. What brought us to Tsumeb was its proximity to Etosha National Park. The unimaginably vast Etosha pan exposes 6,000 square kilometres of blinding white salt flats, the bottom of a mighty, ancient lake now home to dust-devils and shimmering mirages. The animals take refuge from the midday heat in the thickets, but the odd zebra or oryx trekking across a corner of the gleaming saltpan forms a diminutive silhouette against the low, empty horizon.

The Portuguese navigator Diogo Cão was the first European to venture so far south down the African continent. At a point now known as Cape Cross, famed for its seal reserve, 'in the year 6685 after the creation of the world and 1485 after the birth of Christ', he erected a cross in honour of *o excelente e esclarecido Rei Dom João II de Portugal*.

Fog was rolling in off the Atlantic as we approached across desert plains streaked with intricate patterns of flash-flood water courses moulded over millennia. This was the Skeleton Coast, stretching up to Angola, its rocky shores a cemetery for fifteenth-century caravels and modern ships alike. The Benguela current sweeps up from Antarctica, bringing cold air masses which clash with the searing desert heat and form treacherous fogs. They cause deaths at sea, but save lives inland where desert plants, insects and animals harvest this moisture to survive. A tarred road led the way over the grey rocky desert to where Swakopmund basked in evening sunshine, smaller than we imagined from its fame as Namibia's summer resort. We circled for some time in thirty-knot gusts trying to find the landing strip. Bare gravel stretched in all directions beyond the eastern urban limits, dotted with strange circles of green grass. The sight of a man pulling a golf trolley made us realise these were putting greens! When we discovered a long straight scarred with heavier wheel marks, we deduced it was the runway.

As we tied down, a tiny Cessna landed, not on the airstrip, but beside the terminal shack. The wind was so strong that it simply stopped in mid-air, like a helicopter. The pilot, Erick, a German, gave us a lift to town. He had lived in Swakop since 1955 when the population stood at 2,000. It had since grown to 20,000, fingering its way out into the desert. Despite the desert setting, the town is unmistakably Germanic. The railway station, built in 1901, a graceful building topped with a church-like steeple, looks as if it had been plucked from a Bavarian village and dropped on the sand. In a nearby garden, among red cannas, stands the German Colonial War Memorial, a statue of battle-torn soldiers in remembrance of the casualties of the German colonial forces, the Schutztruppe, which used a camel cavalry in its murderous campaign against the rebellious Herero in 1904-5. A solemn group of Germans was gathered before it. To our astonishment, they suddenly burst into the German national anthem. In one of the main streets, we were horrified to find a shop doing a busy trade in SS uniforms, swastikas and posters of Hitler. Most popular were car stickers showing a map of Namibia, described as Deutsch Südwestafrika with the German eagle firmly planted in the middle. Yet, Germany had lost Namibia seventy years before, and true independence was only days away.

Windhoek, the capital, was another world, one of green tree-covered hillsides, snuggled at 5,600 feet in a valley between the Khomas Hochland, the Auas and Eros mountains. A few Germanic buildings remained as isolated eccentricities among functional concrete edifices being raised on addresses such as Kaiserstrasse and Goringstrasse. From the front façade of the Tintenpalast, the seat of central government, hung an enormous yellow canvas inscribed with the new constitution: '. . . Whereas we the people of Namibia have finally emerged victorious in our struggle against colonialism, racism and apartheid . . .' Just yards away, a road sign still pointed towards Administrasie vir Blankes – Administration for Whites – and another to the 'Non-European Hospital.'

On Kaiserstrasse, Nazi memorabilia ceded to an appalling array of wildlife parts. Michèle and I ventured into one such shop, where shrivelled lion heads grinned painfully from pelts spreadeagled on the floor. Snarling baboon faces and surprised ostrich heads stuck out of wooden wall plaques. Bedspreads boasted eighteen jackal pelts, while the skins of cheetahs, despite being listed by CITES (Convention on the International Trade in Endangered Species), cost a mere US$350.

'Zis ees gut example of ze excellent taxidermy,' the shop lady vaunted, pointing to grotesque stools made of severed elephant feet and shiny brass ashtrays glued onto dainty antelope hooves chopped off above the ankle.

'Your shop is like an animal cemetery,' Michèle said.

'Zank you,' the frau replied automatically, believing she had been paid

94

a compliment. She did a double take, and turned puce. 'Vat did you zay?'

'I said your shop is like an animal cemetery,' Michèle repeated.

'Zees animals are legal! Zey are taiken from ze naiture conservaition. From ze parks.' She was blind to the irony of killing animals in their only sanctuaries. 'Zees ees ze conservaition. Ees not poaching, laik zose black men,' she fumed.

'It's a bloody disgrace,' Michèle retorted. We fled, giggling, followed by a volley of curses.

The Namib Desert, reputedly the oldest in the world, is known as the Sand Sea. It stretches from the seasonal Kuiseb River to the perennial Orange River, the border with South Africa. From above, it presents a varied display of colours and textures: beige sand streaked with riverbeds; red sand scarred with massifs of black rock; areas swept completely flat, others rippling with tumultuous dunes.

An engine failure would be a very serious matter. We had ten litres of water, irresponsibly little for four people. It would be impossible to walk out of this *région inhospitalière*. Control's blasé attitude to reporting points was surprising but we breezily preferred not to dwell on the efficiency of search and rescue services. Accidents happen to others. I nevertheless watched anxiously for the Atlantic, where at least our manual water desalinator could be put to use. The coastline, when it came, was harsh and unwelcoming, pounded by vicious waves and offering no shelter, no sign of habitation until, at Hottentot's Bay, a spit of land protected a cove where half a dozen tiny huts and fishing boats staved off isolation. Who could want to live there, so completely cut off by a treacherous ocean and a hostile desert?

Even Lüderitz had the air of a derelict town. Overlooking a natural harbour, a handful of incongruously pretty German houses and a Teutonic church stood defiantly on the bare rocks. The uncontrolled airstrip lay ten kilometres inland. Windhoek had warned of thirty-five-knot crosswinds. Sheets of sand billowed across the tarmac, often obliterating it completely. It was a frightening turbulent landing which Kees and Michèle braved well. They were great company and never complained about the drivers! Lüderitz, the first German settlement in South-west Africa, was founded in 1883 by Franz Lüderitz, a merchant from Bremen who persuaded Bismarck to declare the region a German protectorate. In the museum, a photograph of the town in 1910 showed not a great deal had changed in eighty years. Only the shanty towns on the outskirts were new.

In a safari tours-cum-hardware store, we negotiated a ride to Kolmanskop with a lady called Marion. We asked her how she saw the new Namibia. She did not look upon independence with relish. 'Do you know, I can't even go away on holiday, because when I come back my shop'll be empty. They steal everything, these blacks. So, I'll let my stocks run down, and then I can go to Europe for three months to get away from it all.' She had a more serious dilemma. 'I'm going to apply for a Namibian passport but I tell you, if they want me to give up my German one, forget it. I won't give it up for anything. Then they might make me apply for a work permit. Isn't that ridiculous? A work permit in my own country where I was born!' Patriotism, it seemed, was a veneer as thin as a passport.

Kolmanskop lies near the airport. In 1914, it was a sophisticated town with mod cons – electricity, elegant mansions, an ice-making machine, beer hall, ten-pin bowling, theatre and casino. It boomed on diamonds, discovered glistening on the sand during the laying of the Keetmanshoop railway line in 1908. After the post-war slump in world diamond sales and the discovery of richer deposits in the Orange River, Kolmanskop was abandoned. Although still legislated as a 'Diamond Area' into which no one may trespass without permission from Consolidated Diamond Mines, a subsidiary of de Beers, today it is a ghost town. The panes of imported glass in the porches and bay windows are shattered, and an army of dunes has besieged the town, sending zillions of foot soldiers in the form of grains of sand whistling through the parlours and bedrooms of its erstwhile elegant mansions.

The skyscrapers of Johannesburg rose in the haze beyond the countless baby-blue swimming pools adorning the manorial lawns of the north-western suburbs. Rand airport was an industrious hive of light aircraft, all too first-worldly to believe. There was a neat terminal building with proper waiting-rooms and even loo paper in the toilets. Despite the air of efficiency, however, there were no taxis. In South Africa, we discovered, everyone who mattered had their own car. Obliged to hire one, we joined the fleet of Mercedes-Benz and BMWs on the four-lane highway into the city. We were headed for Bruma, where fashion boutiques and trendy restaurants sprouted beside an artificial lake with a twee mock tower-bridge. It was hard to believe this was not America.

'Where you come from, there are no blacks, are there?' asked Edith, the house-maid at the flat where we were staying.

'Oh yes, almost half the population in Brazil is black.'

'Really?' She was astounded. 'I have never seen white people shake hands with blacks like me before. Like you did when you arrived.' She laughed and went on, 'I once worked for a Portuguese lady. Where she comes from, she said she had a maid who is white! I can't believe it. Imagine telling a white maid to clean shoes! Surely it's not true?'

'It's true, Edith. In Brazil, for example, maids can be white, black or coloured. Everybody mixes. It doesn't matter.'

Her eyes opened wide with incredulity.

Those were the days of white minority rule, when white people did not venture readily into Soweto, South Africa's famous ghetto. We wanted to see for ourselves what conditions were like, but were afraid to drive there alone, so we joined a tour organised by a black businessman. The idea of sitting in a minibus to gawp at people living in a slum was anathema to us, but curiosity overcame us.

Originally established by the government as a dormitory for mine workers, Soweto's population of two and a half million encompasses nine tribes and spreads over a hundred square kilometres. In 1976, over 600 people were killed in the Soweto Uprising, a student protest march against the government ruling that all schoolchildren learn the hated Afrikaans language. Pete, the lively driver, started by showing us the large attractive houses of the wealthier section, which would have been the pride of any white neighbourhood. They had swimming pools, tidy lawns and well-fed dogs, a side of Soweto never portrayed on television. It is how a small minority live, but the only South African on the tour was an Afrikaner receptionist at the Carlton hotel on a famtour. She was flabbergasted to see the smart houses, muttering resentfully that *they* were better off than many whites. It was unacceptable to her that a handful of blacks had, against hefty odds, managed to raise their standard of living. She had hoped to find nothing but hovels, to justify her belief that blacks were good for nothing.

In the 'middle-class' section was Mandela's house, painted in the ANC colours. Close by, on the whitewashed garden wall of Archbishop Desmond Tutu's house, graffiti warned: SOWETO IS NO ZOO FOR WHITE RACIST TOURISTS. GO HOME AND TAKE YOUR STOOGE GUIDE WITH YOU. Tutu's wife had a reputation for throwing things at the tour van if it came by when she was around. We already felt like intruders, so the sign hit a nerve. Pete kept the van rolling.

Lower down the hill, the illegal squatters camps were what we had imagined Soweto to be. One-roomed shacks were constructed of anything – cardboard, corrugated iron, old planks of wood, plastic sheeting. Children played in the refuse in the narrow alleys. Women, armed with plastic containers, waited in a line at the water pumps. It was early evening, and the air thick with nauseating sulphur fumes where supper was being cooked over low-grade coal fires, making the scene infinitely more depressing than Rio's *favelas*.

Then, just fifteen minutes away along the highway, the slum of untouchables evaporated and we were back in Johannesburg's glitzy world of Rolex watches and painted fingernails.

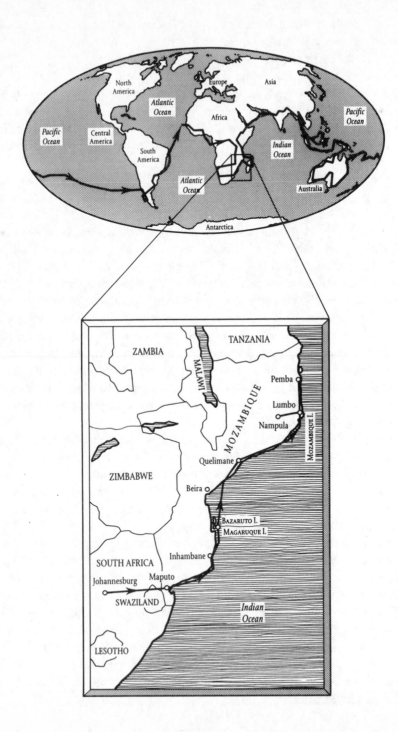

10   *'Abaixo os bandidos armados!'*

It was difficult to believe Mozambique was a country riven by civil war. No soldiers nor security guards patrolled Maputo airport, although the air buzzed with Russian helicopters. For the last fifteen years, Mozambique had been in the grip of a brutal civil war between the Frelimo Marxists, who took power in 1975, and the South African-backed Renamo guerrillas intent on destabilisation. Known in Mozambique as *bandidos armados* for their senseless violence, Renamo targeted schools, hospitals and churches, killing men, women and children with equal vigour.

The manager of a local cargo airliner offered to introduce Gérard to the aeronautical authorities from whom we needed permission to fly within the country. But he warned that in the space of one year, his aircraft had been shot at thirty-five times. Just the week before, a tyre was blown off by a land mine. The incidents could happen in any part of the country at any time, and he believed it would be impossible for us to obtain permission to fly around as tourists. The authorities were understandably strict and the slightest schedule alteration had to be approved. He suggested we claim to represent a relief organisation, but we could not see how to make this sound convincing. On our initial clearance request, we had stipulated the purpose of our visit as 'tourism'.

Paulo Muxanga, the Director General of Civil Aviation, was delighted we could speak Portuguese, unlike most foreign pilots flying in and out of Mozambique. When Gérard produced a copy of an article about our trip in the Brazilian press, he brimmed with enthusiasm. Telling us that Renamo did not have heat-seeking missiles, he gave us carte blanche to fly wherever we wished, though he strictly recommended following the coastline, out at sea, to be on the safe side.

Avenida Julius Nyerere led from the stately Polana Hotel past ministry buildings and placards proclaiming VIVA O PARTIDO SOCIALISTA into the centre. Lourenço Marques, as Maputo used to be called, had been a beautiful city of mansions set in tropical gardens shaded by flamboyants and jacarandas. Now, on the ground level of impersonal Eastern European concrete blocks, with cracked walls, shattered windows and broken lifts, Mozambican women washed dishes, clothes and babies at water pumps. The soiled, foul-smelling water flowed out into the street. No one we met in Maputo had ventured beyond the city limits for years, so we had no idea what to expect in the provinces. We took off for Inhambane, obediently flying out at sea to avoid becoming a target.

'We really must be nuts,' I mused to Gérard. 'Or dead stupid.'

'Why do you say that?'

'What the devil are we doing tootling around a country where everyone's killing each other or dying of hunger?'

'Well, we want to go to Madagascar, right? Mozambique's in the way.'

'So why don't we just fly there direct from Maputo?'

'You don't like flying across water, remember? The shortest feasible route's from Pemba to Mahajanga. We've been through all this already.'

'OK, but I dislike the constant threat of being shot at.'

'We're quite safe over the sea. And over land too, above 8,000 feet where the missiles can't reach us. Don't worry. We'll be lucky. We always are!'

'So is everybody, until their luck runs out.'

Through the binoculars, I scoured the landscape for signs of an enemy. All was quiet. Beyond kilometres of empty white beaches, a wall of dunes carpeted with natural vegetation dropped into blue lagoons where flocks of flamingos glided in pink unison. Behind, sandy unproductive fields and occasional derelict huts.

Inhambane's whitewashed houses and tree-lined streets were remarkably well-kept for a war-torn country. Afternoon sunshine warmed the quicksilver waters of the creek flecked with the dirty white sails of miniature dhows carrying passengers to Maxixe. The two-storey block of Hotel Baia stood unpoetically at right angles to this view. It had seen better days, but the linen was clean and there was a shower in the cupboard. It cost 4,150 meticais (US$1.80).

The manager proudly advised us that an international singer would be performing that evening. What stars, we wondered incredulously, came to Inhambane? Guilherme da Silva, it turned out, was a local boy who lived in Portugal. This elevated him to the rank of *cantor internacional*. We arrived at the hall at midnight and the audience trickled in at one a.m. At last, Guilherme da Silva, dressed in a shiny crimson jacket, arrived. He promptly plugged into a synthesiser and sang a pre-programmed selection of Julio Iglesias tunes! The crowd loved it, but our great expectations of a night of vibrant African music were shattered. A thin, bespectacled man accompanied by a *mulata* joined our table. From his superior manner and Leninist beard (very popular in Mozambique), we guessed he must be a party official. He solemnly introduced himself as Alexandre Luiz Mendes, Provincial Director of Agriculture. Once he had established that we were not aid workers, he dropped his formal pose and invited us to dinner at his house the following day.

We turned up in our travellers' attire of jeans and T-shirts, embarrassed to find him in a smart shirt and tie. He had also invited Antônio, a Brazilian agronomist working with the United Nations, who had undergone a complete culture shock upon arriving in Mozambique.

'You can't imagine the poverty here,' he told us when Alexandre was in the kitchen attending to roast chicken. 'Whole families live in one-roomed huts made of straw, with bare earthen floors.' Being from Paraná, a prosperous agricultural state in southern Brazil, he seemed unaware that many of his own countrymen in the north-eastern Brazil live in similar conditions.

We had given Alexandre a kilo of Brazilian coffee. He was so proud of this gift, he placed it in prime position in a glass-fronted cabinet. Antônio stared at it longingly throughout the meal, but Alexandre preferred to keep it on show. After seven months in Inhambane, Antônio had only been a few kilometres out of town. Nowhere was immune from attack. It was difficult to tell on which side the aggressors were, since Frelimo soldiers took to banditry in their spare time, and Renamo rebels wore stolen Frelimo uniforms. Renamo had attacked Massingo, a nearby town, three days earlier, killing several people at the hospital. But this was all just sensationalism to Alexandre: he had an important post and a difficult job to do; the war was incidental. He was anxious to get on with rebuilding his country, planting casuarina trees to prevent erosion, and eucalyptus for fuel. We admired his dedication.

Even if Gérard was unafraid, my dread of being shot at each time we made a flight did not abate. Having learned that herds of elephant had supposedly taken refuge in the impenetrable swamps of the Zambezi delta, he had a bout of pig-headedness. Contravening the rule of only flying out at sea, he swooped over the estuary in the hopes of seeing some. Fortunately, besides no elephants, there were no *bandidos* about, only a lone male waterbuck standing majestically in a patch of yellow grass.

In fact, Mozambique's elephant herds have been annihilated. Renamo had to exchange something for the arms Pretoria provided. The currency was ivory. Before the CITES ivory ban, South Africa loud-mouthed about the importance of the ivory trade because making the elephant lucrative was its only hope of salvation. It smugly pointed out that other African countries were too corrupt to control poaching, whereas in their police state, elephants were so numerous that they had to be culled 'for their own good'. A glance at South Africa's annual ivory export statistics are self-condemnatory. If the number of elephants culled were truly represented by the tusks they marketed, their own herds would have been wiped out. Much of the ivory they flooded onto the international market came from Mozambique and Angola. In exchange for arms. Culling elephants 'for their own good' is a lie. Elephants are culled for 'our' good, so that we can make trinkets or piano keys of their incisors, and vegetable plots or housing estates out of the bush they have wandered peacefully for millennia. The total African elephant population in 1979 was estimated at 1,300,000; by 1989, only 625,000 remained. If there is not enough room for them, it is because *Homo sapiens* is out of control, not because there are too many elephants.

Ilha de Moçambique, a Portuguese version of Zanzibar, was the country's capital until 1907. This small island, completely covered with buildings, is attached to the mainland by a single-lane causeway, well-guarded and surprisingly still intact. Lumbo airport lies on the mainland nearby. The grass on each side of the tarmac strip rose three metres tall, making us suddenly fearful of an ambush. But there was no one in sight, not even when we rounded the corner to the tiny terminal building, until an old man hobbled onto the patio with two red batons to direct us.

'*Decolar que horas?* What time take off?' he asked by way of welcome.

'We're going to visit Ilha de Moçambique. We'll leave tomorrow.'

'But here no soldiers to guard plane. Me don't know you coming.'

'Is it a problem?'

'*Muito sério.*' He shook his head disapprovingly. '*Bandidos armados* attack here last week. They fire houses, kill the people. Very bad. You must go.'

He urgently encouraged us to leave for Nampula, eighty nautical miles inland. The panic in his voice made it clear that he was serious. For us, it was a gamble. Should we stay and risk having the plane torched, or fly inland and risk being shot down? We chose the latter, taking off immediately and climbing in steep circles over the sea to reach 8,000 feet before daring to fly inland. Knowing that there were active Renamo about, we hoped it was true that their SAM missiles could not reach that height.

The sun was a fiery red ball setting behind dramatic rocky outcrops as we approached Nampula airport. Anti-aircraft guns and military trucks lay in wait at each threshold, the first blatant signs of the war we had seen.

To our acute embarrassment, when we arrived back at Lumbo early the next morning, several dignitaries waited on the steps of the terminal. A crowd had assembled to one side, under a scrawny tree, and numerous soldiers hung around in the background. Beaming, the old man, dressed in smart yellow and navy overalls, rushed out with his red batons and waved us into a corner. A motley bunch of Frelimo soldiers stood guard. One wore tight red trousers, a combat jacket, a straw hat and antique boots. Most were barefoot. Rusty AK47s hung from their shoulders. We were at a loss as to how to approach the waiting crowds when a twin-engined Islander landed, and we realised that the reception was not in our honour at all! The representatives of a relief fund were arriving to examine the damage caused during the Renamo attack. The Administrator of Mozambique Island, Abel Ernesto Safrão (locally referred to as *Presidente*), was there to meet them. For good form, we introduced ourselves and explained we would like to visit the island for the day and would leave for Pemba that evening.

'I shall examine your true intentions in due course. For the present, you follow along behind us,' he advised brusquely, indicating we should climb in the back of the pick-up carrying the German team. It sped us to the village where many women, dressed in threadbare *kitenge*, sat under an enormous mango tree, legs stretched straight out in front of them. Regardless of age, each had a babe in arms.

'*Viva a Frelimo. A luta continua*,' Safrão yelled, a clenched fist thrust upwards. 'The fight goes on!'

'*Continua!*' the crowd echoed, a hundred fists raised.

'*A luta continua,*' he bellowed.

'*Continua, continua, continua!*'

The ritual over, he switched into the local language, Makua, explaining who the visitors were. Clearly, the crowd already knew, which was why they were there. The honoured guest was a blonde girl of about twenty-five employed by the relief organisation. The purpose of the meeting was for her to learn what had happened directly from the victims, thereby assessing their needs. Only after insistence from Safrão did she condescend to address the crowd in hesitant Portuguese. The gist was 'nice to be here. Ummm. We'll try to send you something. Can't promise anything though.' The floor was opened for the ladies to present their grievances. After a long silence, one woman raised the courage to speak. Swaying from side to side like a schoolgirl, eyes to the floor, she said, in Portuguese:

'It was those same people who always come and take our things. I want to know what kind of life our children are going to have?' She looked stonily at the Administrator.

Silence. The shrill hiss of cicadas. The Administrator did not look impressed, and the blonde made no token murmur of sympathy. Finally, the other women applauded. This encouraged an old lady, hunchbacked and probably over eighty, to speak out. She complained that when maize was donated, the needy never received it because those in administration helped themselves or sold it. These audacious remarks generated approbatory laughter from her colleagues, followed by hearty applause. Furious, Safrão immediately wound up the meeting.

'*Viva a Frelimo! Abaixo os bandidos armados!*'

Three times the chants echoed, and clenched fists pounded downwards.

'*Abaixo, abaixo, abaixo!*'

We were all bundled back into the pick-up and raced across the causeway onto Mozambique Island. At a vast mansion reserved for official visitors, the Administrator turned on us. What was the purpose of our visit? He found it suspicious, as indeed it was, that we were mere tourists dropping in by plane.

He needed to be sure we were not spies. Again, the Brazilian newspaper article saved the day. If we were in print, we were OK.

Mozambique Island was a bustling Arab settlement when Vasco da Gama anchored here on his maiden voyage to India in 1498, thus reaching the southern limits of Arab colonisation of the East African coast. He found elaborately dressed merchants, fine workmanship and Arab dhows laden with gold, spices and precious stones. But the islanders, upon discovering the visitors were not Muslims, did not take kindly to them and the Portuguese left on unfriendly terms. Many years later, they returned to occupy the region, transforming half the island into a little Portugal which now lay decaying in the tropical sun. A young man leaning against the crumbling wall of a ruined mansion from which young trees sprouted explained that it was registered as national heritage.

'This building adds beauty to our town,' he told us solemnly. It was an extraordinary sentiment from an unemployed youth in a war-ravaged country.

11 'Vous partirez tout de suite!'

Madagascar is the world's fourth largest island. It is a unique world, a *mélange* of African, Asiatic and Arabian peoples and cultures. The Malagasy are essentially descended from Malays who first arrived in the sixth century. During the ninth century, large waves of immigrants arrived at the time of the Hindu-Sumatran Srivijaya empire. The island had been split into a number of kingdoms which, only with the 'help' of European weapons and advisers in the eighteenth century, were unified under the Merina. By the nineteenth century, a powerful modern state existed with an army and an organised educational system. However, fearing a British occupation, the French invaded in 1895 and deposed the Malagasy queen, Ranavalona III, who was sent to die in exile in Algeria. Revolts against the colonialists sprang up continually and legionnaires were despatched to quell them. Full-scale rebellion broke out in March 1947. Some 100,000 Madagascans paid for this audacity with their lives before the main agitators were executed or imprisoned. Tactics changed. Political solutions were sought, culminating in the declaration of a *république autonome* in 1958. Official independence followed in 1960.

Its capital, Antananarivo, 'City of Thousands', known as Tana, lies at 4,200 feet. From the airport at Ivato, the road to town leads through a medieval film set where street vendors spread their vegetables on the pavements in front of their two-storey red adobe houses with sharply sloping tin roofs. The facial features of the Merina people, of the *hauts plateaux,* are indubitably Asian and the clumps of houses part periodically to reveal Asiatic scenery of flooded rice paddies where ducks swim and bullocks wallow. Tana is dominated by the Palais de la Reine, where a mixture of architectural styles share the hilltop *rova* (royal residence). Sheer cliffs offer stunning views of the countryside beyond and the numerous white parasols of the famous Zoma market below. In a bout of anti-European feeling after invasions by the British and the French, Queen Ranavalona I persecuted Christian converts in the mid-1800s, throwing them off these very cliffs.

In the spa town of Antsirabe, muscular young men dozed under straw hats across the seats of their colourful rickshaws, or *pousse-pousses*. I initially contemplated this age-old mode of transport with horror, preferring to walk than be pulled by a man in a shaft. But the drivers were so assiduous in their pleas, so desperate to earn a few francs, that we ceded. After all, they saw nothing dishonourable about their profession. It was a job which provided them with a living. Local people used their services without a second

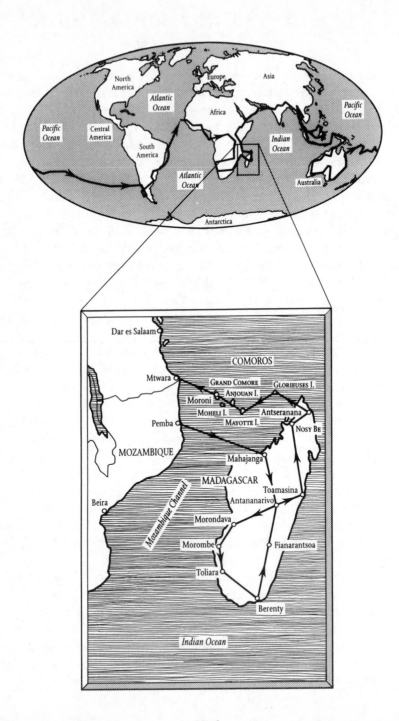

thought. As *vahaza* we paid three times the going rate. It soothed our malaise.

While crossing the Mozambique Channel to reach Madagascar, we had noticed on the charts an airport on a dot surrounded by reefs to the north-west of the island: Iles Glorieuses, the map said and, in brackets below, France. Intrigued, we paid a visit to the French Embassy to obtain permission to fly there. We were channelled to the military attaché, Colonel Jean-Bernard Vialle. A bald, sour-faced individual, he had no time for pesky visitors asking silly questions. The interview was held using, as intermediary, the gendarme seated in a sound-proof, bullet-proof tinted glass kiosk. We bellowed our questions about Glorieuse to the gendarme, who conveyed them to the attaché standing sullenly in a dark doorway behind him.

'*Quelle nationalité êtes-vous?*'

'*Britannique,*' we yelled.

The Colonel made rude go-away gestures.

'Go to the British Embassy!' bawled the gendarme.

'The islands are not British. They're French. *N'est-ce pas?*'

The two Frenchmen conferred.

'*Ecoutez,* the Colonel is very busy.'

'So, who can we speak to instead?'

More unfriendly gesticulations from the shadowy attaché.

'Consult the Malagasy Ministry of Transport.'

'But the islands are not Malagasy!'

'*Excusez-moi, M'sieur,*' the gendarme replied kindly, glancing nervously at the empty doorway where the Colonel had vanished. 'There's nothing I can do. You know, we're very busy here.'

'So, is that the official answer? Consult the Madagascans? Okay, we will. Too bad about the consequences!'

The gendarme shrugged. It was not his problem.

By contrast, Remi Rahagalala in the Malagasy Civil Aviation Department received us warmly, offering us a seat in his office. We told him of our visit to the embassy to request permission to fly to Iles Glorieuses. He laughed heartily and confirmed that, as far as the Malagasy authorities were concerned, we were welcome to go there. So we did.

First, we went exploring *la Grande Ile*. From the air, we witnessed how Madagascar, once cloaked in rich forests, now faces the world's most serious erosion problems. Muddy-brown rivers weave between bald hills scarred by red ravines and carry a precious booty of topsoil to the sea. Only five per cent of the forests remain. In Tana, we had struck up conversation with a logger from La Réunion who had come over in search of *palissandre*, a valuable hardwood much sought after for making furniture. He was in a hurry because he knew that in twenty years' time, there would be nothing left. Timber concessions, he told us proudly, are clear-felled 'to make the land good for agriculture'.

Beyond the gorges of the Tsiribihina River, large stretches of grey-green semi-arid bush were unmolested, except for lot demarcation lines. The Malagasy refer to this area as *le désert*. In fact, it is dry scrubland where slim-line baobabs, cacti and aloes have adapted to the harsh conditions. In the clearings around scattered homesteads, bare earth, sometimes reddish, sometimes sandy, spread like gangrene. Cultivation only deteriorated the land, leading to desertification.

We had given ourselves a wide margin on the flight plan in order to explore the spectacular Manambolo River gorges. When we resumed contact with Tana Control upon approaching Morombe, there was panic in the controller's voice. He reprimanded us for not maintaining contact, but we were having increasing difficulty with the HF radio and began to suspect a fault. After much fiddling with the dials, Gérard turned round and saw that the HF antenna had detached itself. It bounced along the tarmac behind us as we landed at Morombe. Gérard repaired it beside the pole and palm-frond terminal, before an astonished audience of jet black children who squatted respectfully at the edge of the tarmac in the scorching sun.

Albert, who had immediately offered his services as *gardien de nuit*, cycled into town to fetch us a lift. He returned in the car of a smooth young Indian called Assim who told us that Les Dattiers was the only hotel in town. He stopped outside a grocery store in Morombe's sole street, shouted and hooted several times. A skeletal, blond Frenchman emerged, red eyes squinting in the sunlight, and promised to come to the hotel forthwith. We proceeded to a firmly shuttered white house and waited.

'*Le patron arrive ou pas?*' Gérard asked.

'*Le patron, c'est moi*. Patrice is just the manager,' Assim replied curtly.

Faux pas. We had fallen into the trap of presuming the hungover white man was the boss, despite the young Indian's clearly superior possession of his faculties!

Although once united with Africa and Australia in the ancient continent of Gondwanaland, much of Madagascar's fauna and flora is unique. Man's rapaciousness eliminated the flightless elephant bird (over three metres tall and weighing 500 kilos) in the seventeenth century. The giant lemur, the size of a small gorilla, has followed the same sad path. Ninety per cent of the world's lemur species live in Madagascar, where they once flourished because of a lack of predators. They are endearing prosimians, a suborder of primates whose bulging eyes inspired them to be named after the Lemures, the ghosts of the afflicted dead in Roman times who returned to vex the living. Today, the destruction of their habitat is propelling them towards extinction. Considered a local delicacy, they also have to contend with the pot.

We headed to Berenty, a lemur reserve which we knew to be located near a sisal plantation. When we found a grass airstrip surrounded by mile upon spiky mile of sisal, we circled several times in doubt. There was only a tiny patch of forest nearby. Surely this could not be the famous reserve? It was. Visitors generally arrive overland, and are led in circles in the forest, never realising how little has been preserved compared to the vast hectares cleared for sisal. As we entered an avenue through the trees, bands of ring-tailed lemurs, or *maki*, and brown lemurs, accustomed to receiving bananas from visitors, sprang through the trees to meet us. A lone brown female, thin and blind in one eye, adopted us. Her fur was rubbed bare over her hindquarters, where a rope had once been attached. She was clearly on heat but in no mood for hanky panky, so after various rape attempts, she sought refuge on Gérard's shoulders, clutching his hair. That is where she stayed as we meandered through the forest, the randy males following along in a line behind us.

Climbing steeply to pass the 6,000-foot Rebord Manambien, we levelled off at 6,500 feet. Beyond, a cloud layer stretched unbroken over the *hauts plateaux*. With no visual references and no navigational beacons for guidance, we again depended entirely on the SatNav as we penetrated inland. For an hour, there were only rare glimpses of barren hills and valleys beneath, until the stark mountains of Andringitra pierced the cloud layer, shattering it like glass and enabling us to descend into Fianarantsoa.

We hitched into town. A Peugeot 504 taxi stopped to pick us up. It was already loaded with eight adults. We declined, but driver and passengers alike insisted we climb aboard. They were arriving after an eight-hour drive from Tana, but cheerfully squashed up against each other even closer to let us in. Refusing any payment, the driver dropped us in town beside a Swiss-looking railway station, complete with clock, where straw-hatted vendors wrapped in blankets gathered.

Fianar's streets were Dickensian: boys chased hoops; filthy coalmen carried baskets of charcoal suspended on long sticks over their shoulders; old men squatted on the pavements making piggy-banks from Nescafé tins. Others sold oil lamps ingeniously wrought from old light bulbs. Despite the strong sunshine, the men customarily wrapped themselves in a blanket with one end flung over the shoulder. Everyone, including toddlers, wore a hat of sorts, mostly of straw. In their voluminous colourful skirts, the women with their tanned complexions, Asiatic eyes, and long, black plaits looked startlingly Bolivian.

We had last refuelled in Tana, the only place in Madagascar where Avgas was available, and were falling short of reserves to get back. The only option was to mix twenty litres of car petrol into one of the wingtanks to increase our range. Depending upon the petrol/Avgas ratio, the engine performs well for level flight. The other wingtank was kept uncontaminated for climbing. We left Fianarantsoa for Tana knowing we couldn't afford to waste a drop of fuel. It was a resplendent winter morning, with not a cloud to be seen, so we thanked our luck and idly followed the heading calculated by the SatNav. After a while, Gérard began to suspect something was wrong. I rapidly recalculated the heading, and discovered we were already fifty miles off course.

How stupid! It's too easy to be blasé. The skies are as unforgiving as the sea. Headings and fuel supplies have a critical ratio: they should be double-checked. Mountains crinkled away into the distance on all sides, denuded of trees but offering no smooth space for an emergency landing. Why did we make such an error just when we were critically low on fuel? Sod's law! We watched fretfully as the needles of the fuel gauges dipped towards empty. Gérard, beads of sweat on his brow, ill disguised the helpless chill of panic. But Providence sent a tail wind. At last, we spotted the railway to Antsirabe, and Mount Tsiafajavona beyond. Approaching Tana from the south, we swooped joyfully over the Palais de la Reine before landing with ten minutes' fuel to spare.

Our destination on the flight plan was written in full: Iles Glorieuses. No one in Antseranana knew the aeronautical four-letter designator, even though the islands lay only 120 miles away. They were conspicuously absent from the Jeppesen Manual. Subsequent to our visit to the embassy in Tana, we learned that a contingent of the Régiment Parachutiste d'Infantrie de Marine was stationed there. What for?

Forty-five minutes later, two sandy islets encrusted in azure waters lay before us. Glorieuse was a fitting description. We deliberately switched off the radio in case we were prohibited from landing and, not to aggravate the marines into defensive attack, avoided making sight-seeing passes over the pristine beaches on which we could distinguish turtle tracks. A tarred strip stretched smoothly the length of Grande Glorieuse. It clearly catered for major aircraft. As we lost height and swung round on base leg, a number of shirtless white men stared up with astonishment.

'*Vous avez des problèmes mécaniques?*' were the first words shot at us as we opened the cockpit door. They were spoken by a short, balding man, a baby-blue T-shirt stretched tautly across his ample stomach with a single word emblazoned across it in Coca-cola graphics: *Co-Caine*. Various Rambo types with bulging muscles and crew cuts stood to one side watching quietly.

Their interest sharpened when they saw that the plane contained a woman. We disembarked, shook hands, *bonjoured* everyone and had to admit we did not have a problem.

'Are you aware that this is a private airfield?' Cocaine asked guardedly. *'Je suis l'Administrateur.'*

'That's strange. The charts say nothing about it being private. Who does it belong to?'

The question was ignored. Realising we were harmless fools, Cocaine's initial wariness ceded to authoritative indignation. 'What do you want here?'

'Well, we saw the islands on the chart. With a tantalising name like Glorieuses, we decided to come and see. They look lovely. May we look around?'

Military officer that he was, despite his trendy Cocaine disguise, he needed to find a tactful way to be rid of us.

'This is a nature reserve. You need special permission to land here. *Je le regrette* but you must leave immediately.'

'But we're very interested in nature reserves.'

'I cannot allow you to stay here. You must have permission.'

'We asked for permission. We spoke to Colonel Vialle in Tana.'

Cocaine was taken aback. His tone recovered its earlier prudence. 'So where's this permission?'

'Colonel Vialle instructed us to consult the Malagasy authorities. We did. They have no objection to our landing here.'

'Mais, c'est ridicule! It's nothing to do with *les malgashes*! *Ici, c'est la France!* Permission has to be obtained exclusively from La Réunion. You must leave immediately!'

'Ecoutez, Monsieur l'Administrateur,' Gérard argued, 'we consulted your embassy in Tana. Presumably you know Colonel Vialle?' Contempt flashed across Cocaine's face. At least we had something in common! Gérard went on: 'Well, he's the defence attaché, so he should know what he's talking about, *n'est-ce pas?* He made no objections and I did exactly as he instructed. What's the big deal? After all, it's only a nature reserve, isn't it? We've come to see the turtles.'

'I told you, this is a private strip. Nobody is allowed to come here,' Cocaine retorted, verging on foot-stamping. 'I am obliged to advise Réunion of your presence here,' he threatened, as if he was calling the War Office. Perhaps we were supposed to be daunted by this prospect, but we shrugged. This infuriated him.

'Vouz partirez tout de suite. You will leave immediately. Immediately, I say!'

'Can't we look around and leave in the afternoon?'

'*Non! Non! Non!* Out of the question. If you spend more than fifty-nine minutes on the ground here, there will be very serious consequences.'

We were wondering what these might be when a gendarme, hastily buttoning his uniform, rushed onto the scene. It was his unarguable duty, above and beyond Cocaine, to examine our passports, and he invited us to proceed to his office. As we went, one of the marines called out: 'Heh! You're lucky we weren't on target practice down at the firing range!'

They all laughed heartily, but Cocaine spun round with fury.

'There is no firing range here!' he muttered through gritted teeth.

'Of course there is!' the soldier retorted.

Cocaine looked daggers at him. *'Je répète:* there is no firing range. This is a nature reserve!'

'There is,' the soldier nodded at us.

'I tell you, there is no firing range!' Cocaine bellowed.

In the office, we were served tinned fruit juice while the gendarme meticulously copied our passport details into a register. Cocaine, trying to be diplomatic, told us Réunion only granted permission to eminent scientists and similarly distinguished people to visit the island-reserve. To play along with his pantomime, we asked about the turtles he was supposed to protect (when not at the firing range). Funnily enough, despite his position as administrator of a nature reserve, he was unable to name the turtle species that laid eggs there.

'This is a very special reserve,' he insisted. (Special enough for a firing range, we thought.) 'It must be protected from tourists.' (Prying eyes like ours.) 'I am an ecologist,' he lied. 'We have some lizard species here that don't exist anywhere else in the world. They must be preserved at all costs!'

The gendarme stamped our passports and told Cocaine he would escort us back to the plane.

'When you come back with permission,' the amiable gendarme said as we walked out to the patio, 'I will personally show you around the island. Except the military installations, *c'est clair*, but I don't suppose you're interested in those.'

Hadn't he realised we were supposed to believe the island was a nature reserve?

'In any case, you are among very few civilians to have ever set foot on the Iles Glorieuses!' he concluded cheerily.

I asked if we could fly around the island. He agreed. The marine who had so incensed Cocaine earlier invited us to lunch, waving his hand contemptuously in the direction where the latter stood. Furious that we were delaying by chatting to the gendarme and the soldier, Cocaine bellowed at them. We climbed aboard.

112

Cocaine had curtly informed us of the radio frequency, now specifically switched on for our benefit. As we taxied to the threshold, his voice came over the airwaves: 'I warn you that overflying the island is strictly forbidden. *Au revoir, M'sieur-dame, et bon voyage.'*

We never did discover what they were up to on Glorieuse.

The green mountains of Mayotte rise suddenly from the blue ocean. We made our approach over a bright-green crater lake and spectacular cliffs where white tropical birds soared, their long scissor tails flowing behind. Despite its geographical and cultural unity with the three other Comoros islands, Mayotte is classified as French Overseas Territory. Its deep water harbour is a strategic base in the southern Indian Ocean guarding the Mozambique Channel, hence the determination of the French to hold onto it, by fair means or foul. Crew-cut legionnaires with protruding ears stomp round the island like overgrown scouts in beige shorts, long socks and big black boots. In December 1974, a referendum on the four islands resulted in a ninety-four per cent vote in favour of independence. The French, however, declared that on 'their' island, Mayotte, sixty-four per cent had voted in favour of remaining French, and refused to leave.

The Comoros, known as *l'Archipel des Parfums*, take their name from the Arabic Djouzour al Kamar – Islands of the Moon. Roads twine through gnarled ylang-ylang plantations, the scent of their exquisite greenish-yellow flowers, shaped like flat-legged spiders, filling the air like a dream. Their essence is exported to the best perfume houses in France. The other major products are cloves and vanilla. It was here that the discovery of a prehistoric fish caused great excitement among ichthyologists. This was regarded with bemusement by the Comorians, who commonly eat the awesome, 300-million-year-old coelacanth, believed extinct until identified by a South African in 1938.

Ahmed Abdallah unilaterally declared the independence of the three other islands, forming the République Fédérale Islamique des Comores in July 1975. Moroni, the capital, lies on Grande Comore (Ngazidja) Island, dominated by the 7,000-foot Karthala, a volcano with the pudding-like bulge of Kilimanjaro. Legend claims that spirits hid the Queen of Sheba's throne in its active crater. Strombolic cones, fumaroles and craters pimple the face of the entire island like teenage acne. The arched and crenellated Friday Mosque shines bright white against the dark slopes of Karthala. It adorns the port where crude mastless wooden *boutres* lie like beached whales on the muddy bottom at low tide. They are used to collect supplies from ships moored off the coast. The narrow streets were a-bustle with vendors. Women in colourful *chiromani* and black veils struggled under heavy baskets or large bunches of green bananas, while their menfolk, in white *khanzus* and Swahili caps, walked empty-handed beside them.

We asked for directions in French from a handsome bronze-skinned young man. He replied in English. Mohammed was a Kenyan who lived in Moroni. He led us to a bar run by Tanzanians, where everyone spoke Kiswahili and English, and they were soon recounting the island's political intrigues: tales of French mercenaries (the main star being the infamous Bob Denard), *coups d'état*, two presidential assassinations (with the support, they say, of the French government and its secret service) . . . plots worthy of spy novels. During our stay on the islands, we found a remarkable consistency to the tales, whether we spoke to government officials, shopkeepers, students, or even French expatriates. Young Comorians would approach us in the street wanting to know what the world thought of their dramas.

The world thought nothing. Mostly, it did not know. Certainly, it did not care.

12 'You are making history in Ethiopia!'

As we headed back up towards the Horn of Africa, the Middle East loomed across our path. We knew visas for Yemen and Oman would be difficult to obtain and were happy to discover a Brazilian Embassy in Dar es Salaam. The amiable acting ambassador, Antônio Luz, immediately agreed to write a letter of introduction for us. Despite only being Brazilian residents, not nationals, we found their diplomatic staff welcoming and helpful whereas the British or Swiss consular personnel tend to receive travellers disturbing their brief working hours with indignant irritation.

The Third Secretary at the Embassy of the People's Democratic Republic of Yemen (the two Yemens were just uniting) listened disbelievingly to our wish to travel to Yemen in a small plane until we produced Antônio's letter on smart embassy paper. Our visas were ready the next day.

Oman has ancient colonial ties with Zanzibar, so it prefers to locate its embassy on the island, a mere twenty-minute flight from Dar. Since Antônio had never been there, we invited him to come with us. Upon entering old Zanzibar, known as Stone Town, our 1955 Austin taxi-driver (who had driven sedately on the open road) put his foot to the floor and raced through the winding alleyways, scattering pedestrians. We felt uncomfortably colonial as the natives scuttled aside to avoid being run over, but they were clearly used to it. When the car could squeeze no further, it halted before the Aga Khan mosque, a splendid primrose building with an imposing carved door. It was a rare pearl gleaming amid dilapidated four-storey buildings which, under coats of pastel paint, fended off mildew and decay. We had to proceed on foot. In the alleys, we stepped from black shadows into yellow sunlight, peering into minuscule stores and workshops where young men chiselled at famous Zanzibari chests. Women in black veils swished past us, the men, in less of a hurry, meandered by in *khanzus* or striped *kikois* and *kufias*, a sort of intricately embroidered cotton fez. In the heart of it all stood the Spice Inn, an old Zanzibari house overlooking the maze of alleys, with a wooden staircase leading up to airy balconies and rooms with slow, hypnotic ceiling fans.

Zanzibar is derived from the Arabic, *zenj* meaning black, and *ba* land. But the Land of Blacks is famed as the Spice Isle. Its cloves, introduced from the Moluccas in 1918, once supplied eighty per cent of the world market. Their heady fragrance still emanates from the clove warehouses that line the port.

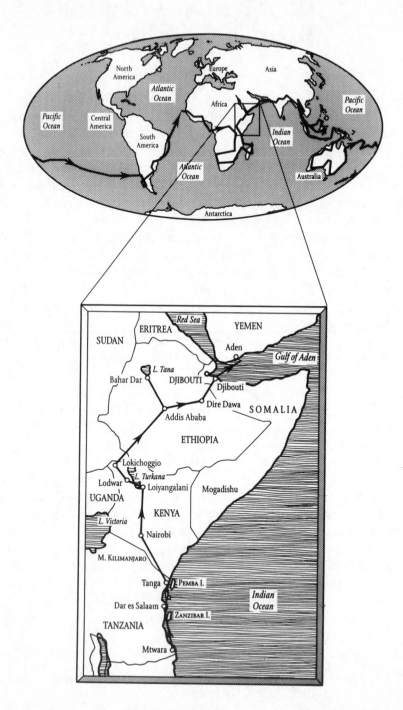

In the harbour, massive dhows, built entirely of wood, including nails and sail pulleys, still load up with people and produce for Mombasa, Tanga, Pemba, Dar and the Comoros. Crates of Coca-cola and sacks of rice are unloaded and replaced with spices and coconuts in jute sacks. Like the Comoros, Zanzibar was a seat of Shirazi princes in the eleventh century. Palatial Arab ruins, complete with Turkish baths, dot the island. After a brief spell under the Portuguese in the sixteenth century, the Omanis arrived. In 1832, the Sultan of Muscat and Oman moved his capital to Zanzibar, from where he commanded a vast empire. Zanzibar became a Sultanate in its own right in 1860, thriving on the trade of slaves and ivory until, in 1873, the British threatened Sultan Barghash with naval bombardment unless he outlawed slavery.

In our least crumpled clothes, we trailed behind António into the Omani Embassy. The Consul-General, in voluminous robes and turban, offered us tea and *petit-fours*. Regardless of what he thought of our pesky travel plans, he did not wish to appear unhelpful in front of a Brazilian diplomat. A beautiful Omani secretary, swathed in full-length, figure-hugging, green-and-black dress, completed our visa applications in Arabic script, while the Consul grilled António on which projects Brazil was financing for the Tanzanians. He was unimpressed by the reply that Brazil was not in a position to help anyone, they were in need of help themselves!

Kilimanjaro, the highest free-standing mountain in the world, rose majestically ahead of us as we flew from Tanga to Nairobi. It brought back vivid memories. Weeks before, as we had been setting off on the five-day trek, we passed a weary climber on his way down.

'It's easier just to shoot yourself,' he said.

Some thirty climbers set out each day for the 19,340-foot summit but, with insufficient time to adjust to the rarefied atmosphere, most are overcome by altitude sickness. Frederick, our guide, had lectured us: the secret is *pole pole*, go slowly, allowing the body to adjust, he said. It starts as a delightful walk through the sunny rainforest, home to groups of curious blue monkeys and the African violet. Higher up, in the alpine woodland, mist wafts through the curtains of old man's beard hanging from the lichen-covered branches. On the moorlands beyond the tree line, giant lobelias thrive in gullies among the heathers. It is a long, steady slog with stupendous views out over the whole of Africa, while the snowy summit peers down, taunting. Half our group faded out with severe headaches and palpitations (even Frederick asked for an aspirin) so that only Gérard, Hugo and Liz made it to the top.

Now flying alongside the mountain, we struggled up as high as we could go, to 14,000 feet. I took photos from the back while Gérard, headsets on, filmed from the cockpit. Brrrrup! The engine made a sort of splutter. My heart stopped cold. I looked to see if Gérard had reacted, but he continued filming. Had I imagined it? Brrrrup! There it was again. Should I say something? He would tell me not to be a fool. Although mentally prepared for an engine stoppage at some time ('We'll just glide down and land somewhere'), those engine coughs set my pulse racing.

Brrrrrruuuup! Brrrup! Brrup! Silence. Uncanny silence. Golden silence. The mountain stood there, waiting to receive us.

Gérard moved like lightning. The moment he did so, I remembered we were deliberately running the ferry tank dry. He whipped the fuel pump on and pushed the nose down to avoid stalling. After several heart-stopping splutters the purring of the engine resumed, but our pulse rates took longer to return to normal.

On 2 August 1990, Iraq invaded Kuwait. For days, we listened anxiously to news bulletins. If full-scale war broke out, our route to Asia would be blocked. There would be fuel shortages. *Revista Geográfica* in Brazil was serialising our story as a circumnavigation – it would be embarrassing if we had to stop. We resolved to continue to Ethiopia and, in the hope that war would be avoided, applied for Pakistani visas in Nairobi. We discovered a campaign against British passport holders who were charged 800 shillings (US$35) per visa, whereas a Swiss would pay a mere US$5. Similarly, an Indian visa cost Britons US$60 per entry, while a Swiss paid US$20.

In a hostile landscape of desert and lava fields pimpled with tired volcanoes in northern Kenya lies Lake Turkana, known as the Jade Sea because of the vibrant colour of its water. It is immense – 250 kilometres long – but due to the alkaline content of the water, its barren shores are not lined with grateful trees.

Loiyangalani is an oasis a short distance from the lake. Its name, Place of Trees, refers to the sudden verdure inspired by gushing hot springs which fill a swimming pool at the Oasis Lodge. When the temperature drops at night, and the Jade Sea's famous gales start to blow, its steaming water is truly inviting. Tin-roofed stores and bars line the single street upon which stands an incongruous bright-red telephone box. Behind the buildings are small straw huts, and thorn-bush *bomas* into which livestock is herded at night. Various nomadic tribes wander this desolate area and drift into town: Turkana, El Molo, Samburu, Somali and Rendille. Their spartan attire, embellished with colourful bead necklaces and bracelets, add splashes of colour to the desert landscape. Along the lake shore, flamingos, pelicans, Egyptian geese and African skimmers waded peacefully, unperturbed by the approach of the small boat which took us to the village of the El Molo. Only some 200 members of this placid, age-old tribe survive. They live in tiny, round, igloo-like palm-leaf huts beside the lake, fishing for their staple diet of Nile perch, tilapia and crocodiles. Colourful bead necklaces festoon the jet black complexions of the women and girls, sometimes marred by the adoption of handed-down rags of Western clothing.

Inbreeding is a serious problem, resulting in numerous cross-eyed and handicapped children. A tall, good-looking woman with five children, two of whom were handicapped, invited me into her hut, its diameter no more than eight feet. A cowhide lay on the floor – it was the bed she would share with the children. Motley trinkets hung on the wall, but all that was precious was carefully stored in a cardboard shoe-box. A solitary blackened pot sat on a cold hearth of three stones inside the hut. An open fire in a straw hut spelled potential tragedy to me, but it was their custom, and a reflection of the care that was taken.

From Lodwar, a Godforsaken outpost of corrugated iron roofs perched on adobe walls tucked in beside black volcanic pyramids, a tarred road led west towards blue mountain ranges. Overcome by lethargy in the suffocating heat, we figured the road must lead to our destination, Lokichoggio, which lies in a gap between Sogot Mountain and the Mogila range near the Sudanese border. Where else could it go in these desolate parts?

Sandy riverbeds streaked the spartan scrub beneath us. When a murram road turned off towards a mountain gap, we followed it. It led to a rough airstrip beside a meagre collection of huts and a large concrete building, no way resembling the UN camp we had expected, with a proper runway. As we dipped over the houses, surprised men ran out of the building in seeming panic. Rapid map consultations indicated a wrong turn. This was Oropoi. We veered away to the north. Lokichoggio airport was indeed a broad smear of well-maintained gravel running the entire distance of the village. From here, the UN was flying relief supplies into southern Sudan. We intended to clear formalities and leave immediately for Addis Ababa. Customs and immigration were based at the police post controlling the road to the Sudanese border.

'Eef you leavi now, you pay 175 shillings overtime. Ees lunch hour from one o'clocks to three o'clocks,' the officer said.

Having refuelled in Lodwar, we only had ninety Kenya shillings left. There was nowhere to change money – in fact, the village seemed quite dead.

'It's only five past one. Please, can't you help us? We don't have 175 shillings,' I pleaded.

'Eef I saach plane between one and three, you pay overtime,' he barked.

'But you don't need to search the plane. You said yourself that if we arrived from somewhere in Kenya, it did not need to be searched. We have already cleared Customs at Wilson Airport.'

He was narked. 'Of corse I must to saach the plen! Eet ees law of the laand.'

Drat! If we waited till three o'clock, it would be dark by the time we reached Addis. I strode back to the runway where Gérard waited. To hell, I thought, let's just take off – after all, what could the customs officer do? I resolved to pretend to Gérard all was in order and only confess once we were airborne.

A shadow fell across my path. There stood a police officer.

'Betta you follow me,' he ordered. Inside his tin shed office, he proceeded. 'Did you flying over anudder airport before landing here?' he asked.

So Oropoi must have radioed him! I explained we had gone there by mistake.

'You waar lucky. It is high security area. They could shoot you. Not good to go thaar. Uganda borda.'

I thought he was going to make a big issue of it, but he extended his hand.

'You may leave for Addis. Have a good flight!'

For most of the three-hour flight, the southern Ethiopian highlands were hidden. Sudden gaps in the stodgy layer of cloud would reveal them, a thousand feet below, denuded of trees like those of Madagascar but splashed with green between the scant settlements and the black scars of burn-offs. Occasionally, the sun pierced biblically through the clouds to illuminate green valleys where streams cascaded over waterfalls to join the mighty Omo River. The en route chart minimum altitudes for the highlands vary between 13,400 and 14,200 feet. We were at 12,500 feet, making periodic detours to stay visual or avoid a peak looming suddenly out of the cloud.

Addis lies at 7,700 feet on a huge, bare plateau, a serene patchwork of greens and browns speckled with thatched rondavels. The city's extensive suburbs glinted in the afternoon sunlight as we joined the downwind leg for the 3.7-kilometre runway at Bole International. It was clearly too short, for there were wrecked jets at each threshold. An Ethiopian Airlines 707 was neatly split in two. Beyond it lay the remains of a Mig. Solemn reminders of the dangers of high-altitude airports.

Addis is the seat of the sumptuous headquarters of the Organisation of African Unity. Its car park was jammed with the Mercedes and BMWs that apparently no diplomat can live without. African presidents meet here annually to discuss African issues. Each year, they agree something must be done to fight poverty. Then they go away in presidential jets to fill their Swiss bank accounts. Shades of South America! Meanwhile, the Mercato, the largest market in Africa, was the direst we had seen. We felt horribly conspicuous in the seething mass of begging children, lepers, and war amputees. Shoppers wrapped in white *shamma* shawls to stave off the morning chill moseyed between colourful *injera* baskets, coarse sheep wool carpets, ancient silver coins, tools and brushes. Fruit and vegetables were displayed on the ground. The impoverished and the hungry gazed longingly at produce they could not afford. Two young lads had acquired a pair of bathroom scales and charged a few pence for people to weigh themselves. No one stopped. They did not need to know what their bones weighed. To give them some business, I climbed on board and a group crowded round to chant out the kilos. I felt shamefully obese among a people scourged by famine. A month eating Ethiopia's national dish would have knocked off a few kilos. *Injera* is a huge spongy pancake made from a fermented Ethiopian cereal called *t'eff*. A piece is broken off and used like a handkerchief to scoop up dollops of vegetable or meat relishes. Its acrid taste is hardly inspiring, but its clammy wet-towel feel makes it quite unpalatable.

Formerly Abyssinia, Ethiopia is an ancient kingdom which escaped colonisation and was only briefly occupied by the Italians. The last emperor, Ras Tafari aka Haile Selassie, is the revered model of Rastafarians worldwide. His family tree boasted such notables as Soloman, the Queen of Sheba and Emperor Memelik II. He was ousted in 1974 (and subsequently murdered) by Mengistu Haile-Mariam. There followed years of war, violence and repression in the name of Marxism-Leninism.

Immigration ordered us to register at the Tourist Commission in order to obtain a letter for Internal Security, from whom we required permission to fly within the war-torn country. The office displayed flashy leaflets about the magical northern towns of Gondar and Lalibela, out-of-bounds to tourists. We were aiming for Bahar Dar, on the banks of Lake Tana, where exquisite thirteenth-century monasteries, stuffed with ancient Coptic treasures and writings, dot various islands. The Commissioner's secretary insisted it was the National Tourist Office's job to provide the letter.

At the NTO, there was another blank wall. 'I cannot write this letter,' the lady said. 'The Tourist Commission must do it. In any case, if you wanted to travel around Ethiopia, why didn't you book a tour like everybody else?'

'We are travelling by small plane.'

'Nobody comes to Ethiopia for tourism in their own plane,' she retorted crossly, 'so I can't solve your problem.'

'All we need is a letter for Internal Security.'

'I cannot write such a letter, and the manager is away,' she said, showing us to the door.

We decided to tackle the issue from the other end. The man responsible for clearances at the Civil Aviation Department had agreed we could fly to Bahar Dar provided we kept to the airway. He phoned the intransigent lady at the NTO to instruct her how to prepare the letter we needed. Over the phone, she agreed. But when we arrived back there, she refused once again. It was forbidden for foreigners to travel to Bahar Dar, she said. Fortunately, the manager, Mr Johanes Berhanu, arrived. He was all charm and courtesy, explaining that it was the first time that such a request had been made in Ethiopia since the 1974 revolution, so it took people by surprise. But he was the epitome of helpfulness, and the vital letter was sent to Internal Security. As we waited for an answer, we showed him the *Revista Geográfica* articles on our trip.

'Ah, so you do this for adventure? Let me see.' He studied each map and photo with intent. 'You have been to all these places? For adventure! It's incredible.'

Inspired to adopt our crusade, he assailed various people in Amharic on the telephone, during which we could distinguish only one word, repeated several times: adventure. Suddenly, he jumped to his feet and thrust out his hand.

'Congratulations!' he beamed excitedly. 'You've done it! I never thought it was possible. You are making history in Ethiopia! I didn't think they would let you go to Bahar Dar. Just one thing though: one of our guides must go with you.'

'It's all thanks to you, Mr Berhanu. I'm very grateful, but I'm afraid we can't take a passenger. It's a small plane. There isn't room—'

'Find room. Even if you have to unload equipment and leave it here. He has to go with you, even if he sits on a box.' Internal Security's permission depended upon one of their men accompanying us. They did not want snoopers flying about.

The next day, Berhanu introduced us to our 'guide', GT, describing him as working in the domestic sector. GT was a tall, solemn fellow clearly not enthralled with the prospect of a trip to Bahar Dar in a small plane. His apprehension was reflected in such suggestions as making a hotel booking. Even Berhanu laughed at the notion that the hotels might be full, since no tourists were allowed there.

GT's disguise as a humble guide was flimsy. All the office personnel bowed low upon shaking his hand, and treated him with utmost respect. When we piled into his bright-blue VW Beetle and headed for the airport, his severity mellowed and he verged on becoming chatty. The crashed 707, he told us, had aborted take-off after a bird strike in one engine. The other large wreck was that of an overloaded Antonov that had stalled with deadly results.

We duly lined up for take-off, and Gérard put on full power. Not much happened. After an interminable ground roll, *Romeo* became reluctantly airborne. At 7,700 feet and 18°C, the density altitude must have been well over 10,000 feet. GT stared stoically ahead with a for-king-and-country expression as the stall alarm screamed. We imagined his job was to prevent us from seeing or photographing sensitive military material. Gérard insisted he sat in the co-pilot's seat, knowing that with the earphones on and bouncing through the turbulence, his eyes would be riveted forward and I would be free to take photographs in the rear. It worked, but we discovered no secrets flying over that astounding terrain. The winding course of the Blue Nile (the Brown Nile would be an apter name) carves a path through magnificent gorges, joined by tributaries cascading down sheer cliffs. It hardly looked the same country where Sebastião Salgado had photographed appalling misery and starvation. Not an inch of land was uncultivated. No trees remained either – a serious cause of diminished rainfall and erosion – but the fields were a radiant green. Ethiopia was exporting vegetables to Europe, while Europe sent food to the starving in Tigray and Eritrea.

At Bahar Dar airport, two planes awaited a human cargo: rows of young recruits sat on the hot tarmac, headed for Asmara, today capital of Eritrea but at that time desperately held by the Ethiopian Army. In Addis, just before the nightly curfew at eleven p.m., we had seen convoys of buses on the nigh-deserted streets. At each window, the unforgettable face of a frightened young boy. These children, collected off the streets or dragged from their homes, were forcibly transported to the front as gun fodder. We had landed at what amounted to a military airport actively engaged in warlike operations, and understood Berhanu's amazement that we had been permitted to do so. Rebel forces had taken the city a year before and had only recently been repelled by the Army. Yet GT staunchly denied the rebels had ever been there. The airport building had collapsed on one side, the windows were shattered, and bullet and rocket holes punctured the walls. GT dismissed our assumption that these had been caused by rebel action: it was the result of an earthquake, he claimed. We waited for a lift in the shade of the only tree to escape the axe. Pigeons and long-tailed glossy starlings competed noisily for its berries. Seven army trucks arrived. In the back, teenage soldiers were singing: not crude aggressive war songs, but a gentle, harmonious tune, a sort of Amharic lullaby. They had nothing to sing about. The BBC that morning had reported Eritrean rebels' claims to have killed or wounded 11,000 Ethiopian soldiers in Asmara in recent months.

We set about arranging to visit the monasteries. The Marine Transport Offices were the government body responsible for transport on the lake. They were inflexible. A boat would cost 250 birr per hour, the four-hour trip to the monasteries would set us back US$500. Perhaps a fisherman could take us to the islands? Certainly not! It was prohibited for them to take tourists in their boats, made of papyrus like those of the Indians on Lake Titicaca. With GT along, we were tied to the regulations. Gérard went to investigate alone. He was adopted by Goshu, a toothless teenager who knew where a boat was available: at the Orthodox church two kilometres out of town. Priests in colourful medieval flowing robes greeted Gérard and led him to the abbot. Wearing a long bright yellow garment and purple hat, the latter explained that we could use their boat as long as it was authorised in writing. Last time he had taken visitors to the monasteries, the Marine Transport Company had threatened to forbid the church from using their boat on the lake ever again.

By that time, the office was closed. GT offered to contact Internal Security, discovering an old buddy in charge. A letter was promised first thing next day. We celebrated over a few beers on the terrace of the empty Ghion Hotel overlooking a park of centennial trees and flowerbeds of roses, marigolds and busy-lizzies which led to the lake. GT relaxed and talked about Ethiopia's problems. The image in the Western press of valiant Eritrean freedomfighters trying to break away from a ruthless Marxist-Leninist dictatorship, he said, was not fair. Ethiopia had been a fervently Christian country since the fourth century. It was besieged by Muslims who wanted to force it along their track, finding easy support and weapons from Libya and Iraq. But it really boiled down to economics. If Eritrea and Tigray seceded, Ethiopia would become a landlocked country in a stranglehold and would have to pay dearly for port facilities. GT believed it was right to fight. I wonder what he thinks today.

'I wake early. The birds, they are shouting,' he complained at breakfast next morning. Amazingly, the letter of authorisation had already arrived. We proceeded forthwith to the church.

'You have the letter?' the chief priest asked anxiously when we arrived. He glanced at it and shook his head. Approval from Internal Security was not enough. We needed permission from Marine Transport. Accompanied by the priest, GT and Gérard returned to town. To no avail! None of the Marine Transport directors were at work. This was not surprising, since we had seen them, very drunk, at the hotel bar the night before. The secretary had also scarpered. It was a small town. They knew what we wanted and how to foil us. Our flight clearances in Ethiopia were pre-fixed; we couldn't wait around indefinitely. So we concluded that, like our flight to Gabú in Guinea-Bissau, this trip had been in vain. Back to Addis.

'Yaaaaaw. Yaaaaaaawww.'

Beyond the sturdy city walls of Harrar, the Hyena Man sat with a sack of putrid entrails and yowled into the night. Slanted yellow eyes glowed in the darkness as wild hyenas advanced, a dozen of them skulking timorously on the rim of light cast by the headlights of a car. Braver ones approached within metres of him as he cajoled, howling, holding aloft pieces of tripe, and throwing them just beyond his skinny outstretched legs. Massive jaws would snatch the morsel and the hulk would skulk off into the darkness. Any sudden move sent them scurrying, so Hyena Man called to them continuously, wooing them to take meat from his hand. For generations, his butcher family has fed the hyenas with the leftovers. I joined him, timorously holding out the meat to watch the ferocious jaws close with surprising gentleness. It was like a last offering to Africa.

Nearby Dire Dawa, founded a century ago as a depot during the construction of the Djibouti/Addis railway, was a different Ethiopia – one of nomads' tents and camel herds. Abyssinians were building castles and writing manuscripts when Europeans were still marauding barbarians, yet nowhere in Africa had we seen so much suffering. One man, head and torso hidden under a blanket, lay sprawled on the pavement exposing testicles swollen to the size of a rugby ball. Another dragged a completely rotten leg upon which flies feasted. It was no longer black like his good leg, but white.

When we departed from Dire Dawa for Djibouti, Gérard was extra worried about an engine failure. Indeed, there was nothing comforting about the landscape beneath: rugged brown mountains whittled down by millennia of wind erosion, glaring-white salt pans, sudden lava flows and sand, endless sand. But his anxiety was not because of the desert. A local Italian resident had told us of an ancient ritual between the Afar, Issa, and Karayu nomads, arch enemies who wander these desert wastes. To prove his manhood and win a bride, a young man must slay another to cut off the testicles. Subsequently sun-dried, these would adorn both brides and camels. Perhaps the Italian had been taking the mickey, but the testicle-cropping story made Gérard more nervous on this flight than crossing the Atlantic.

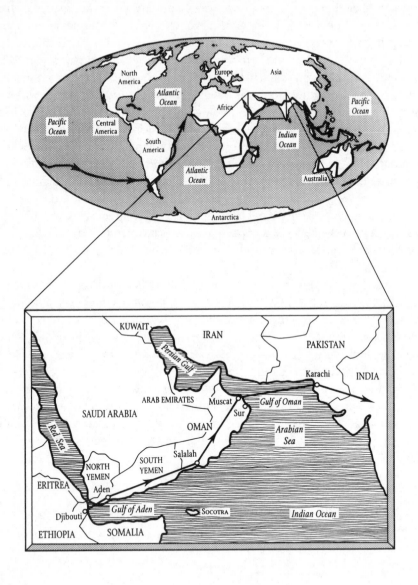

13 FAILURE TO COMPLY . . .
MAY PLACE THE AIRCRAFT AT RISK

The altimeter read five hundred feet below sea level. *Below* sea level. We were taking a subterranean flight inside the fiery bowl of Lake Assal, a vast depression of blinding white salt flats hemmed in by bare brown mountains. Its crimson saline waters form intricate patterns where they meet outstretched fingers of black lava, encrusting them with white crystals. Volcanic build-ups at the end of the Ghoubet Kharab (Devil's Throat) inlet prevent the sea from flooding the depression, but water still infiltrates. It evaporates in the excruciating heat, leaving a thick crust of gleaming salt which is mined by Afar nomads.

There was severe risk of overheating the engine in this inferno, which would result in a loss of climbing power. We knew some aircraft had come to grief trying to climb back up to sea level, and though we stayed only fifteen minutes, the oil temperature soared. Over the volcano-punctured lip of the bowl, we were duly buffeted by violent turbulence. A clear-cut fault line, where two continental plates are drawing apart, appeared in 1978. Lava seeps up to fill the gap, increasing Djibouti's land mass and making it the fastest-growing country in Africa!

From childhood stamp-collecting days, I remembered when Djibouti went by the name of Territoire Français des Afars et des Issas, evocative of Arabian Nights. But, as we came in to land, we were faced by the stark reality of the modern world and a war in the making: legionnaires were busy installing anti-aircraft weaponry.

'So, you're on honeymoon?' asked Abdul, the marshal, as we emerged from the cockpit into an overpowering sauna. 'Like that other couple who passed through here?'

We lethargically agreed. If that's what pleased him, well and good. In Flight Operations, he insisted on showing us an address sticker on the back of his locker door. It read Flemming Pedersen. Flemming and Angela are friends of ours who had flown from Geneva to Nairobi in their *Honey Mooney* in 1988. Abdul was not surprised we knew them – he expected it. He told us French Air Force pilots had spotted Iraqi Migs and Mirages in Yemeni skies. Pilots arriving from Yemen reported that fuel was only sold to aircraft from countries supportive of Iraq and that Westerners were harassed in the streets. Things in the Middle East were heating up.

We had come to a crossroads. Should we continue to Asia or not? We chewed over the dilemma at lunch and agreed to let Fate decide on our behalf. The war had not started. If Yemen granted overflying permission, and Oman allowed us to land, we would proceed. Deep down, we felt sure the way would be blocked. It didn't matter, really: we believed in silver linings. Claiming extenuating circumstances, we could turn back and enjoy more of Africa. We sent off the clearance requests and waited.

Fate made her move. When both countries gave their approval, we felt trapped because we had made the Middle East into a danger zone in our minds. Suddenly the way was clear. We had to go on.

Future sources of fuel were still a major concern. A war or sanctions against Iraq would jeopardise supplies. Muscat consistently ignored our queries about Avgas. It lay 1,200 miles from Djibouti and would leave us one hour's reserves. Abdul discovered Avgas was available at Salalah, Oman's southernmost city. Refuelling there would enable us to reach Muscat and even continue to Karachi.

I rang my mother. She was in a panic, torn between relief that we had survived war-torn Ethiopia and terror over what awaited us in the Gulf. I tried to reassure her (and myself) that Oman was a long way from Kuwait.

'But what about all those aircraft?' she asked.

'What aircraft?'

'The British fighter jets!'

'British jets won't shoot a little plane flying the other way,' I said, wondering if there was any truth in that.

'Well, I don't like it,' she announced. 'In fact, I've been asked to tell you not to go. They say, Don't go.'

'Who's they, Mum?'

'Your sisters! And me.'

'Don't worry, we'll be fine.'

'I wish you wouldn't do this.'

'Everything's fine in Oman. I'll call you from Muscat.'

French Air Force Mirages took off on patrol with earth-tremoring roars as we held short of the runway. Then it was our turn, and Djibouti was soon lost in sandy haze as we climbed sluggishly to 7,500 feet across the Gulf of Aden at the mouth of the Red Sea.

'Aircraft entering OYP7 will be fired upon without warning' warned the ONC chart for Yemen, with unusual severity. No-go areas are customarily demarcated with R, P or D: Restricted, Prohibited or Dangerous. This permanent injunction was indicative of tensions in the area unrelated to the Gulf crisis. Aden materialised, its docks pricking outwards from arid mountains. Beyond, the desolate desert – sometimes rock, sometimes sand – was punctured with volcanoes and tracts of

Buzzing Eighty-Mile Beach, Western Australia. Not a soul in sight for its entire length, only seagulls.

The spectacular Olga Mountains, Australia.

Take-off from dirt strip at Victoria River, Northern Territory, Australia.

Gizo airport, like an aircraft-carrier!

The grass strip at Gimbat, where shortly after setting up camp, a park ranger tried to move us on.

'. . . a row of leaping kangaroos on the red Qantas tails.' Dawn at Cairns as we prepare the first leg across the Pacific.

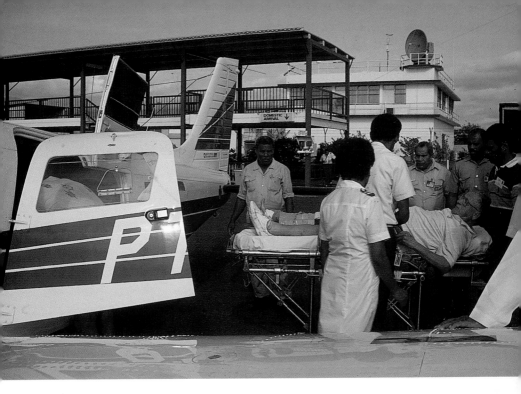

Medical evacuation. The patient is off-loaded at Nadi airport, Fiji.

Stopped for the usual spaghetti lunch at the deserted strip of North-West Santo, Espiritu Santo island, Vanuatu.

Bad weather complicates
the approach to Taveuni,
Fiji.

Sandstorm.

Romeo still tied to the baggage trolleys on the morning the hurricane in Apia, Western Samoa, subsided. The hangar is a wreck.

Reitoro Atoll, Tuamotu, Polynesia.

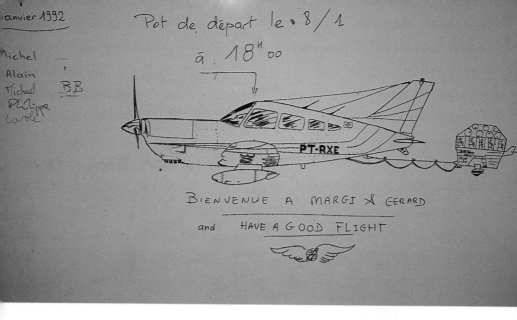

anvier 1992

Michel
Alain
Michael   BB
Philippe
Carole

Pot de départ le 8/1
à 18ʰ oo

PT-RXE

BIENVENUE A MARGI & GERARD

and   HAVE A GOOD FLIGHT

A talented student pilot drew this sketch to announce the send-off party at Tahiti Aeroclub. Tahiti had given us the warmest welcome and departure we had received anywhere.

Refuelling at Easter Island. The seal had been broken on one of our 'specially' ordered barrels, none of which was new.

Cabin interior showing single extra tank (150 litres) after removing second one in Dak and before installing another in Sydney. Note GPS (acquired by the time we reache Nepal) on windshield.

Romeo on the wing.

black lava. The engine oil temperature was high, but it was not surprising since the outside air temperature at 9,500 feet read 22°C.

Muscat Control cleared us direct to Salalah where the weather was given as broken at 2,000 feet, complete overcast at 3,500 feet. It sounded like London. The met report received in Djibouti had surprised us by forecasting drizzle, but we naively assumed it was a passing shower. Gérard asked for an instrument approach. We descended from cheery haze into gloomy soup, continually expecting to break through any moment. There was no break. Control vectored us down and cleared us to join base leg at 1,600 feet to intercept the localiser. Still in the soup.

Salalah lies on a narrow plain behind which rise the 3,000-foot Dhofar mountains, home of frankincense trees. Terrain rose to 1,000 feet just three miles from the runway. We could see nothing. Tense silence filled the cockpit. Instrument landings require constant practice, which Gérard had not had for over a year. He concentrated on the instruments, beads of sweat glistening on his forehead. In his diary, he later wrote: 'I had a hesitation regarding the glide slope, whether I was entering too high or too low. The corrections I was making were too large, but I managed to avoid pegging the needles, descending lower and lower, my eyes nervously skimming the altimeter – 1,400, 1,200, 1,000, 800, still in fog, 500, 400, 300, still totally blind and close to panic. When the layer broke at 250 feet, and the runway lights glinted like a welcoming carpet ahead, we were scraping over the buildings.'

'Is the weather often like this?' I asked the Filipino fuel attendant who rushed over as the engine stopped.

'You have chosen the best time to come to Salalah,' he announced, extolling the virtues of such weather. Salalah, we learned, lives in the clouds from June to September, when moist monsoon winds clash against the Dhofar mountains. Arabs flock here on holiday to get away from eternal sunshine.

Upon emerging from the terminal, a cheerful gentleman introduced himself as Abdallah and offered us a lift to town. Wary of overfriendly strangers, we were wondering if it was a trick when a car drew up, a beautiful lady swathed in a colourful shawl at the wheel. It was Abdallah's wife. With a warm smile, she greeted us in immaculate English and invited us to join them for a lamb dinner after a tour of the night *souq*. First, though, they dropped us at the modest Redam Hotel in the city centre where the receptionist was astounded. Didn't we want to go to the Holiday Inn, where all other Westerners stayed? No, we didn't.

A stroll through Salalah's spotless streets made it blatantly clear we were off the impoverished African continent and in a rich Gulf state. Shops displayed French perfumes, giant TVs and computers. All vehicles were spanking new: gone were the rusty heaps, held together with string, that hobble along African roads.

Muscat Control maintained continuous radio contact as we crossed the vast empty desert where occasional concrete settlements would suddenly appear beside remote oil wells. Air navigation equipment was of the highest quality – another phenomenon after eighteen months in Africa. At Seeb airport, US Air Force transport planes were stationed on patios along the runway, a reminder that war was brewing nearby. Two police officers sped over to keep vigil as we unpacked, chocked and blanketed the plane. Was such intense security standard practice or due to the Gulf crisis?

An Oman Aviation Services Fokker 28 drew up alongside. Its Australian pilot, Peter Vasey, came to greet us, inviting us to his home in Madinat Qaboos for a drink. As we entered, he called out to his wife that he had arrived with guests. Lindy bounced down the stairs, and took one look at us.

'Hello. You just flown into Muscat in a small plane?'

'How did you guess?'

'Just by looking at you!' Our half-cocked uniforms were not convincing to a pilot's wife! She warned that I would have to find something longer to wear than my knee-length bermudas. Elbows border on the audacious, but knees and shoulders are offensive. Even men out jogging must not wear shorts. After all, Omani men habitually wear *dishdasha*, long Wee Willie Winkie night-dresses.

As the evening sun illuminated the mountains behind the city, they drove us along kilometres of irrigated highway gardens into Muscat. It was a far cry from a hectic scenario of desert armies amassing for war. The Corniche in Muttrah, its whitewashed merchants' houses embellished with filigree balconies overlooking the bright blue bay, is stunning. Glowing mosque domes, arabesque arches, crenellated towers and carved doors are tucked between steep rocky mountains scattered with sixteenth-century Portuguese forts. The Portuguese had arrived in 1507, dominating Muscat and other coastal areas until expelled by the Yaaribah rulers in 1650. Oman subsequently became a significant power in Arabia and East Africa.

The *souq* was not a film-set maze of dark alleys swarming with thieves. Women wrapped in black veils lingered longingly before the gold merchants' exuberant window displays. The men wore cheerful red-checked turbans, some being neatly bound and tucked in, others worn untidily, odd ends left dangling. An atmosphere of opulence pervaded the city.

His Majesty Sultan Qaboos bin Said al Said deposed his father, Sayyid Said bin Taimur, in 1970. Educated at Sandhurst, he was poignantly aware that his country needed to be brought into the twentieth century. He had the advantage of the wherewithal provided by oil reserves to do it. Roads, schools and hospitals were built by an expatriate labour force of Pakistanis, Indians and Filipinos, supervised by British technicians. Thanks to Qaboos' sensitivity to his country's history and culture, its numerous medieval forts are being restored. Rigid legislation, unprecedented in the Middle East, protects fauna and flora. It is illegal to hunt or otherwise disturb wildlife or birds, spear fish, collect turtle eggs or even live shells. The Arabian oryx had become extinct in Arabia in the fifties, when the once plentiful herds were annihilated by motorised hunting parties using automatic weapons for the pure pleasure of killing. In 1980, ten animals from a World Herd bred in Phoenix, Arizona, were donated to form the core of new herds for Oman. Released into the wild in the Jiddat al-Harasis, they are now strictly protected by Harasis rangers.

Peter Vasey had told us that it was an offence to drive a dirty car, which reminded us that *Romeo* was long overdue a bath. It was too hot to do this during the day, so he arranged for us to use Oman Aviation's hose one night. It was not easy convincing the Royal Omani police to let us airside to wash our plane. They reacted with contempt. No self-respecting aircraft-owning Omani would ever do such a thing: that was what immigrant labour was for. After a long discussion, a policeman accompanied us. He stood guard for two hours as we splashed, soaped and scrubbed, muttering into his walkie-talkie every ten minutes. A group of Pakistani and Filipino airport employees on their way off-duty were amazed at the sight of white manual labour in action. They sat quietly on the tarmac to watch.

The Jabal Akhdar rises precipitously from the desert, carved by deep valleys leading into pebble-strewn wadis where long-haired goats chew on dry grasses and thorn bushes. Occasionally, the low wall of a *falaj* springs from nowhere, gouged in a black gorge from which life-giving water emerges, leading to a small settlement huddled under date palms, beside a sun-baked watchtower. For 1,000 years, Omani villagers have tapped ingeniously into the underground water table, constructing complex irrigation ditches known as *falaj*.

At Misfat al Ibriyeen, perched high up a hillside, we *salaamed* the old men in white *dishdasha* who chatted quietly in the shade. They gestured for us to enter their village through its ancient archway. An all-embracing sense of timelessness wafted through the tidy alleys between reddish adobe terraced houses with colourful metalwork doors. Clay water pots, framed in small black windows, caught the sunlight. Three girls in colourful robes returning from the well, plastic bowls of water balanced on their heads, giggled coyly. A white-bearded elder waved us towards a gorge vibrant with bird song where, under lofty date palms, the gurgling of the *falaj* water was punctuated with the periodic plop of contented frogs. The air was heavy with the bitter-sweet scent of limes drying in the sun.

The Honda Civic we had hired became bogged down in Mintrib, a village on the edge of the Wahibah Sands. Before we had time to ask for help, several robed villagers lifted the car bodily out of its sandy pit. They ushered us to the residence of a one-eyed storekeeper where we were offered water and *qahwa*, delicious coffee spruced with herbs. A tray with oranges and fresh dates was set before us and we were bidden to eat while the old man told us proudly of his progeny of fifteen children. The youngest of his three wives arrived with her four daughters. Much giggling ensued as, in sign language, we were bidden to take photos of the family.

Continuing to Sūr, we picked up Nasser, a medical student from Oman's only university named, like most things, after Sultan Qaboos. When Qaboos took over in 1970, Nasser said, the country only had schools educating 900 boys to primary level. He had placed an emphasis on education, giving equal opportunities for girls, a revolutionary move for an Arab country. Nasser showed us round his hometown of Bilad Bani Bu Ali where there was an ancient multi-domed mosque, like an upside-down egg box. At his home, we were seated on a red carpet in a room devoid of furniture, the walls lined with cushions, and offered melon, date meat and oranges prepared by his womenfolk kept safely out of sight. He kept insisting we should eat. We forced ourselves to do so in order not to offend him (the family at Mintrib had already stuffed us full) while he poured cups of *qahwa*. When I asked if he was not going to join us, he explained that tradition dictated that he should only drink once his guests had finished, unless bidden to accompany them. It was also Arab hospitality to insist guests always eat more, though it did not mean we were supposed to!

'You cannot go to Flight Operations unless your company manager sends us a letter,' the security chief at Seeb airport decided.

'There is no company. It is a private plane. I am the pilot and I have to make a flight plan. What do you mean I can't go through?' Gérard asked indignantly.

A uniform was proving irrelevant in Oman. So was the AOPA crew card. A tantrum worked better. In the inner sanctum of the briefing room, a telex from Karachi awaited: KINDLY ELABORATE THE PURPOSE OF YOUR STAY IN KARACHI FOR 09 DAYS. ALSO SPECIFY THE ROUTE WITH ENTRY/EXIT POINTS AND TIMINGS IN PAKISTAN AIR SPACE. This information had already been sent twice. The option was to telephone Karachi.

'What is the purpose of your trip?' the Pakistani asked.

'Tourism – it's on the telex.'

'Yes, but what purpose?'

'Tourism. You know, visit your country . . .'

'Send a telex—'

'I have sent three telexes . . .' The call was cut off twice, but eventually approval was granted. We could move on.

Allied forces were already patrolling the waters of the Gulf of Oman, over which we would fly. A Notam on the wall in the briefing room made chilling reading:

US MILITARY FORCES ARE OPERATING NORTH OF 20 DEGREES NORTH LATITUDE IN THE AREA OF THE ARABIAN SEA, GULF OF OMAN, STRAIT OF HORMUZ AND THE GULF WEST OF STRAIT OF HORMUZ.

THE ACCURATE IDENTIFICATION OF AIRCRAFT IN THIS AREA IS ESSENTIAL TO PRECLUDE THE INADVERTENT USE OF MILITARY FORCE AGAINST CIVILIAN AIRCRAFT. THE U.S. HAS STATED THAT ITS MILITARY FORCES ARE PREPARED TO EXERCISE SELF-DEFENCE MEASURES AS THEY ARE APPROACHED BY UNIDENTIFIED AIRCRAFT – FIXED WING OR HELICOPTER – OR AIRCRAFT WHOSE INTENTIONS ARE UNCLEAR . . . ALL AIRCRAFT FLYING WITHIN OR ENTERING THIS AREA SHOULD MAINTAIN A CONTINUOUS LISTENING WATCH ON ONE OR BOTH INTERNATIONAL EMERGENCY FREQUENCIES VHF 121 500 AND/OR UHF 247 000 MHZ. AIRCRAFT EQUIPPED WITH A CIVIL WEATHER AVOIDANCE RADAR AND/OR AN OPERATIONAL CIVIL TYPE TRANSPONDER SHOULD OPERATE BOTH CONTINUOUSLY WHEN TRANSITING THIS AREA. UNIDENTIFIED AIRCRAFT AND THOSE WHOSE INTENTIONS ARE UNCLEAR TO U.S. MILITARY FORCES WILL BE CONTACTED USING THE ENGLISH LANGUAGE . . . REQUESTED TO IDENTIFY THEMSELVES AND TO STATE THEIR INTENTIONS. SUCH CONTACTS MAY ORIGINATE FROM MILITARY SURFACE AND/OR AIRBORNE UNITS.

AIRCRAFT RECEIVING ADVISORY CALLS SHOULD ACKNOWLEDGE RECEIPT AND UNDERSTANDING OF THE WARNING ON THE FREQUENCY RECEIVED, AND PROVIDE THE INFORMATION REQUESTED. IN THE EVENT THE AIRCRAFT IN QUESTION REMAINS UNIDENTIFIED AND/OR IS DEEMED TO POSE THREAT TO U.S. MILITARY FORCES, AN EMERGENCY SITUATION EXISTS. THE PILOT MUST BE PREPARED TO EXERCISE HIS EMERGENCY AUTHORITY TO DEVIATE FROM ATC CLEARANCE, COMPLY WITH RECOMMENDED HEADING OR ALTITUDE CHANGES PROVIDED BY U.S. MILITARY FORCES, AND NOTIFY THE APPROPRIATE ATC FACILITY OF THE DEVIATION. FLIGHT CREWS ARE FURTHER ADVISED THAT FAILURE TO RESPOND TO RADIO TRANSMISSION OR TO RESPOND TO OR COMPLY WITH THE ADVICE GIVEN MAY PLACE THE AIRCRAFT AT RISK. AIRCRAFT TRANSITING THE AREAS MENTIONED ABOVE MAY MINIMISE THEIR EXPOSURE TO THE ADVISORY PROCEDURE BY MAINTAINING AN ALTITUDE ABOVE FL250, BY AVOIDING OFF AIRWAYS ROUTING, AND BY AVOIDING ABRUPT AND UNUSUAL CHANGES OF HEADING AND/OR ALTITUDE WHICH MAY BE CONSIDERED AS INCONSISTENT WITH NORMAL CIVIL AIRCRAFT FLIGHT PATTERNS. ILLUMINATION OF A U.S. MILITARY UNIT WITH A WEAPONS TYPE FIRE CONTROL RADAR WILL BE VIEWED WITH SUSPICION AND COULD RESULT IN AN IMMEDIATE MILITARY DEFENSIVE ACTION.

The military jargon made our flesh creep. Under the ominous shadow of this Notam, we contemplated the flight with some trepidation. Ever conscious that the recommended minimum altitude was 25,000 feet, we struggled painfully for a tense thirty minutes to reach 9,500 feet: the oil temperature was high, the oil pressure approaching the yellow, so we climbed in stages. Our eyes nervously scanned sky and sea for signs of patrol aircraft or the American fleet. The words 'friendly fire' revererated in my head. Concern about interception by American fighter jets or, worse still, Iranians (we did not have a clearance to clip the thirty miles of Iranian airspace), only faded once Pakistan's rugged coastline came into view.

Karachi airport terminal was dirty, airless mayhem. Pakistani families and their extensive collections of boxes and suitcases tied with string, occupied all available floor space. Ubiquitous children bawled. In no African country had we beheld such chaos. The authorities soon made it clear that we were strictly forbidden to fly anywhere in Pakistan. Islamabad, Lahore, Gilgit – all out of the question. There was no reason to stay in Karachi's jumble of shanty towns any longer than necessary for acquiring Indian visas and clearances. The former were processed in one day. Flight clearances were another story.

We sent a total of seven telexes to New Delhi. Not one was acknowledged. The only solution was to phone. At the airport post office, it was obligatory to pre-pay a three-minute call to India, more expensive than one to Europe. Four such calls in the morning were a waste of time and money. Once connected, the telephonist at the CAA in Delhi would curtly say there was no one in the department and hang up before another word could be said.

Thomas Casey, an American pilot Gérard met in the briefing room, advised that only one gentleman in all India could authorise a flight clearance. This Mr Saha could only be caught after 14:30. Gérard eventually tracked down the elusive man who naturally claimed he had never seen any of our telexes. So yet another telex was sent, in exchange for a promise that a clearance number would be sent that afternoon.

But our problems were negligible compared to Casey's. Attempting the first circumnavigation by float plane, a single-engine Cessna 206 exclusively able to land on water, he required clearances from aeronautical authorities, because it flew, and naval authorities, because it landed on water. He had been trying for a clearance for Bombay for seven days. We wondered if we would ever hear of him again.

134

14 'We are not having Avgas for thirty-five years!'

The difficulty experienced in obtaining clearances for India was surely a harbinger of a battery of bureaucratic battles ahead. With a sense of tired foreboding, we landed at Ahmadabad for entry formalities. Despite being the only aircraft, we were instructed to park at Bay 5, as far as possible from the terminal building. This gave me time to empty the pee bottle onto the grass before the arrival of five Customs and Immigration employees sweating heavily from the long walk in the torrid heat.

Gérard accompanied them back to the Customs office to complete endless forms with irrelevant questions: How many wristwatches on board? How many litres of engine oil on board? How many of gasoline? How many will you have on departure? (Was there a lucrative business in India trafficking fuel and engine oil?) Where did you start your journey? Where will it end? (We had no idea.) Name all airports in between. That made 119 in our case. The form was not big enough. On the telephone from Karachi, Mr Saha had advised that foreign aircraft could not remain in India for more than fifteen days. We could stay in the country, but not *Romeo*, lest we were tempted to set up an air-taxi company and steal customers from Indian Airlines. Our original plan to criss-cross the whole subcontinent was reduced to a fleeting visit to a handful of cities.

We had hoped to proceed immediately to Udaipur, but Control advised its airport would close in fifteen minutes. For each additional hour it stayed open for us, we would be charged 1,400 rupees (US$700). When we opted to wait till morning, Customs claimed that if we stayed overnight in Ahmadabad, *Romeo* must be guarded and kept in bond even though fully cleared by this time.

'It is being the regulations,' they said. 'The aircraft doors must be bond-sealed.'

A roll of cellotape was produced for this purpose. Gérard, who has a special hatred for people who idly drum their fingers on the preciously waxed fuselage, refused to allow them to stick this 'deterrent' on the paint-work. A compromise was reached. We 'sealed' the doors with Marlboro stickers, equally farcical as a deterrent, but which would peal off without leaving a sticky mark. This tomfoolery seemed to satisfy them.

* * *

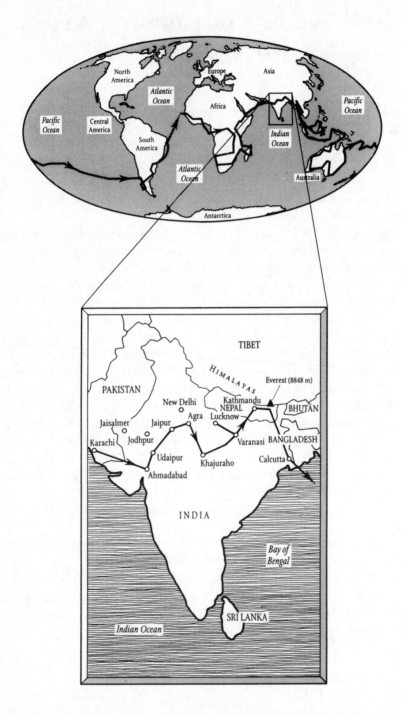

Rajasthan, Land of Kings, is an ideal place for a gentle meeting with India. Udaipur is a web of crooked streets winding through a jumble of temples, ghats and tiny stores. The Lake Palace Hotel, a sort of terrestrial passenger liner cemented onto an island in Lake Pichola, was built as the summer palace of the Mewar princes. From its tranquil rooftop cupolas, we gazed at the city panorama radiating in the golden rays of sunset, and felt a great sense of peace. The white-arched City Palace, a rambling building begun in 1559 by the city's founder, Maharaja Udai (hence Udaipur) Singh, dominates the skyline. We could happily have spent days exploring Udaipur and neighbouring Chittaurgarh, a medieval fortress-city once home to chivalrous warriors and ravishing princesses. But the time restrictions on *Romeo* forced us into continual telephone battles with Mr Saha in New Delhi. He was unable to confirm a clearance beyond one single flight. Both Jodhpur and Jaisalmer would require special Air Force permission, a hurdle too unbearable to contemplate. Finally, approval was granted for Jaipur, 162 nautical miles away.

As we drove to the airport in the early morning, the sun peered coyly through a fine mist. Landing would have been one thing, but we were to take off. In India, it is compulsory to receive the weather before making a flight plan. While we ostensibly waited for the met report from Bombay, the controller descended from his lofty fishbowl to examine *Romeo*.

'How long being your autonomy?' he asked.

'Twelve hours.'

'Without stopping, is it?'

'Autonomy means without stopping. How long does Bombay take to send a weather report?' Gérard asked, squinting in the sunlight and anxious to proceed.

'Frankly, I not worrying about Bombay. The visibility here is being my worry. Are you seeing those mountains over there?' He pointed to some hills, clearly visible, fifteen kilometres away. 'That's being the danger. Only when we can be seeing those mountains, then the visibility is good.'

'Wonderful. We can see them perfectly. So we'll be off.'

'No, no, no. You are not understanding. Only when I, Controller, am telling you visibility is good, then you can be leaving.' Logic is not the forte of civil servants in any country. He only released us when there was not a wisp of cloud in the sky.

While I sat in the rear to photograph rural India, an interminable flatness partitioned into fields, dams and villages, Gérard spent most of the flight trying to raise Jaipur Control. He finally succeeded when we were only thirty miles away.

'Maintain Flight Level 055. Report field in sight,' he was instructed.

We chugged on.

'Get the video ready. Quick – out of the right window,' he yelled suddenly. Assuming I was to film on the ground, I pointed the lens down.

'No, not down! A plane's going to pass the window.'

He never said how close. Whoooooooosh! It passed within a hundred feet. We could see the surprised faces of the pilots. I gasped. Mid-air collisions were another nightmare of mine. I could just see us, ablaze, falling through the empty skies of Rajasthan, to sizzle out in one of those green village ponds. We were ten miles from Jaipur when Gérard had spotted that Indian Air Force Avro. He took avoiding action but the Avro captain only caught sight of us once he was abeam. Shocked, he demanded, in tremulous voice, an explanation from Jaipur Tower. The tower was strangely silent. Gérard, with the cynical composure of one in control of the situation, replied directly. We had been cleared to proceed on track. He asked the tower to corroborate. Silence.

'What is your registration? There will be a full investigation!' the Air Force captain threatened accusingly.

We looked at each other in dismay. We were having enough problems in India with a foreign aircraft without being blamed for an air traffic incident when, for once, we were in the right place at the right time. Why was it so readily presumed that we were in the wrong? An investigation could result in *Romeo* being impounded, pending weeks of legal disputes. And where the hell was the controller? After all, it was his fault. He had cleared two aircraft on a collision course and abandoned his post. Gérard called persistently as we continued approach and entered the circuit. Nothing. Then, seconds before we were to touch down, 'Cleared to land' was grumbled over the airwaves. So the controller hadn't died of a heart attack. The prop had barely stopped spinning, and we were already climbing the staircase, stained with betel nut spittle, up to the tower. He must have heard the furious footsteps.

'What is your clearance number?' he fired in self-defence.

'Where have you been? I was trying to call you for ages. How did you clear that Avro straight on course with us?'

'I am asking your clearance number,' the controller rebutted, tight black moustache twitching nervously, trying to assert his authority.

'Stuff the clearance, where the hell were you?' Gérard's voice began to rise dangerously. 'We almost had a mid-air collision up there. Do you hear me? This is very serious. You cleared me, and the Avro, and then just disappeared. He wants an investigation.'

'No worry. Nothing happen.'

'What happened to you? Why didn't you answer?'

'Plees, no worry. I having to go toilet.'

So! He wandered off for a pee after setting two aircraft on a collision course. Only a handful of planes fly into Jaipur per day and even then, he ballsed up.

'Listen here. The other pilot demanded my registration. He blames *me!*'

'No worry. He do nothing. I am taking care.'

Unconvinced, we sincerely hoped he could placate the Avro captain. We knew any investigation would find us, the foreigners, to be guilty.

Jaipur, capital of Rajasthan, is known as the Pink City. Founded by Sawai Jai Singh II in 1727, it is set out in gridfashion within rosy fortified walls. Along the main bazaar, between the exuberant russet-coloured buildings, weaves an incredible jumble of animals and vehicles. Elephants, antiquated Ambassador cars, scooters and bicycles contend with carts pulled by camels, bullocks, horses, or donkeys. Tractor-rickshaws, scooter-rickshaws and bicycle-rickshaws weave between dirty buses with passengers inside and piled aloft. Behind every truck, a painted sign reads PLEASE HORN. No one needs any encouragement. Horn, they do. Incessantly.

On the phone to Mr Saha, we received another blow. Agra was out of bounds. Despite its constant civilian use by Indian Airlines, Saha claimed it was a military airport. Dreams of buzzing the Taj Mahal drowned in disappointment. Flying in India was a chain of frustrations. Our time had been restricted to two weeks, the National Parks were all closed until 1 October, and now we were prohibited from flying to Agra. Loath to miss the Taj, we opted for the train, a mode of transport more suited to India. Ragged families slept on every inch of the station platform. Puddles of urine moistened the corners and the raw stench of human excrement wafted up from the railtrack. This drove us to the arrogance of first-class tickets which entitled us to a filthy berth. The bunks were black with grime, as if the train was arriving from a coal mine. But it was a delightful experience to slip through the countryside instead of over it. Water buffaloes wallowed in luminous green ponds, oxen dragged ploughs over misty furrows and peacocks, indigenous to India, strode proprietorially along the hedgerows dragging their majestic rainbow tails.

Then, behold, there was Agra. Opulence unashamedly staring dire poverty in the face. Architectural magnificence stands aloof from the filth. A majestic red sandstone gateway, encrusted with ornate mosaics, frames the gleaming Taj Mahal, the clichéd epitome of love which draws millions of sighing visitors from all over the world. This building moves the sensibilities in a way no other does. Shah Jahan, the Moghul emperor who built this mausoleum for his favourite wife, Mumtaz Mahal (Ornament of the Palace), lies entombed beside her in the torrid basement. Outside, a percussion of international camera buttons accompanies the serenade of bands of screeching green-and-pink parakeets.

Back in Jaipur to collect *Romeo*, it was essential to establish which airports ahead stocked Avgas. Gérard visited the manager of Indian Oil.

'You can be buying fuel in Varanasi,' he suggested.

'Are you sure they have fuel in stock? Couldn't you call or send a telex to your colleague there to confirm?' Gérard asked, ever cautious.

'Not necessary. I am working twenty years with Indian Oil Company. I am knowing company, and I am telling you plenty Avgas in Varanasi.'

How to doubt such conviction? We made a flight plan to Khajuraho, prepared the flight and lined up on the runway.

'ROMEO-XRAY-ECHO cleared for take-off. Climb to Flight Level 050 direct Agra VOR,' the controller announced. Did he say Agra?

'Jaipur ROMEO-XRAY-ECHO. We are bound to Khajuraho VFR.'

'You are obliged to take the airway. You are cleared to Agra. Upon reaching, intercept Airway W33 to Khajuraho.'

We looked at each other in amazed delight. For once, things had worked in our favour. Having been refused permission to fly to Agra, we were now being sent there! A detour to any other city would have been infuriating, but this was our chance to overfly the Taj.

An hour later, abeam Agra airport, no special instructions were issued. The Taj glimmered in the haze ahead. Reduce speed, nose up, gear down. Descent at 1,500 feet per minute, to 1,000 feet. Gear up. Flaps one notch. Lowest speed possible. We swooped between vultures along the muddy Jumna River until the Taj, a white jewel radiating on its banks, floated past the window. This time we were breaking the law! It was worth it; we felt avenged. Full power. Flaps up. Back to 5,500 feet. No remarks from Control. We quietly resumed the correct heading.

At dawn in the holy city of Varanasi, hundreds of men, women and children descend to the ghats to bathe in the hallowed water of the Mother Ganges. Some take quick pragmatic baths; for most, it is a profound religious experience, as they stand waist deep in the thick brown water, hands joined in prayer, gazing with ecstasy at the glow of the rising sun. In the gentle morning light, the houses and maharaja palaces formed a poetic backdrop to the scene. We became absorbed in the profound ancient ritual, watching a *sadhu*, with unkempt hair and wild eyes, chanting and bowing in worship. A young woman, her long black hair flowing free, stared in intense adoration at the sun, eyes filled with inner peace.

Reality returned with a thump as our shallow boat was rocked in an eddy, bringing our attention sharply to the insalubrious water. A corpse swathed in white bandages, one stiff arm raised in protest, bobbed by ten feet from where bathers submerged themselves, gargling in the muddy water. The ashes and physical remains of bodies cremated at the burning ghats are cast into the water to float past women washing clothes or dishes, and bathers scooping up water to clean their teeth. Upstream, for a thousand kilometres, Indians had been dumping their refuse, sewage and dead into the river.

To be cremated at Varanasi and have your ashes flung into the Ganges is the sure way to Nirvana and an escape from the eternal cycle of life and death. Families unable to afford to cremate a loved one slip backsheesh to a rickshaw driver to dispose of the body directly in the river. Dead animals are also flung in – an illegal but common practice.

'Putting bodies in Ganga no good. Some peoples drinking water, getting sick,' our boat man said. 'Job of cowman putting in ground. Putting in river more easy. But very problem.'

As if on cue, the carcass of a cow floated past. Two crows perched on its back argued over the pickings.

The magic had faded for us. After thirteen days in India, Varanasi's maze of crowded backstreets were no longer picturesque, they were infernal. Full concentration was required for each footstep, for the stone paving was slippery with urine, slops and cowpats. Cows meandering the narrow alleys to forage force pedestrians into doorways. Complacent in their sanctity, they lie in the road chewing the indigestible cud of the refuse they eat. Vehicles pass within inches of their noses or legs, but they do not flinch.

'You'll never guess what's happened now,' Gérard exclaimed upon return from the Indian Oil office. (Well, I could guess, because he was livid.) 'That's right! No bloody Avgas. I told him his bloody colleague in Jaipur assured me that it was available in Varanasi, and what does he say? "I cannot be helping, sir. We are not having Avgas for thirty-five years!" Can you believe it. Thirty-five bloody years. I could strangle that pig-headed fool in Jaipur.'

It wasn't really funny, but I had to chuckle. It was difficult to get more definitive than thirty-five years. The nearest source of fuel was Allahabad. It was a military field, so we would never be allowed to land there. The closest civilian fuel depot was Lucknow, 130 miles away, but the tower would not allow us even to make a technical flight without authorisation from New Delhi. We only had a day to leave the country. Perhaps we could take a taxi to Allahabad, 120 kilometres away, and collect Avgas in drums. Or mix car fuel in one tank for straight and level flying, saving the other tank uncontaminated for full climbing power over the mountains to Kathmandu. We slept on it.

The next day, both options were eliminated. In a sudden public relations move, the Hindu government had announced a public holiday in honour of a Muslim festivity, and the fuel stations closed. But Varanasi Tower personnel were the kindest we had encountered in India. The controller radioed Lucknow to confirm that fuel was available and miraculously provided the home number of Mr Saha, who did not seem to mind being disturbed on a holiday and immediately sent instructions okaying our flight.

Back in Varanasi after refuelling, Gérard advised Customs of our intention to leave for Nepal early next morning when turbulence over the mountains would be minimal.

'Impossible!' the customs chief retorted. 'We are only coming on duty at 13:00 for Kathmandu flight.'

'Fine. We'll leave in the afternoon.'

'I cannot be clearing you without special permission, in writing, from Finance Ministry in Delhi.'

'Why not? Varanasi is a recognised Airport of Entry. You are obliged to clear all aircraft,' Gérard argued.

'Show me your arrival documents.' Papers were produced.

'This form no good. From immigration.'

'But, sir, look hard. It is stamped by a customs officer.'

The customs personnel gathered round to interrogate us, talking excitedly in Hindi and rotating their heads in the unique Indian fashion, before firing questions in English.

'Why are you entering India at Ahmadabad?'

'Because it is an Airport of Entry.'

'Ahmadabad is not possible. I am knowing very well that there is no customs in Ahmadabad. You are tricking me. Where are you entering India? Show me your passports!'

It was absurd. The chief refused to believe we had entered at Ahmadabad, despite the irrefutable proof of the immigration stamps in our passports. There followed half an hour of ludicrous argument and accusations of spying. Reining in his temper, Gérard advised through gritted teeth that our flight was authorised by New Delhi, and that we would take off at 13.30 the next day, regardless. They had twenty-four hours to decide whether we had forged our entry stamps or not.

Next day, a telex from Ahmadabad had duly confirmed our story and the customs chief had to eat humble pie. India, we concluded, was definitely no place to go with a private plane. The hassles had coloured our impressions of the country.

It was a relief to fly away, up to 11,500 feet, towards the crispy Himalayan peaks. The weather in Kathmandu, 192 nautical miles away, was reported as scattered cumulus at 2,500 feet AGL. Fine, but the Mahabharat Range blocked the way, shutting the Kathmandu valley off from the outside world. Cumulus clouds bunched together in conspiracy, forming a formidable wall soaring to 20,000 feet. Mid-afternoon was no time for mountain flying.

Was it worth the risk? Gérard was not keen to fly instrument in such cloud. A gap appeared thirty degrees left of course. With seatbelts securely tightened for heavy-duty turbulence, we dived into it. Swirling clouds swatted at the droning fly that was *Romeo*. Clammy veils swept the windscreen as we pierced towards the brightest spot, scouring the whiteness below for dangerous terrain. Sheer green mountainsides would lunge at us, frighteningly close. Their precipitous sides were not too much for industrious Nepalese farmers who had stratified them with rice paddies. Then, with the swoop of a magical theatre curtain, we burst clear over an inviting valley stretched like a cat in the sunshine. Red brick houses, green paddies, the smudge of a city ahead.

Kathmandu is a city of surprises, preserving its ancient jumble of charm in medieval alleys and crowded streets which radiate out from Durbar Square. Crimson-robed monks with Tibetan faces strode among scraggy *sadhus* and ladies in glorious saris buying vegetables. Dogs soaked up doorstep sunshine. Boys hawked tiny Buddhas and garish portraits of Hindu gods. One lad hand-fed a basket of vegetable leftovers to a fat white cow meditating on the steps of a stupa. Further along, a monstrous black bull blocked an alley as he faced two beggars crouched over a bowl of rice. He tossed his head, gazing at the food and insinuating in a fearsome manner. Unperturbed, they looked up periodically from shovelling rice into their mouths to make shooing motions at him.

In Thamel district, tourist lodges and restaurants compete hotly for the backpacker-trekker market. Stores drape climbing gear out into the street where T-shirts hang like bandannas, and touts jovially assault passers-by with offers of treks, tours, hashish and money-changing. After two weeks of curries, we gorged on steak au poivre and lemon meringue pie in a babel of pokey cafés.

Our trek would take us towards Helambu. Tika Ram Puri, our shy, clean-shaven guide, collected us with Krishna, the jovial cook, for a bumpy taxi ride to Sundarijal where the road ended abruptly against a sheer mountainside. Four porters packed equipment and six days' supplies into triangular wicker baskets to be suspended from a strap across their foreheads.

Climbing began, up through villages of thatched, red-brick cottages where corn cobs hung from the rafters to dry. Every square inch was cultivated with millet and corn, the terraces climbing on all sides like eternal staircases to heaven. Nepalese women wrapped in voluminous robes wore chunky gold earrings and nose-rings. They ignored us clambering clumsily through their villages. If we called out *Namaste*, they would smile sweetly and return the greeting. Little girls with wild, unkempt hair would make the *namaste* gesture as we passed, hands joined, as if in prayer, by the chest as we passed. 'One photo!' they would call, and scamper away. None asked for money.

Compared to the ragged, barefoot porters on Kilimanjaro, the Nepalese were well-dressed in jeans, gym shoes or flip-flops. Crew-cut Bhima, despite being exceedingly skinny, carried the largest load. Another Krishna, a Tibetan and a mimic of animal noises, constantly crinkled his face in laughter. Playful tiny Shyam, who looked Japanese, was the youngest. Tik, a thick-set Mongolian-looking young man, was on his first trek. By midday, his legs ached and he was mercilessly heckled by his colleagues. Although none of the four spoke English, a fun rapport developed. They staggered uncomplainingly under heavy baskets, singing increasingly louder versions of the same song. We could not understand the words, and to their amusement, made up our own 'sounds-like' equivalent:

Resam firiri, resam firiri
You are a donkey, I am a monkey
Resam firiri.

They roared with laughter and soon adopted our version.

Gérard and I once dawdled taking photographs. When we rushed to catch up, we rounded a bend to discover the baskets scattered in the path and no sign of any of them. We had heard stories of porters who, fed up with heavy loads and bad pay, dumped their burdens and went home. The abandoned loads glared at us in condemnation. What on earth should we do? Snickering noises came from above. There, dangling on the branches of a tree, six faces peered down, creased with pain to hold back giggles. Raucous laughter broke out, tears rolled down in pleasure at our self-conscious foolishness.

Beyond the village of Chepu Bhanjyang, swirling mists descended. The path hugged the precipitous hillside, and we hugged the path, seeing only a few steps ahead, groping along at the edge of a world that plunged into a white chasm. The eeriness was amplified by an announcement from Tika: dacoits had robbed and killed three Nepalese on that very path two weeks earlier. He pointed sorrowfully at the ashes of the camp fire where the men had slept the night they were murdered.

It was still foggy when we arrived at Chisapani (Cold Water), where a few red-brick thatched houses stood by new concrete housing built for the military dacoit deterrent. Supper was brought to us inside our cosy tent. We were given bland Western food and looked on enviously as Tika tucked into perfumed curry.

He was a good-looking lad who studied economics at university when not working as a guide to pay for his education. Realistically aware that there was little likelihood of finding a job in economics, he confessed he would probably end his days as a guide. Not much older than the others, he took his job seriously and was scrupulously fair.

Chisapani is perched on a crest. When we peeped out through the tent zipper at dawn, the proud horizon was formed by a row of pink snowy peaks which briefly turned liquid gold as the sun illuminated them. The valleys were in deep shadow and their floors obscured by lakes of cloud. As sun and temperature rose, the mist mounted the valley walls and swept over us. The rays gradually penetrated deep inside the gulleys, spotlighting small hamlets while all around remained in mysterious darkness. We sipped hot tea on the edge of the precipice, gazing in silent awe as Tika sang out the names of the peaks: Langtang Lirung, Ganesh Himal, Lapsang . . .

Golfu Bhanjyang, at 2,142 metres, was fog-bound and damn cold. We decided against the heroics of a tent and opted for lodgings, sharing a six-bunk dormitory of a mud-walled tin-roofed house with a French couple, Tika and Krishna. The porters found an outhouse in which to sleep and cook dinner. We joined them on the beaten-earth verandah. They were in high spirits, and after dinner started a sing-song. Krishna danced, hopping and genuflecting, waving his arms with oriental grace, for hours. Gérard sportingly survived a few rounds before collapsing. They all sang heartily and clapped noisily, regardless of the silence of the dark village. An old lady and her grand-daughter materialised on the periphery, and grandpa brought his *maadal* drum, which increased the animation until a thunderstorm drove us all to bed.

In the primrose light of dawn, hacking coughs announced early risers. At the well, barefoot teenage girls collected water in brass pots.

'I never been in Nepal,' a young man told us earnestly. It was not the first time we heard that extraordinary statement on the trek. Was it a joke? Tika explained that country folk refer to Kathmandu as Nepal.

A treacherous, wet path led along the side of a steep valley. It was no place for a haemophiliac to take a stroll. Heat-seeking missiles an inch long lay on the path, one end fixed to the ground, the other tasting the air. Leeches! We all gave blood. They home in on warm-blooded mammals by heat, not smell, and climb aboard unnoticed, their touch of great gentleness. Clinging to any shoes, they make their way over the rim or take a shortcut through the lace-holes and socks to attach themselves to the warm, succulent flesh beneath. Injecting an anti-coagulant to ease the flow of blood, the power of their sucking is such that love-bite bruises subsequently surround the bites, which bleed for some time. Ideally, they gorge until full, and then let go, but those inside boots find it less easy to squeeze out when bloated. The pressure of the walking foot bursts them. Live ones should not be ripped off, as the head would remain entrenched in the skin. The leech itself retracts its suckers if a lighted cigarette is held against it. Gérard diligently watched his boots, stopping frequently to fend off the assault. I kept a vague eye on my shoes, but only realised I had been attacked when tell-tale red stains appeared. Tika disgusted us all with a tale of how, as a young boy herding cows, he had fallen asleep in the grass and woken up to find his mouth full of leeches.

It was so hot in the valleys that, crossing one river, Gérard and I were tempted by an inviting pool below. We suggested a swim and met with blank fear. For once, we had the upper hand. We cajoled and tried to persuade. No way, people never swam in the rivers because they were afraid of the water, Tika said, admitting he could not swim. Water cascaded into the pool from surrounding boulders, but it was only knee deep. When he saw that we were determined to bathe, Tika felt obliged to join us and, in spite of himself, was soon splashing happily like a baby, while Krishna and the four porters sat on the bridge, watching with astonishment. Since we did not drown, Krishna could not bear to be left out. He joined us with wary bravado, and was soon laughing merrily. This persuaded Shyam, the daredevil who loved to sway the suspension bridges as we crossed them just to scare me. Tik came next. But Bhima and Tibetan Krishna were not convinced, though they looked increasingly tempted and might have joined us if we had withstood the cold water any longer.

Our final trek meal spelled the end of *kukra*, a chicken bought in a market that morning and carried, on my insistence and to their amusement, on top of the basket instead of dangling upside down by its feet. Krishna produced a coffee and chocolate cake, cooked to perfection on the campfire embers and decorated with flowers and candles. We were deeply moved and the evening rounded off with another *maadal* drum session.

A few days after returning to Kathmandu, we had a chance encounter with Tika. He warmly embraced us both, in a demonstrativeness out of character for a Nepalese. We took him for a meal, after which he produced two fine white scarves from his pocket and tied them round our necks in a traditional Tibetan good-luck gesture. He said he had already written to us in Rio.

We read his letter over a year later: 'Where is Brazil from Nepal? Can I see? 12 hour different oposit from Nepal. Land divide by the ocean but heart join by the love. I am getting worm love from you like ray of sun. When you return in Nepal or not? Mt. Everest inviting to you. Mountains are asking with me Where are Gerard and Margi? When they come to see us? I am saying soon-soon.'

15 'You will be intercepted by fighter jets'

The impressive wall of the Himalayas faded away like an old photograph and India spread her threadbare carpet under a cloudless sky up to the fringe of Calcutta. One of the most polluted cities on earth, it was hidden by a midday smog so thick that the runway lights only became visible one mile from the airfield.

We dreaded having to face Indian Customs again, but were waved ceremoniously towards the exit without any problems. The briefing room was a dingy office with a nauseous green carpet upon which lay sedentary deposits dated from the stone age. The window panes were so grimy that electric light was necessary all day. Having received a definitive No from New Delhi regarding our request to proceed to the Andaman Islands in the Bay of Bengal, we drafted telex messages to Rangoon and Bangkok. A couple of days and a dose of Delhi Belly later, a helpful man in the radio room talked to Rangoon Control, discovering that landing was out of the question in Burma, but that overflight was approved. Furthermore, he said Rangoon had spoken to the Thai authorities, who confirmed all was in order and that our clearance number would be given to us once airborne.

To simplify our lives on departure, we started lodging the flight plan a day ahead. This involved the collection of five different departmental signatures, in the right order. In a major airport like Calcutta, this meant several kilometres of footwork. It was unlikely that a flight plan and a flight could be made on the same day. Just to calculate the landing fees took an hour and a half.

On departure day, the formalities were effected in a record two hours, by which time the sun was drilling through the smog and we were aboard, engine running, requesting permission to taxi to the threshold. There arose a pesky problem of visibility. According to the controller, the RVR (Runway Visual Range) was 800 metres (300 more than we needed for take-off) and we must wait until it reached 1,500 metres. Gérard asked for an instrument departure. Refused. Three Indian Airlines 737s took off. Gérard pointed this out. Ah, but PT-RXE was not registered in New Delhi, as Indian Airlines was, for instrument departures below the minimums. Just wait. Gérard pleaded: we faced a six-hour flight east, with a two-hour time difference, and wanted to reach Bangkok before nightfall. Overhearing the discussion, an incoming Indian Airlines captain tried to help by confirming to Control that the entire runway was visible four miles out. It made no difference. The controller adamantly refused to budge.

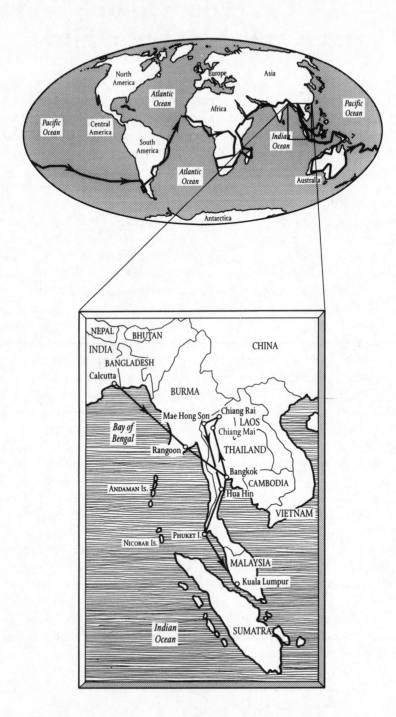

In India, we had been warned, it served no purpose to lose one's temper; only patient persistence would win through. But Gérard blew his top. Fuming, he stormed the terminal, spitting wasps and yelling unseemly insults about Mother India and her inhabitants, especially controllers, all the way down the admin block to the tower. Rows of little heads ducked behind desks. He bellowed, as he entered the control room, that he happened to know that the RVR system of Runway 19 was inoperative. What did they think they were playing at? An Indian Airlines pilot had confirmed full visibility four miles out.

'I just want to leave this bloody country, and never set foot in it again,' he roared. Perhaps Ganesh or Shiva heard him.

'Oooh! Look, the visibility has just improved,' the controller said sheepishly. 'I am thinking you can depart now.'

We fled, south over the grey-brown waters of the Ganges delta and its mangrove islands, and then south-south-east across the Bay of Bengal.

'XRAY-ECHO, you have negative, repeat negative, clearance to land in Bangkok,' Rangoon advised over the HF two hours later.

'There must be a misunderstanding,' Gérard explained. 'Your station advised Calcutta yesterday that the Thai authorisation number would be given once airborne. Please try again.'

'Stand-by.' Long moments passed. 'XRAY-ECHO, Bangkok maintains negative and advises that if you persist on current course and violate Thai airspace, you will be intercepted by Thai Air Force fighter jets.'

We stared at each other in disbelief. The Indian radio operator had assured us that all was in order. Burma was already visible ahead, pretty islands dotted on a clean blue sea. We requested a technical landing in Rangoon. The authorities were consulted. Permission refused. Rejection on all sides.

Surely the Thais would not shoot us down? Or would they? Burma was frustratingly close. Political turmoil and the intransigence of the military regime made it unwise to disobey. Malaysia, for which we had a clearance for a later date, was out of range at this stage. Bangladesh was nearby, but we had never even requested a clearance from them. That left . . . India! After Gérard's tirade, she would probably not let us back. Nay, she would no doubt rejoice in our predicament. Worse, we had no re-entry clearance.

We finally managed to contact Bangkok directly on the HF. A sympathetic Thai with an American accent agreed to plead with the authorities on our behalf. The final result was that we could proceed to Bangkok, subject to a strict investigation as to why we were entering Thai airspace illegally. Would the gravity of such a crime entail life imprisonment or death sentences, we wondered. The choice was ours. The Indians, for all their sins, were perhaps less likely to imprison us

149

than the Thais or Burmese. After three hours airborne, we decided to turn back. Calcutta did not query our intention to land. A different controller was on duty, but no doubt he had heard all about the bad-mannered Swiss pilot!

The only practical result of that six-hour flight to nowhere had been obtaining the elusive phone number of the DCA in Bangkok. We joined the interminable telephone queue at the airport. When the call finally went through, a Mr Sawat bollocked Gérard for entering Thailand illegally. He thought we were calling from Bangkok airport. It took some time to interrupt his tirade and explain we were back in Calcutta. A clearance was grumpily given, and the warning still stood: we were to report to headquarters on arrival in Bangkok.

Next day, buzzing like a gnat on the fringe of a locust storm, we were vectored in to land at Bangkok International with the big boys. We felt very grown up as a British Airways 747 held short of the runway to await our landing. It was thrilling to taxi behind a line of Airbuses and Jumbos but, just to cut us down to size, the tower sent us to park in the last bay beyond the domestic terminal where two marshals waited with chocks larger than our wheels. They had obviously rehearsed the only phrase they knew in English: 'You leport DCA tomolow.'

'You are Captain Moss,' announced a perspicacious young man with prominent ears who greeted us with smiles at Non-Regional Operations.

'There seems to have been some confusion. Calcutta assured us that-'

'Write a report,' he interrupted, pushing pen and paper before Gérard as if he was to do detention. After a while, the departmental head, an elegant lady in her thirties with a beatific smile, came over to see how the report was progressing. Again, Gérard tried to explain what had happened. She did not want to know.

'Just write it down,' she said.

The calligraphy exercise over, we enquired (not without trepidation) about flying to northern Thailand and the infamous Golden Triangle. There were absolutely no restrictions! Provided we flew instrument, we could go where we wanted. So why had there been such a fuss over our entry into Thailand? We were not even reprimanded. Puzzled, we set off to explore the city, weaving between the army of two-stroke three-wheeler putt-putts and throngs of street vendors flogging imitation designer underwear and cheap silk blouses. We marvelled at the exotic *wats, chedis* and stupas, with their resplendent golden or multi-coloured spires encasing mammoth Buddhas. Away from the traffic, we rippled up the Chao Phraya River and peeked at suburban life along the web of *klongs*, or canals.

Robert Schmidt, of the Thai Flying Club, invited us to join with the members that weekend in Chaing Rai, northern Thailand. Vanity got the better of us. We hastily gave *Romeo* a bath so that when we arrived, the Thai pilots would say 'Aaaahhh,' instead of, 'You crossed the Atlantic in that?' They had the best collection of private aircraft we had seen on our trip. Private ownership of aircraft was not permitted in Thailand, so the planes were technically owned by the club, though bought by individual pilots. Money was clearly no object. The planes were in excellent condition and equipped with the latest instruments, even though not one pilot was instrument-rated. They gave us a great welcome and, as we had expected, crowded round *Romeo* flooding us with questions. Pride swelled inside us. None of their fancy Tobagos, Mooneys or 172s could combine range with the space, comfort and payload we had. The Sertanejo was by far the best choice for what we were doing.

Teak-forested mountain ranges leaned against the horizon, crinkling increasingly paler into the haze. Mae Hong Son nestles in a valley in north-western Thailand, close to the Burmese border. Its one-way airstrip ends disconcertingly against a hill.

At a guest house beside a duck-filled lake overlooked by the colourful stupas of Wat Chong Kham, we met Crazy Ed. A balding, portly flower-power American grandfather with six stud earrings in one ear, he had first visited Thailand after shaking off a mega-cocaine habit, and fallen in love with it. To justify continual visits, he had set up a travel agency called Paradise Found. Ed's factotum was a young Thai called Kol who, when talking to Gérard, referred to me as 'your wife'. Overhearing this, Ed interrupted, telling Kol that just because we were travelling together did not mean we were husband and wife. He advised him in future to say 'your friend'. I pointed out that Kol was right.

'You're kidding me? You really are married?'

'What's so strange about that?'

'You seem too happy to be married.'

He had a point. Our trip had only been possible because, first and foremost, we were firm friends. To be constantly in each other's company could have resulted in blinding rows; instead, we had a lifetime of bonding memories.

Kyaw, a gaunt permanently smiling Burmese, joined our beer-laden table. When he heard from Ed that we had a plane, he beamed excitedly. He lived by a Kayan refugee village in the forests near the border. The village chief had never been in a plane, so he suggested we spent a night at the village and then took the chief flying. We agreed.

Next morning, we hired two motorbikes, one for us and one for hungover Kyaw, so that he could bring the chief down to Mae Hong Son. The morning mists had dissipated, leaving the mountain air as crispy as cornflakes. We whizzed through tranquil rural scenes where women, crouched under broad straw hats, planted new lurid-green rice. Buffalo munched in fawn-coloured harvested paddies between villages of wooden houses on stilts. Near the border, the dust was so bad we hung well back from Kyaw's bike and wondered what heavy traffic could have churned the road to powder dust. Log-trucks, of course, taking teak out of Burma! Logging is banned in Thailand, so the Thais, like the Japanese who have forests of their own but prefer to destroy those of poorer countries, buy logs from Burma.

In the forest, we came across a band of elephants and their *mahouts* off for a day's browsing, accompanied by several calves. We stopped to watch but Kyaw, bored by it all, sped on with a cheery 'you can't miss it – keep going straight on'. No fences mark the Thai–Burmese border in this area. Various tracks led off into the forest in all directions. So much for straight on. After several kilometres, we feared having inadvertently crossed the border. Trekkers have been known to wander unwittingly into Burma, with dire consequences. We anxiously monitored our progress by checking the dust for Kyaw's bike tracks. When at last we reached the village, Kyaw gave a whoop of delight as if he had not expected to see us again. He insisted we sat down for a rest, so we politely felt tired. The village chief, Shay Reh, a good-looking young man with a round face and flowing black hair, greeted us warmly. Kyaw had already told him about his pending flight.

A long neck is considered a sign of beauty in many parts of the world, but the Padaung have taken this one stage further. Otherwise known as the Long-Neck tribe, Padaung women stretch their necks by the gradual application of brass rings. Eight rings in a single coil are placed round a little girl's neck at six years old. More coils are added each year until, by the time a girl is twenty, they weigh up to four kilos. They cannot be removed unless the neck is bound because the atrophied muscles are unable to support the weight of the head. There were many more women in the camp than men. They wore traditional dress, a long shirt-tunic over a black skirt, and brightly coloured head-dresses they weave themselves. Apart from the brass neck coils, which gave them a stiff pose as if they had pulled a back muscle, more metal bangles weighed down their arms and upper calves. They had fled Burma two years earlier, abandoning their homes and fields to make the dangerous mine-spiked trek into Thailand. The village consisted of a dozen bamboo houses on stilts scattered under the trees. It had been named Bang Mai (New Village in Thai), but they called it Doh Selle, New Village in Karenni. Built of bamboo, each house had an open terrace, a kitchen corner, and a master bedroom with split-bamboo walls.

That night, sitting on the split-bamboo floor, we dined with Shay Reh and his family on cabbage soup, rice, chilli and tiny birds shot for our benefit with a home-made rifle. There was not a gram of flesh on them. They crunched their way through the whole thing, head and all, while we nibbled reluctantly.

After dinner, Kyaw led us by torchlight up a narrow path through the forest to the nearby Karenni (or Red Karen) refugee camp. On the terrace of the hut where his two children studied by candlelight, a guerrilla back from the battlefield told us of their forty-year struggle to make Burma into a federation of autonomous states.

'Politics is like the weather,' he remarked. 'Some days are cloudy, sometimes it rains, but the sunshine always comes out in the end.'

Such optimism keeps the agile rebels ambushing the heavily equipped government army when impossible odds should force them to desist. Their unilaterally declared independent Karenni government places great emphasis on education. He pointed out the rustic schoolhouse where over a hundred kids under twelve were educated.

'Who knows, one even might become president!' he said.

We had been billeted by Shay Reh in the house of an old lady who, despite the cloth round her brass-ringed neck, clanged like a bell each time she turned over on the floor beyond the flimsy bamboo partition that separated us. Icy air whistled up between the floorboards, piercing our summer-weight sleeping bags. Hacking coughs roused us at dawn. The Padaung women, their throats surrounded by cold metal, are susceptible to throat infections. Huddled in a jacket, a woollen hat pulled over his ears, Kyaw summoned us to Chief Shay Reh's home for hot coffee with condensed milk. It was cheering to think that there is still one drink more universal than Coca-cola.

When it was time to leave for town, Shay Reh, in his habitual blue-grey sarong and clutching a plastic bag, climbed onto the bike behind Kyaw. We arrived in Mae Hong Son unavoidably caked with dust. Kyaw and Shay Reh refused to fly without having a bath. We just brushed the dust off as best we could and prepared the plane while, on a pretext of returning the bikes, they vanished and reappeared squeaky clean. The plastic bag Shay Reh had clutched to his chest on the motorbike had contained a smart pair of jeans for the occasion.

The flight was memorable for us all. Our grinning passengers showed not the slightest fear. Both gazed out of the windows, nudging each other at the familiar landmarks. In minutes, we were above Nai Soi and circling Kyaw's house on the river bend, where his wife waved from the courtyard. Then following the dirt track where we could discern it through the trees, we found Doh Selle. Disappointment clouded Shay Reh's face as he saw how insignificant his chiefdom was compared to the immensity of the forest. But the excited chattering soon resumed and, upon landing, they thanked us profusely and sped away to tell their friends all about it.

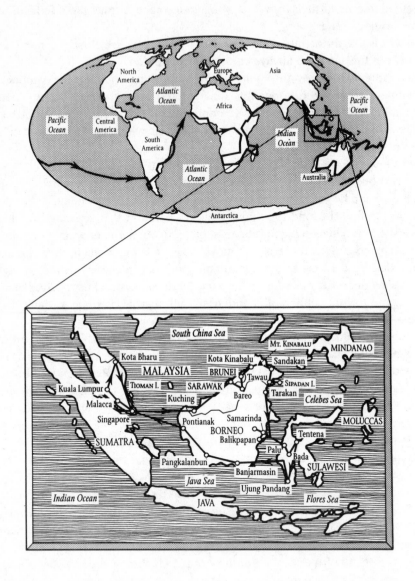

16 'We're on fire!'

At the tip of Peninsular Malaysia, beyond the oil palm plantations set out like rows of green starfish, fields of skyscrapers rose in the distance. An efficient controller vectored us towards Seletar airport. Singapore's first prime minister, Lee Kwan Yew, brought the island from sultry chaos in 1959 into a little Switzerland in just twenty-five years. His harsh tactics have given Singaporeans the high standard of living in which they now revel, despite a lack of certain personal liberties (chewing gum and over-eating are illegal). The national sport is shopping.

Ted and Susie Nation, friends who had moved from Rio to Singapore, were our patient hosts. Together with another friend, Jonathan Scherer, we set off one weekend for Tioman Island, off the east coast of Malaysia. Touted as one of the world's top ten islands, Tioman was the idyllic setting for *South Pacific*. Lush forested mountains rose out of the sapphire blue South China Sea, which turned aquamarine as it broke on the white beaches. Susie, a petite, blonde, fun-loving Australian, ill-disguised her aversion to small planes. She climbed aboard and immediately reached for the protective hand of tall, dark, handsome Ted. They had flown with us once in Brazil, from Rio to São Félix do Araguaia where we had camped on the river's sandbanks. On the return journey, beset by bad weather and engine problems, we had abandoned the plane in Anápolis. However, since we had successfully negotiated half the globe to reach Singapore, she banished her apprehensions and agreed to come along.

We knew that Tioman had a difficult one-way airstrip with mountains at either end. The only possible approach was to make a crooked base leg to avoid the hill behind Kampong Tekek and dive sharply towards the runway while maintaining sufficient height to clear the palm trees growing right up to the threshold. The length of the strip was effectively shortened by the fact that landings and take-offs are made with a tailwind, while heading for a sheer hillside. Every attempted landing must succeed. There is no second chance. A glance at the runway confirmed the warnings were not exaggerated. Fortunately, Ted and Susie were distracted by the view of the beaches. Jonathan, who was plugged into the headphones beside Gerard, looked like a small boy in the engine compartment of a train with his dad. To make room for us all, Gérard had removed the extra fuel-tank, and I sat on the floor in its place, with no seat nor seatbelt, fighting the momentum as he fought with the breaks. An acrid smell of burnt rubber filled the cabin.

On the Sunday evening, it was a tired, happy bunch that climbed aboard for Singapore. The heavens to the south were obliterated by a mega-Cb, its gunmetal grey ablaze with flashes of lightning. At the sight of it, Susie's blood pressure rose alarmingly, but the storm thankfully moved on over the Straits of Malacca.

I only noticed we had a different problem when I heard the landing gear being lowered for the second time. Why, I wondered, had Gérard raised the wheels again, so close to the airport? I peered over his shoulder to look for the 'three greens', the lights which indicate that each wheel is firmly locked in place. Only two lights were on. Gérard had done some maintenance on the landing gear a few days before. Perhaps some bolt was not sufficiently tightened? Or maybe the light bulb had blown? No point in mentioning anything to Ted and Susie – they were already nervous because of the thunderstorm. Gérard continued the approach. I didn't want to distract him with silly questions, nor give the Nations the impression I was worried. However, when I saw we were not lined up with the runway, I guessed we were to buzz the tower, standard practice to enable the controller to see if all wheels are down.

'What are we doing?' Ted asked.

I felt like a doctor avoiding a terminal patient's inquisitive eyes.

'Ummm, we're going to fly over the tower,' I replied nonchalantly.

'I see. Do you always do that?' His voice quivered.

'Not always.' It was only a little lie: we never did. But I didn't want to make them unnecessarily afraid.

We duly buzzed the tower and Gérard continued fiddling with the gear lever, up and down, up and down. Jonathan, who was wearing headphones and knew what was going on, watched like a hungry hawk. There was no more avoiding the subject.

'It seems there's a doubt whether one of the wheels is locked,' I ventured casually.

Susie's blue eyes swelled to the size of ping-pong balls as Gérard turned to make a captain's announcement.

'I am going to jolt the plane sideways to see if the wheel locks, so hold tight.'

He turned back to the job in hand. Susie didn't need telling twice. Her nails were already dug deep into Ted's thigh. On base leg, Gérard shuddered *Romeo* a few times before descending fast over the runway. Ted and Susie held each other in an octopus grasp while I, not having a seat-belt, tried to find a hand-hold. The wheels bumped two or three times on the ground and whooooossh! We took off again, full throttle, passed a fire engine with flashing red lights, the sight of which did nothing to appease Susie. As we aborted the landing, she stared at me in blank terror. What could I say? Things looked bad.

Gérard pulled aside his headphones. 'The gear seems to be holding,' he announced. The responsibility of other lives in his hands had made him tense. 'I'm going in for the proper landing.'

So, he hadn't intended to land the first time, he was simply gauging the gear while maintaining a good speed. I asked if I should unlock the back door for a quick getaway. When he shook his head, I knew he was sure the wheels were safe.

Susie's face was ashen. She tormented herself how her baby Sarah would manage as an orphan. Her concern contaminated Ted, whose air of bravado had dropped. I felt complete confidence in Gerard's decision and ability and tried to reassure them. If there was any doubt about the landing gear, he would have opted for a harmless wheels-up landing on the grass beside the runway. So, when all three wheels touched down smoothly, enthusiastic clapping and excited babbling filled the cabin. Wow! We're still alive! When we clambered out, Gérard and Jonathan were in stitches. As we had buzzed the tower, it transpired, the nervous controller was convinced his end was nigh. 'Mind the tower! Mind the tower!' he had bellowed down the mike. Presumably, he had dived under the table as, after our passage, he was unable to say if the gear was down or not.

'That has decidedly put me off small planes for ever!' Susie announced, tight-lipped.

Technically, Malaysia is a secular state, with Islam as the official religion. Only half its population are Malays, true sons of the earth, or *bumiputra* as they are known. Chinese make up about thirty-seven per cent, the balance being Indians and indigenous tribes.

Tucked between the glass and concrete of Kuala Lumpur's modern multi-storey town centre, a few terraced shopfronts still overlook traditional covered pavements, or five-foot ways. There is a vibrant intimacy in these backstreets, where real people walk and laugh, and buy orchids or fish from street vendors. Nearby, the Sri Mahamariaman Temple squats unobtrusively. When it was built in 1873, its remarkable dome, a jumble of multi-coloured figurines, no doubt dominated the houses which surrounded it. Today, you espy it quite by chance, when standing face-to-face. It is the starting point of the annual Thaipusan procession to the Batu Caves, when devotees pay their respects and request favours which they vow to recompense with penance the following year. The procession is a living spectacle bordering on the macabre. We joined it about a mile from the caves, at dawn. Hundreds of Hindu families, laden with baskets and plastic bags, were also arriving. They lay out their utensils of torture (fish-hooks, skewers) and magic (potions, powders and fruit) while the devotee about to fulfil his penance would work himself into a frenzy. One good-looking lad chatted merrily until I asked what his vow was.

'Let us just say it's to do with education,' he said secretively. 'Excuse me, I have to go into a trance.' Off he went to have his cheeks skewered.

In order to suffer the insertion of skewers (like those for making kebabs) and hooks (yes, fish-hooks) into their faces, arms and backs, devotees enter into a trance after chewing betel nut, sniffing camphor fumes and smoking powerful cheroots. Like medieval madmen, their eyes roll backwards and their bellows rent the air. They bite hard on their protruding tongues as skewers, sterilised with banana skins and lime juice, are driven through one cheek, through the tongue, and out through the other cheek. Their mouths are rinsed with soothing milk which, mixed with a sacred red powder, dribbles out like frothy blood. Many male devotees bear *kavadis*, metal frames of great weight and massive proportions decorated with an abundance of peacock feathers, suspended over their shoulders. The skin of their bare backs and chests is pierced by fish-hooks upon which limes, apples, oranges and little copper milk pots hang. Some add to their torture by dragging behind a brother or two whose task is to pull against metal chains connected to fish-hooks inserted in the penitent's skin, thereby increasing his suffering. Barefoot and wearing simple sarongs, they shuffle along the avenue leading to the caves, tongues hanging out, salivating. Family members follow, urging on each devotee with chants and drums. Female devotees, wearing yellow saris and bearing heavy brass urns full of milk on their heads or shoulders, mainly pray for sons. Half the milk is given to the priests, the remainder blessed and taken home.

The colourful procession arrived already weary at the flight of 272 steps rising to the caves. Despite the bizarre frenzy, behaviour was orderly as they struggled on. The caves were filled with the smoke of flaming torches and a roaring fire fed with camphor which belched black fumes towards a hole in the roof. It was like a medieval painting of a scene from hell. Devotees queued to have the skewers removed by a handful of appointed men. Drums beat out powerful rhythms. The trances had worn off and, faced with the painful extraction, devotees were given courage by their families to face the extractor, who moistened the skewer with his saliva before yanking it out in one swift movement. Some penitents had such swollen tongues that they were unable to close their mouths. Several fainted.

Sarawak and Sabah, two states in Borneo, the world's third largest island, joined the Federation of Malaysia in 1963. Sarawak, Land of the Hornbill, thus became Malaysia's largest state. Once part of the Brunei Sultanate, in 1841 it became the kingdom of Rajah James Brooke, an Englishman who helped the Sultan quell secessionists. It was the seat of intense rebellion against occupying Japanese forces during World War II. Its name is evocative of dense jungles, head-hunting tribes, orang-utans and the world's largest flower, the elusive rafflesia which can reach one metre in diameter. Tribal peoples – Ibans, Land Dayaks, Melanau, Penan – make up fifty per cent of Sarawak's inhabitants. They have lived in the great forests for hundreds of years without destroying them. But now, primary rainforest is being converted into plywood, scaffolding and disposable chopsticks. The federal government (not the Sarawak State Government) is plundering this treasure at such a devastating rate that even the International Timber Association has voiced alarm. Brazil is constantly criticised about the Amazon, but world opinion keeps strangely quiet about all the destruction in Malaysia and Indonesia.

Sarawak's capital, Kuching ('cat' in Malay), is a graceful town which straddles the Kuching River. Its clean streets wind between imposing colonial buildings, such as a post office with Corinthian columns and the stately law courts. The majestic palace, or Astana, built in 1870 by Rajah Charles Brooke, continues as the official residence of the head of Sarawak state. In the market, buxom women in wide-rimmed palm hats sold crinkled crimson rambuttans and pungent durians (not unlike jack-fruit). We first thought the nauseous smell of durians emanated from a pile of gas cylinders stashed on the dock. There are those who adore its thick, putrid flavour, but many abhor it. NO DURIANS PLEASE notices are prominent in public places, for the rotten smell contaminates the whole building.

The numerous airfields dotting our 1978 ONC chart were no indication of landing options. Many had been closed after the suspension of missionary aviation services by the government concerned that the tribes were being led down a Christian rather than Islamic path. Thereby ended an invaluable service for peoples previously disdained by the authorities. So we headed north-north-east at 3,500 feet across flat lowlands, patchily deforested, periodically catching sight of longhouse settlements. Those closest to 'civilisation' had substituted traditional palm-thatch roofs with shiny corrugated iron. Near Miri, acres upon acres of rainforest had been clear-felled, leaving the land desolate and unused. From above, wanton destruction of the rainforest is a despairing sight.

We landed at Marudi, a one-street town with pastel-coloured wooden houses on stilts nestled on a bend of the muddy Baram River. A Twin Otter was parked on the tarmac beside us. A small crowd in their Sunday best assembled to watch the harassed pilot, who sat cross-legged in the shade of the wing beside a huge set of scales. He noted down the weights of numerous boxes and bundles, a metal filing cabinet and sheets of corrugated iron to be loaded for Long Lellang, in the Tama Abu mountains beyond road access. In the end, an argument broke out. The pilot refused to take off with the cargo because some boxes had been loaded surreptitiously into the plane behind his back. In addition, the owner of the cargo insisted that his wife should go along. The pilot maintained it was a cargo flight, but finally agreed to take her in the co-pilot's seat. She refused to board without her children, who refused to go without the grandparents, who refused to let the cargo go without them!

Marudi was clouded over in the morning, but the weather report announced that Bario, our destination in the highlands, was clear. We climbed above the layer and passed 7,800-foot Mount Mulu which the clouds, in argumentative confusion, fought to suffocate. Being a National Park, it was thickly coated with trees, but the surrounding hills bore the eyesore scars of loggers' destruction. Exposed, the bare soil glared like eczema and washed into the rivers, turning them muddy brown. In virgin valleys still awaiting the whine of the chainsaw, the rivers were as black as the Rio Negro: black from decomposing vegetation, not pollution.

Bario, a glint of corrugated iron along one side of the grass airstrip, reposes in a broad valley at 3,500 feet. There were only two ways to reach it: a week-long walk through the forest, or by light aircraft. Kelabit villagers had gathered in the shade of a wooden shack entitled Kelabit Highlands Bario Co-operative Multi-Purpose Society Limited. The older men and women had extended loopy earlobes in which hung massive chunks of brass. The men wore straw hats like baseball caps, with a design improvement of an additional shade for the back of the neck.

The daily Twin Otter flight was due in. It pulled up in 300 metres, putting *Romeo* to shame – we required the whole runway. Boxes, baskets and crates of cans were unloaded and carted off in wheelbarrows. Each passenger was weighed with his luggage so that precise calculations could be made to establish how many sacks of Bario's fragrant rice and famous pineapples could be air-freighted to Miri.

Together with Mike Puleston, a cheery Australian teacher working in the Sultanate of Brunei, we took a mad-dogs-and-Englishmen stroll in the muggy afternoon to Arur Dalan, a longhouse village a few kilometres away. A buxom young girl called Serena invited us into the longhouse for coffee. The sun peeped through the side windows, illuminating the length of the wooden-floored hall, a communal area for the many families who lived in the longhouse in compartments along one side. It exuded a sense of unity and sharing. Most residents were working in the fields. Serena, who was minding some toddlers, bade us sit on raffia mats and produced delicious coffee enriched with condensed milk and slices of juicy pineapple. She lived in Kuching and was on holiday to visit her grandparents. She dreamed of leaving the city and returning to live in a longhouse.

On the way to Sabah, we stopped to refuel on Malaysia's oil-rich island of Labuan. In the arrivals hall, beside a warning that the penalty for drug-trafficking was death, was another prominent sign: 'IMMIGRATION WARNING: Malaysia welcomes bona fide tourists but not hippies. You are therefore advised at all

160

times to dress, behave and live decently in hotels as becoming a bona fide tourist. If you are found dressed in shabby, dirty or indecent clothes, or living in temporary or makeshift shelters, you will be deemed to be a hippy. Your visit pass will be cancelled and you will be ordered to leave Malaysia within 24 hours . . .' So, no camping in Malaysia!

Mount Kinabalu, or 'Aki Nabilu', Home of Departed Spirits to the local Kadazan tribe, soars majestically out of the jungle to 13,500 feet. It is a two-day climb from the National Park entrance at 6,500 feet. One of the species of pitcher plants found in abundance on the trail is named after Sir Hugh Low, who made the first recorded climb in 1851. Unable to extract sufficient nutrients from the poor soil, these plants have a leaf which bends back forming a pitcher which fills with rainwater. The plant absorbs the nutrients from the bodies of drowned insects attracted by its smell.

By 9,000 feet, my heart was thumping like a base drum. Each step on the dusty path through wild rhododendrons was a terrific effort. Gérard cajoled me, pushed and shoved until we staggered over the ledge to Laban Rata rest house, at 10,500 feet, in time to catch the sunset glowing on layers of cloud stretched out way below us. Climbing Kilimanjaro, we had taken two days to reach 10,000 feet, thus allowing the body to acclimatise. I vowed to go not a step further.

High altitude brings on insomnia, so by the 3:30 a.m. wake-up call I was game to try again. Tightly wrapped against the bitter cold, we scrambled by torchlight up sheer rock on rudimentary wooden rung ladders where stunted trees typical of high altitude struggled for rootholds on the granite. The dawn finally illuminated the summit plateau, striated millennia ago by glaciers that had spared the awe-inspiring crags of South Peak, Ugly Sister, Donkey's Ears, Dragon's Tail. Although made of solid granite, our guide told us, Kinabalu grows by five centimetres per year! It is being pushed upwards by two colliding tectonic plates. We leaned against enormous boulders at the summit in full sunshine, and tried to feel it grow as we gazed at the view beyond the sheer abyss on three sides.

Not content with having climbed the mountain, Gérard wanted to soar around it in the plane on our way to Sandakan. When we took off just after dawn from Kota Kinabalu, there the mountain stood, proud dark-blue on a duvet of mist just thirty nautical miles away. We circled it, climbing slowly past the climbers breakfasting on the terrace at Laban Rata. On foot, we had seen only a tiny part of the whole jagged spectacle. From the air, the bulk of the mountain and its numerous inaccessible crags were impressive. Gérard swooped closer and ever closer, inspired by the same thrill of testing limits that made him enjoy racing cars. He loves this kind of flying. I hate it.

161

'Okay, we've seen it now. Let's go. I'm scared.'

'Don't be silly. There's no problem.'

'How d'you know?' His self-confidence annoyed me. 'You can't see turbulence. We could get sucked down by a massive down-draught.'

'Trust me. There's no wind. Just look at that! It's great!'

'What makes you so damn smart? Even big planes with radar hit windshear. We've seen the damned mountain. We've even climbed it. That's enough!' In my memory was the story of the newly licensed chopper pilot who went to wave at his girlfriend in her high-rise apartment. The down-draught on the leeward side smashed him to the ground. A similar fate befell a well-qualified pilot on a sight-seeing trip at Fujiyama.

'Oh, come on. Don't be daft. Would I do it if it was risky? You know me. It's all right, I tell you.'

'Everyone thinks they know what they're doing till they crash.'

He ignored me. On we went, up to 13,500 feet, swooping over the crags like an eagle. Fuming, heart racing, I tried to concentrate on filming because the mountain seemed farther away through the camera lens. Then I sulked all the way to Sandakan.

A young orang-utan (literally, 'man of the forest') was pulling up fence posts for fun. We were trekking through a hot, humid patch of forest at the Sepilok Orang-utan Rehabilitation Centre on the way to a feeding platform where orphaned orang-utans have their diet supplemented on bananas and milk whilst they learn to survive in the forest on their own. They were usually victims of logging or rescued from animal traffickers.

My leg muscles ached horribly from the Kinabalu climb so Gérard went ahead while I dragged behind, groaning up and down the slopes. I rounded a bend in the track, to behold a puce, terrified Scotsman trying to shake off a juvenile orang-utan which had wrapped its jaws round his calf. Gérard was looking on with some bemusement. He had, it transpired, already encountered a similar scene. The same orang-utan had first rugger-tackled an English girl who had promptly lost her balance and fallen over in the mud. Her weedy boyfriend looked on from a safe distance behind a tree. Gérard went to the maiden's rescue, and the tackle was promptly transferred to his own legs. It was not painful, because no pressure was applied with the formidable teeth. It was simply disconcerting to look down and see an orang-utan's face wrapped round your socks. Without a word of thanks, the damsel had scarpered, boyfriend in tow, leaving Gérard to sort himself out. He had just prised open the ape's mouth when the Scotsman arrived to take centre-stage. I produced a banana, and waved it in the orang-utan's face as an exciting alternative to Aberdeen

Angus steak. Its interest aroused, I chucked it a safe distance into the bushes. The orang-utan dived after it, and we all beat a hasty retreat.

A speck in the Celebes Sea off the coast of Sabah, Sipadan is a mushroom atoll topped with a tuft of green vegetation rising behind perfect white sands. Three metres beyond the gin-clear shallows, the sea floor plunges 2,800 feet and the water turns an intense navy blue. When Jacques Cousteau visited the island in the mid-80s, he remarked that he had not seen such an unspoiled place for forty-five years. That Cousteau could be astounded by the beauty of its underwater world says it all. An abundance of fish of all sizes and colours put on an outlandish parade against the kaleidoscopic backdrop of corals, all tangibly close with a snorkel. And then whoomph! . . . a breathtaking plunge into a bottomless pit, a cliff edge along which sharks glide, barracudas shimmer and green turtles flap in slow motion like prehistoric UFOs.

We invited Douglas Leong, the Malaysian-Chinese owner of Pulau Sipadan Resort, a handful of bamboo huts where we stayed, to join us making a flight over the island. The mainland was already lost from view and we were ten minutes short of Sipadan, when Gérard brusquely turned on Douglas.

'Sorry Douglas, no smoking in here.'

'But, I'm not smoking!'

'Surely . . . but – can't you smell smoke?' There was an unmistakable smell of burning. '*Meeeerde!* We're on fire!'

Fumes filled the cockpit and the acrid smell of burning became stronger. A fire in the engine! My pulse set off at a gallop. I soon visualised a blazing aircraft hitting the water with a sizzle. Christ, just when we had a passenger on board *and* were over the sea, a sea in which we had already seen many sharks. Even if we survived the crash, the life-raft could barely hold two.

Gérard immediately switched off all the radios, in case there was a short circuit, and headed back towards land. His decision tormented me. Wasn't it better to fly close to Sipadan, and swim to the island, rather than head for the invisible mainland and fall in the water halfway there, too far to swim either way? Gérard's first thoughts were to save the plane. He figured we could all swim. It was only a sea, not an ocean. Douglas uttered not one word. He stared ahead. Resigned.

Within moments, the fumes had cleared and the smell faded. Clearly one of the radios was to blame. We cheered up. Since there was nothing wrong with the engine, we made another U-turn and buzzed Sipadan before returning to Tawau. We parked beside a Trilander, an ugly three-prop-engined plane which looks like a bullet train. It belonged to Bali Air and was departing for Tarakan, our next destination. Its Indonesian pilots informed us that Customs only operated in

163

Tarakan when the Bali Air flight landed there, thrice a week. We needed to leave immediately or wait three days. Never mind the damaged radio! We rushed to clear Malaysian exit formalities and left Douglas in the airport cafeteria to recover from his traumatic experience.

Oil-rich Tarakan Island was only sixty miles away. We crossed into the Indonesian state of East Kalimantan. Beyond, acres of Borneo were alight, the smoke impairing the visibility as it does when acres of Amazon are similarly burned. Gérard had asked the Indonesian pilots to warn Customs that another aircraft would be arriving. They hadn't bothered. The immigration officer had gone home. He received us at his house, in sarong and slippers.

'Vely plobrem. No visa,' he announced, glancing at the passports.

'We checked with your consulate in Singapore. Swiss passports don't need visas.'

'Need. Vely plobrem. Tarakan need visa. You go visa Tawau.'

'Swiss no need.'

'Need.' He pointed to a paragraph on the visa regulations which listed the points of entry not requiring visas. Tarakan was not one of them. Damn! We had blown it this time. It was almost dark, too late to return to Tawau. We vacillated.

'I help you!' he announced suddenly, disappearing into a back-room and emerging with stamps and papers. He took the Gen Decs, thumped them with bureaucratic ink, did the same with the passports and proudly handed them back. We were astounded and grateful. How easy it had been. How kind of him. Gérard glanced into one passport. Across a Crew visa, was meticulously written: Entry 14MAR 1991, Exit 15MAR 1991. One day!

'Never mind,' he maintained, 'you stay one month. You clew. No plobrem. Now, plis, to excuse me. I must play tennis.'

So that was why he had found a quick solution! We were no longer his 'vely plobrem'. We knew the Crew stamp would cause headaches if we ignored it. Balikpapan, which did qualify as an entry point not requiring visas, was a two-hour flight south. We could make our official entry there, having landed 'for technical reasons' (fuel) in Tarakan.

Before departure the next day, we were curious to discover which radio wire had burned out. But underneath the engine cowling, we were in for a surprise. A complete bird's nest, slightly charred at the edges, lay cosily arranged above the rear cylinder. We burst out laughing. It took some time to remove all the hay, between chortles and pity for the industrious bird. Presumably the 130-knot winds in flight had put out the flames. We had continued to Sipadan, flown to Tawau, and even on to Tarakan with the nest intact!

In Balikpapan, we tried to explain to three dour immigration officers that we needed entry stamps, having stopped in Tarakan only for refuelling. They refused.

'Not possible. Go Tawau. For visa.'

'Listen, Balikpapan is an official Airport of Entry, isn't it? We've seen the list. Swiss passports don't require visas.'

To show that we wouldn't be easily deterred or intimidated, we found immigration forms and filled them in while they argued amongst themselves about us. If we were pilots, we could not be tourists, even if we were on holiday. They suggested giving us another Crew stamp, and advised that we would have to report to Immigration in every town we visited. Then, suddenly, the mood changed: entry stamps pounded into our passports, smiles flashed, and wishes for a pleasant stay boomed over hearty handshakes. In a trice, all three picked up their jackets and hats and rushed out to where a jeep was pulling up. Lunchtime! It seemed that timing was crucial to solving plobrems in Indonesia.

We had wanted to follow the muddy Mahakam River into the Apo Kayan highlands and visit longhouse settlements where head-hunting is not entirely a sport of the past. However, a pilot from Mission Aviation Fellowship (MAF) at Samarinda warned that then, in the wet season, the inland airstrips were out of the question for an aircraft like ours. So we abandoned Borneo in the clutches of rainstorms, and crossed the Makassar Strait to Palu, an attractive town at the end of a long inlet between mountain ranges on the island of Sulawesi, former Celebes.

One morning, under a watery blue sky, we proceeded south over a confused landscape of dried-up savannah, luminous-green paddies and luxuriant forest, climbing over a cloudy mountain pass to Bada. We crossed in the air with a MAF pilot flying the opposite direction, who warned that the strip at Bada was not good, describing it as an overgrown banana, curved with ditches at the end. We decided to judge for ourselves. The spectacular Bada Valley was dotted with paddies and villages with steep A-roofs. A large river wound lazily between them. The grass strip looked inviting. A crowd gathered at the terminal hut watched in bemusement as we buzzed three times to check the runway surface.

'Why the hell do we do this?' Gérard exploded in fury as he struggled to break before we ploughed into the long grass hiding the ditches at the end of the runway. The strip was very short. Too damn short. Despite the warning, the stunning valley had enticed us down. It was going to be impossible to take off again with the weight we had on board. Villagers crowded round. They were used to high-wing Cessnas, but had never seen a bird like ours. Gérard's head was spinning with equations of how we could lift off at an altitude of 2,500 feet, at 25 °C, on a rough, curved airstrip 400 metres long. With a sombre face, he paced the field, measuring and remeasuring each feasible clump of grass and worn patch of clay. He hired a team of volunteers to scythe the longer grass, thereby extending the usable runway. They thought he was mad, because the Cessna could land and take off with five passengers and luggage, no problem. Why couldn't ours make it with only two?

We were still fretting when we heard the drone of the returning Cessna. Its pilot, an Indonesian named Dar Bone, was kind and friendly (he could have said 'I told you so') and admitted that even in his STOL Cessna 185, he took off from Bada fifty kilos under maximum weight. Part of our problem was that we had filled up in Balikpapan. We suggested Dar brought some empty drums on his next flight, so that we could fill them with Avgas and leave them as a stock for him.

Charles Dupa, a middle-aged man who spoke a little English, offered to take us to see Bada's famous megalith stones. Since this was the objective of our visit, I managed to distract Gérard from his concerns about the take-off predicament to go along. I climbed on the rear of Charles's motorbike, and Gérard went with Salang Hambali, a laughing Muslim lad with flowing black locks. Regardless of the potholes and puddles, each tried to be the macho ahead. The track became a narrow, rutted footpath. Our bare calves were scratched by thorns and twigs as Charles and Salang continued their race to a grassy plain where the famous megalith stood, tilted at sixty degrees. Sculpted in pale grey rock, its simple lines and calm face evoke modern art. The arms curve round two flat circles, which protrude as breasts, to clutch at an erect penis. Charles and Salang grinned.

Back at the airport, it was a long, slow process bleeding fuel into Dar's drums. We offered to fill up the motorbikes. I told Charles that he would be able to take off. He was wary, visualising his bike up with the birds, but Salam immediately sped out on the runway. The response of his engine so delighted him that he rushed away to fetch another jerry-can. Meanwhile, I jettisoned all our food supplies (rice, milk powder, sugar, tins) plus some clothes and toiletries, giving them to the villagers who finally believed we did have weight problems.

We decided to camp at the airstrip and attempt a take-off at first light when the temperature would be lowest and, hopefully, there would be no wind. Until then, the only direction in which take-off was feasible – i.e. downhill – was with a tailwind which exacerbated the problem. Then, early evening, heavy clouds closed in on all sides and the temperature dropped to twenty degrees. An approaching storm changed the wind direction in our favour.

'Come on! We've got to try now. Now or never,' Gérard said suddenly. 'Throw everything in. Quick. It's our chance.'

We climbed aboard. He was very serious, very tense.

'Right, Margi. This is it,' he gulped. Shiny beads of sweat had formed on his brow. For once, I felt quite relaxed, confident in his skill and *Romeo*'s knack of defying gravity. The engine purred normally, blissfully unaware of our misgivings as we taxied to the last square inch of runway above the river bank.

'Right, this is really it.'

I had never seen him so nervous. We tightened the seatbelts. As the engine warmed up, we contemplated the miserable patch of lawn impersonating a runway. He leant over to give me a farewell kiss. Wow! It was serious. I felt strangely aloof, as if in a dream, unable to believe our destiny lay in a ditch in the mountains of Sulawesi. He pushed the throttle forward, holding *Romeo* on the brakes.

'This is it.' For the third time, the same phrase, the same finality.

We jolted forward. Twenty knots, thirty, forty, forty-five, fifty. The bushes sped closer. Fifty-five knots in the long grass that held us down. Sixty knots. Gérard yanked on full flaps, forcing *Romeo* into the air before the wings were ready to fly, but just in time to skim the bushes at the end of the airfield.

'Come on, *Romeo,* up we go. Come on, please. Fly. Fly, babe!'

We dropped into a small dip, gaining the precious knots needed to stay airborne.

'Pheeeeeew!' he sighed, taking long, deep breaths. 'That was tight!' He gently lifted my hand and placed it on his racing heart. Thump! Thump! Thump! He really had thought we would kill ourselves. My fearless calm was pure ignorance.

Once airborne, flying seemed effortless. We wound in circles, gaining height over the valley. Dar had warned that to reach Tentena we had to cross a 6,000-foot pass in the Tineba mountains rising on either side to 7,500 feet. Swirling clouds had formed a wall all round the valley, making it impossible to stay visual. Tentena was only a tantalising twenty miles away . . .

The charts were not fail-safe. Much of the area, blank and uncharted, read 'Maximum Elevation Figures believed not to exceed 9,100 feet'. What if we couldn't find Tentena? Or if it was cut off by bad weather? It was my turn to panic.

Gérard persevered through the whiteness, confident of finding a route. With no visual ground contact, we blindly trusted our newly acquired GPS (a reliable satellite navigation system in place of the SatNav) to keep us safe until, suddenly, a dark-grey flatness spread below: Lake Poso. If we were over the lake, we could safely circle down and skim across it towards Tentena in the north-eastern corner. For the second time in twenty minutes, waves of relief, mine this time, swept the cockpit.

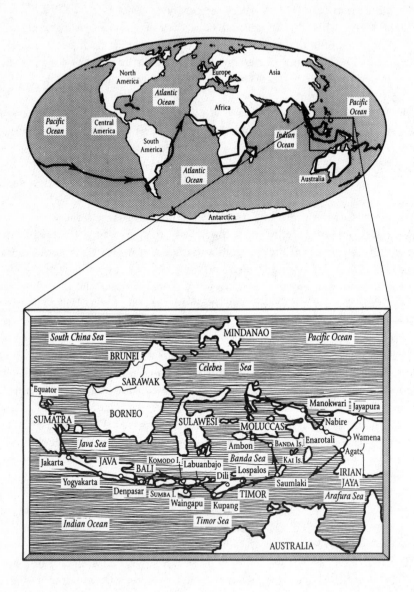

17 'Why did you go to Lospalos?'

Indonesia is the most volcanic country in the world: 128 of its more than 400 volcanoes are still active. They bring destruction, but they also provide mineral-rich soil. Java is extremely fertile. It is also one of the most densely populated places on earth: 100 million people on an island the size of Ireland. Rather than encouraging some sort of family planning, the government has a trans-migration policy, uprooting (initially forcibly, now voluntarily) low income Javanese families and fobbing them off to less populated islands where they disrupt local cultures.

At dawn, poetic wisps of pink smoke emerged from Mount Merapi, Indonesia's most volatile volcano, rising in a perfect cone near the vast Buddhist stupa at Borobudur. Built near Yogyakarta between AD 775 and 850 by kings of the Sailendra dynasty, it was mysteriously abandoned six years after completion. The jungle engulfed it. Subsidence and humidity gnawed at it for 1,000 years until its rediscovery for the outside world in 1814. UNESCO undertook a massive painstaking reconstruction programme. It regained its former glory in 1983.

We were privileged to circle it from above, absorbing its geometrical design of dog-toothed squares within squares moulded onto a hillock and topped with four circular tiers. This pattern is lost to visitors on the ground who enter by the eastern gate, and climb up the tiers of the stupa, lined with intricate carved stone panels depicting the life of Buddha in historic battles and family scenes. The upper tiers become simpler, representing Buddha's approximation to enlightenment. Three layers of stone lattice stupas, like petrified bells, once each housed a statue of Buddha. Few remain; most were stolen for art collectors.

Labuanbajo, a picturesque Muslim village at the western tip of Flores Island, is the starting point for boat excursions to the Komodo Islands, home territory of the feared Komodo dragons. We chugged out across the silver mirror of Bajo bay as the sun rose, its mellow light moulded sensuously round the eroded hills. The luxuriant vegetation typical of Borneo, Sumatra and Java had become a dry landscape of savannahs and palms. We passed several yellow isles with *kampong ayer* (water villages) standing resolutely on their stilts in the sea, until at last, Komodo loomed, intimidating, ahead.

The Komodo dragon, *Varanus komodoensis*, is the world's largest lizard. Locally known as *ora*, it is a vicious carnivore measuring up to four metres in length. Four metres! Dangerous for all warm-blooded creatures including man, it has been eliminated from most of its habitat and now lives chiefly on Komodo, where a National Park has been created to protect it. An official guide led us through the forest trail to the feeding platform, an hour's walk along a dry riverbed with scant shade. He had an eagle eye, spotting a flying lizard camouflaged against a tree trunk and a green snake coiled up in a totally green bush. He gave a headache to a 'very poison' dark-brown snake lying on the trail by throwing a pebble at it. Furious, it curled up in a tight circle to strike, before deciding it was more prudent to move on. As we progressed, he pointed out the enormous footprints and scraping tracks of the *ora's* tail in the sand. We might meet the creatures face to face at any moment. Our only weapon was a long forked wooden staff which he carried. At last we reached the fenced-off wooden *pondok* on a cliff above a dry creek, where a dozen dragons, not exactly cute, lay in waiting. Scales flaked off their pimpled reptilian skins and ominous forked yellow tongues regularly tasted the air while stony-black eyes kept track of our movements. In times gone by, visitors would take along a goat to attract the reptiles, but this easy banquet has been regulated to twice weekly, to force them to lead natural lives hunting deer, wild pig, birds and fish. Even so, the dragons have learned they can lie around all week beside the *pondok* and are still guaranteed two good meals.

One of the guide's colleagues had been attacked while leaning over the railing, but he had been lucky. The doctor of a cruise ship in the bay had treated his mangled arm. *Ora's* teeth are small, but they are razor sharp on one side. They rip off the flesh rather than bite. Even if a dragon cannot defeat a large animal immediately, it is sure to die after being bitten because their saliva is impregnated with bacteria which cause massive infection. Strong digestive juices enable them to eat the whole corpse of their prey – bones, hair, horns. No trace was left of a Swiss naturalist, Baron Rudolf von Reding Biberegg, who disappeared in July 1974. Only his unappetising camera and glasses were found. The tactic for dealing with a dragon attached to your leg or arm is, they say, much the same as for sharks. Wait calmly (!) until the animal opens its mouth for a larger bite, and pull the limb away.

To goad the lethargic *ora* into action, the guide made goat bleating noises and we saw first hand how they moved with surprising alacrity and agility. Upon leaving, we followed the normal track down the hill across open savannah. I traipsed nervously between the guide and Gérard, keeping a wary eye on the surroundings. Suddenly, the guide lashed out with his forked staff into the shade under a bush by the path where a giant *ora* lay, licking its lips. After a couple of prods, it waddled away. Had it not been for the guide's acute attention, Gérard, who was bringing up the rear, could have been the second Swiss to succumb.

170

Indonesia's 13,000 islands languish over 5,000 kilometres of tropical waters, dividing the Indian from the Pacific Ocean. These islands harbour an enormous diversity of cultures – the Tanatoraja of Sulawesi, the Batak and the Minangkabau in Sumatra. Sumba, home to Indonesia's greatest horsemen, was another cultural treasure. Yohanis Dakumbera, a neat Sumbanese we adopted in Waikabubak, led us to visit traditional villages. The houses, or *uma*, with spire-like thatched roofs which descend almost to the ground, are set around massive rock tombstones. The pillars of the shady verandahs where women weave priceless *ikat* textiles are decorated with the buffalo horns and pig tusks of sacrificed animals. The teeth of adult villagers were stained red from chewing betel nut. After years of sucking tobacco, the older women's upper lips were grotesquely distorted as if they had been punched in a marital row. It was sad to think that the young girls, exquisitely beautiful, would inevitably become deformed in this way.

The Sumbanese *marapu* religion, or ancestor-worship, means that life is centred round the dead. Funerals are great celebrations, at which vast numbers of buffaloes, pigs, horses and dogs are sacrificed to honour the departed. In former times, slaves were also put to the knife. Despite my horror of the subject, I found myself morbidly asking Yohanis how all this killing was carried out. A specific knife, or *parang,* is used by specially qualified people. When large animals, such as buffaloes or horses, are sacrificed, teams of men pull on either side forcing the animal's head up so that the jugular is exposed for the slash. Horses die quickly, Yohanis said, but a buffalo can take up to an hour to bleed to death, collapsing slowly as the blood drains out. Pigs are slain with a spear through the heart, as there is too much flesh on their necks for a clean cut to the jugular. Dogs are sacrificed by a bridegroom in honour of the parents of the bride. All animals slaughtered are eaten.

It was the custom to offer betel nut to visitors arriving in the villages. We avoided having to eat it by putting the customary 1,000 rupiah in the basket, as an exchange of gifts. At Tarong, a village on a rocky outcrop overlooking the paddy fields, we were invited into the chief's *uma*. Adi, the chief's son, had broken his leg in a motorbike accident. Prostrate in the darkness of the *uma*, he greeted us warmly. When our eyes finally focused, we could see his knee, twisted to one side, was swollen like a melon. When he moved his leg, the lower half clicked out of place. Various scabs showed where the bone had broken through the flesh. After a week in hospital, he had discharged himself because he was not cured, and resorted to traditional medicine. A special medicine-man slays an animal: if the animal's heart is healthy, it is a good sign that a sick person will recover. After three weeks of sacrifices, there had been no improvement. His father had gone that morning to consult

171

the spirits of the dead. We offered to take Adi with us to hospital at Waingapu, the main city.

'But they have no money,' Yohanis said.

Adi's father was the chief, we argued. He must have plenty of buffaloes to sell. His son's future depended on it. But, Yohanis said, he would never sell them. Instead, he would continue sacrificing them to make his son well. We tried to persuade Adi to come with us.

'I cannot leave until my father returns from talking to the dead persons,' he said resignedly.

Powerlessly frustrated, we wished him well. He beamed, as if our wish was a magic wand.

The authorities in Jakarta had refused us permission to fly in our own plane to Dili, the capital of East Timor. Upon the illegal occupation of this former Portuguese colony by Indonesian forces, there had been much rebellion, cruelly repressed. Determined to see for ourselves what was going on, we bought tickets on a Garuda flight from Kupang.

As we waited for our bag in Dili's tiny terminal, Carlos, a tall ebullient man with a complexion of dark honey, chatted to us in Portuguese. He worked for the Department of Statistics and recommended we stayed at Hotel Turismo. The pretty, white-pillared governor's palace was a prominent reminder of Portuguese colonisation, but most buildings in Dili ostentatiously displayed the red-and-white flag of Indonesia. When we asked directions, few people would speak Portuguese. They were either afraid to do so, or were immigrants from Java, Sumatra and Sulawesi, transmigrated by the government to outnumber the rebellious East Timorese.

That evening, Carlos showed up at the hotel bar. He offered to take us to a wonderful restaurant with the best Portuguese food. With its green walls, strip lighting and plastic furniture, it had none of the charm he had described. We sceptically ordered *peixe cozido* and sat back to wait. Carlos was so curious about us that it seemed like an interrogation, but we responded cheerfully and, in turn, quizzed him on the subject of military abuses in East Timor, and the problems of the guerrilla resistance movement. He was evasive. No problems, he said. The Indonesian government was doing a great job building roads, schools and hospitals. The Portuguese had left nothing in Dili after 450 years of colonisation, just a tarmac road from the governor's office to his residence, a handful of schools and one hospital. The glowing picture he painted contradicted other people's furtively whispered comments.

An hour later, when we had begun to despair of the restaurant, an exquisitely baked fish, with the right touch of herbs and olive oil, arrived accompanied by

172

a litre of *vinho verde* decanted into a whisky bottle. It was unexpectedly the best meal of our entire trip.

A *bemo* (passenger-carrying pick-up) took us up to the impoverished villages commanding sweeping views of Dili. We stopped at a tiny graveyard where an old man with a long white beard stood pensively beside a fresh grave.

'My wife died last week,' he said, filled with sadness.

Gérard offered him a cigarette, which he readily accepted and beckoned us to follow down the hillside. As we reached a broad stretch of open ground around which the thatched houses stood, his smile faded. Inside a new open-sided wooden hall, male villagers were being lectured by a panel of four men in city attire who glared at us. Their paler skins identified them as Javanese. The villagers dared not deviate their attention. They were clearly afraid.

We followed the old man down the slope into the heart of the village. Hot on our tail came a sour-faced soldier with an opaque eye and a bulging belly hanging over his fatigues. He stuck to us like chewing gum. The old man clearly loathed him, but still led us on to his tiny wooden house where he insisted I rest on the only chair. Above his head was a photo in which he posed beside a young man. Gérard asked if it was his son. He nodded, combining pride with profound grief.

'Papapapapapapa,' he said, imitating rifle fire.

Then he turned away as the boots of the soldier stomped into the room and one eye went to peer at the photo. The mood was bitter resentment. Afraid that he could be chastised for showing us hospitality, we excused ourselves so that the soldier would follow us and leave him alone. He stood on his doorstep waving as we made our way back along the dirt alleys, the soldier on our heels.

Carlos had recommended a visit to the traditional *adat* houses at Raça near Lospalos, 200 kilometres away. We made a deal with a driver (I avoid mentioning his name, as the government reprisals are brutal) to take us there. Wearing his best trousers and shirt, he collected us just before sunrise, and we drove out into scenery reminiscent of Africa – flat-topped trees, wild sisal, yellow savannahs on which buffalo grazed. The country folk were extremely poor, their houses made of woven palm or bamboo, with thatched roofs. It was a tough arid climate. Many are said to have died of starvation since the Indonesian invasion. There was substantial military presence we had not seen elsewhere in Indonesia. Armed soldiers stalked every village and patrolled the roadsides, alert against ambush.

Portuguese-style churches prevailed in all villages. In the graveyards, tombs were painted bright blue and the inscriptions bore Portuguese names. The number of new graves did not correspond to a natural death rate compatible with such small villages. We descended the sharp escarpment to Baucau, formerly Vila Salazar. It was not the pretty town we had imagined. In the dirty market place, a cowed old man in string vest and ragged shorts, *parang* in hand, addressed me.

'*Pelo amor de Deus, senhora*, please give me some money.' He began a tirade in Tetum, the local language. I asked a young man what he was saying

'He's asking for money, *senhora*, any small amount. But he's mad. He said he's going to kill everybody.'

The *parang* twitched menacingly in one hand as the beggar gesticulated.

'Why everybody?'

'Well,' the young man whispered, '*ele quer dizer os indonésios*. They've killed his whole family.'

I gave the afflicted man some rupiah. It was small compensation for Indonesian brutality. The Australian military attaché we had met in the hotel bar in Dili had said that four Indonesian battalions were stationed in Timor, of which only two were active. It was nonsense, he said, that any guerrilla activity was still going on because if there was, he would know all about it. It sounded like a policy decision. If he recognised that rebel activity continued (as we all know it does), then logically the Indonesian army would be repressing it with torture and violence. It would therefore be incumbent on the Australian government to protest. Easier to pretend it was not happening. Australia is quick to call the democratic government of Malaysia barbaric for hanging the odd antipodean drug trafficker, who is well aware of the risks he runs. But criticise the genocide in East Timor? It wasn't worth upsetting a military dictatorship neighbour for the sake of a few illiterate peasants. The rest of the world shares the blame. Kissinger had been in Jakarta the day before the invasion in December 1975. The USA agreed to look the other way. Yet, in 1991, it had merrily gone to war to protect the homeland of a handful of rich Kuwaitis.

The traditional *adat* houses we had come to see stood in the village of Raça. They were large wooden boxes on stilts with tall thatched roofs. The villagers thronged round us, not to ask for anything, but to chat. They were delighted we spoke Portuguese, and led us off to visit their graveyard, insisting that we took photos together. They were so open, we broached the subject of the war.

'Many, many people have been killed.'

'Is it still going on?'

'Oh yes, indeed. Out there, in the bush. They would rather die than give up to these Indonesians.'

The Indonesian government had prohibited the use of Portuguese and the writing of names in anything but Bahasa Indonesia, the official Indonesian language spoken as the mother tongue by a tiny percentage of the population

of the entire archipelago. Over the village church, large letters read: GEREJA
BUNDA MARIA which, in Bahasa, means the Church of Mother Mary. *Bunda* is an
affectionate Indonesian word for mother. Unfortunately, in Portuguese it means
backside. The villagers were understandably scandalised by this blasphemy.

Lospalos, the largest village in the area, lay twenty kilometres beyond Raça
across savannahs where horses and miniature Bali cattle grazed. The driver
advised that we were obliged to report at the police station, from where we
were sent to stay at a large private house near the market. A certain Cristóvão,
claiming to be a student, approached Gérard to chat. He spoke excellent English
and Portuguese and asked exactly the same questions as Carlos had in Dili.
In fact, they looked remarkably similar – tall, muscular, clean-shaven, short
military hair cuts. When, as if by coincidence, he joined our table at the Padang
restaurant where we dined on indescribable globules of something that tasted
like a shortcut to hepatitis, the penny dropped. Cristóvão was a government
agent, keeping tabs on us! He knew things about us that we hadn't told him
or the driver. We concluded that Carlos had also been spying on us in Dili.
The driver, who was more switched on to these matters than we were, was
singularly unimpressed by Cristóvão's intrusion on to our table. He huddled
into his jacket, and said not another word. We realised that he was afraid:
'they' might see him as conniving with Timorese-separatist sympathisers.

By candlelight, the room allocated to us had looked fine. However, rain fell
all night through the broken roof tiles onto our beds and flooded the floor. Not
in the best of moods, we were woken by the gay squeals of foraging piglets.
I asked the driver if he had slept well.

'No. I couldn't sleep. I miss my baby son,' he replied glumly. What he really
meant was: 'hurry up, I don't like this place and want to go home'.

The Banda Sea was a sheet of wrinkled satin. Infant cumulus lined up like tin
soldiers to the west, while other clouds lunged at us for a fluffy embrace. We
knew we had arrived at the Banda Islands, part of the Moluccas, when we
spotted a thick dark cloud glued to the protuberances of an island ahead.
As we ducked into heavy turbulence below the cloud base at 2,000 feet,
the sea became choppy and thrashed ominously at the dark hulk of Banda
Besar. Beyond lay Pulau Neira, where the main village, Bandaneira, cowered
uncomfortably close to Gunung Api, a 2,200-foot volcano which had erupted
in 1988. Fierce gusts tossed us spitefully. The lower we descended, the worse
the turbulence became.

The volcano blocked a direct approach, causing orographical wind waves
which further complicated things. A wall of rain was fast approaching. Preparing
for a rough landing, we added the over-shoulder seatbelts and came in, scraping

over the palms on Api's eastern flank. The humpbacked airstrip ran right across the island, the threshold atop a sheer cliff. Gérard maintained height in case of a treacherous down-draught. Too high. Wrestling with the controls, he had chewed up half the runway before touching down, already on the downward slope. Breaking proved ineffectual on the wet tarmac. We aquaplaned towards unhappy oblivion in the pounding waves at the end of the runway.

'Can't stop. Got to abort.' Gérard applied full throttle and fought to stay airborne.

'Damn,' I thought, 'now we'll have to do it again.'

Powerful winds from the oncoming squall brought us perilously close to the cliffs of Banda Besar across the bay. We bounced over an angry sea and, looking back, saw that rain had already engulfed the runway.

'Better go to Ambon. It's an hour away,' Gérard resolved.

'Let's circle for a while, it might pass,' I suggested

'Lucky we have fuel to play with,' Gérard said pointedly.

I had wanted to stop at the Kai Islands, home of the famed birds of paradise, but this would have left us perilously short of fuel. Fortunately, Gérard had been more prudent. We circled for ten minutes until the squall moved on.

'Right, let's try again before the next one hits. I'll make the approach closer to Api this time,' Gérard announced.

The palms had already been in touching distance the last time. I secretly wished he would keep well away from Api, but just nodded dumbly. The second approach was no better. I was more nervous than at the first attempt and Gérard, admittedly, a little tense. We came in slower, with full flaps. It took full aileron and rudder control correction to keep vaguely on the axis and high enough over the cliff. As the threshold whizzed underneath, Gérard cut the engine and fought to prevent a wingtip from landing first. This time, we touched down on the upslope and managed to stop easily.

A young man, in white shirt and black trousers, introduced himself as Man. After hearing our first attempt at landing, he had come to wait for us, bringing a gift of exquisitely arranged nutmeg fruit, carved to look like flower petals. The fruit flesh had a strong nutmeg taste, a little acrid but not unpleasant. He led us into the village, pointing out the historical sites, and took us to a small hotel overlooking the narrow strait separating Bandaneira from the volcano Api.

The Banda Islands had once been the pot at the end of the rainbow. Because of their nutmeg and mace (nutmeg husk), the Dutch and British hotly disputed them in the seventeenth century. The Banda islanders were finally coerced by the Dutch into signing monopoly contracts they did not understand. When they sold spices to the British as well, they were chastised with brutality. A gory painting in the museum depicts the punishment. Samurais were imported from Japan to behead recalcitrant Bandanese, because the Dutch felt it would be unchristian to do the deed themselves. During 200 years of ruthless domination, the Dutch East Indies Company was responsible for a virtual genocide on the Banda Islands. However, greed to dominate the nutmeg market led the Dutch to make a gross real estate error. As part of the 1667 Treaty of Breda, the outer Banda island of Run, held by the British, was exchanged for an insignificant isle by the name of New Amsterdam, off the coast of North America: today's Manhattan.

We came in low over Manokwari, a pleasant town tucked under towering mountains on Irian Jaya's Vogelkop or Bird's Head, as we approached its grass airstrip. We knew very well that Melanesians were dark, but after so long in Asia, it came as a surprise to look down and see the streets populated with black people.

That the Melanesians are an entirely different race, with their own culture, languages and religions, would seem reason enough to allow them to rule their own land. Understandably, the occupation of their country by the Javanese-dominated Indonesian government is bitterly resented. It would have been more logical to have reunited the whole island of New Guinea. But upon independence in 1945, the new Indonesian government claimed that all Dutch possessions in the region should form one country. They were particularly anxious not to let go of Dutch West New Guinea, which Jakarta renamed Irian Jaya, because they could not bear to let the vast resources of gold, diamonds, oil, and timber escape them. After much bickering, the matter was to be resolved by the Act of Free Choice, a trumped-up referendum held in 1969. One thousand Irianese delegates were hand-picked *by the Indonesians* (!) to vote on behalf of the whole population of 800,000. They were bribed to vote in favour of Indonesia. The great majority, not consulted, were primitive tribesmen living according to their own traditions for hundreds of years. When the Melanesians rebelled, it was too late and the Indonesian army showed no pity. It was war. Subtle tactics were employed: diseases to which the tribal peoples had no immunity were deliberately introduced (a shameful method of genocide also used against Indian tribes in Brazil).

In Manokwari, we sought out Dave Rask, the locally based MAF pilot, for advice on weather patterns and airstrips. We knew that flying in the mountains was extremely dangerous. Surprisingly, he did not discourage us.

'It is essential,' he advised, 'to fly in the early morning. Always make sure your path back is clear. There's a long valley between two mountain ranges which we pilots call the Freeway. That's the route to Wamena. The passes lie at seven to eight thousand feet. Be very careful on the Wamena-Jayapura sector. Cloud formations build-up over the city. This could force you back into

177

the mountains with nowhere to land.' He marked the Freeway on our ONC chart. 'By the way, we don't let our pilots fly here alone until they have had three months' dual training,' he added as a parting shot.

We promised to study our route carefully and only fly in good weather. In Nabire, the MAF pilot Herman Jus suggested we visit Enarotali, a beautiful village on Lake Paniai in the mountains. It had been out of bounds to foreigners for some time because it was an area of OPM (Free Papua Movement) rebel activity. But he had dropped a couple of tourists there the week before and it was now open. The controller had no objection to our going there, as long as we secured a clearance from the regional capital, Jayapura, and a *surat jalan*, or *laissez-passer*, from the police station.

In the street, Gérard was picked up by another young man purporting to be a student. We had learned to recognise this as a euphemism for spy. He spoke excellent English, and despite already having a surprisingly accurate in-depth knowledge of our life history, fired numerous questions: who owns your plane, where is it from, where are you going?

'You require a letter from the police to visit Enarotali,' he announced. (Gérard had not even told him we wanted to go there!) 'The police station is open till five o'clock,' he added.

The immediate reaction of the police was to refuse our request. Gérard, who went there alone, tried persuasion. Since Jakarta had authorised us to fly to Irian Jaya, clearly there was no objection to our being in the region. The Commandant insisted the regional capital, Jayapura, be consulted and bade Gérard to wait.

Half an hour later, he was summoned back into the office. With a big smile, the Commandant regretted that Enarotali was out of the question. Jayapura had refused. Accepting defeat, Gérard shook hands and turned to go.

'Why did you go to Lospalos?'

The question ricocheted across the room like a rubber bullet. How did he know we had been to Lospalos, and what the hell did it have to do with Enarotali? A fat file lay open on the table before the Commandant. It traced all our movements since entering Indonesia!

'Why shouldn't we go to Lospalos?'

He did not answer.

'We went there because we wanted to see the *adat* houses.'

'I see your wife is Swiss,' he accused.

We had opted to be Swiss in Indonesia precisely because no one had anything against Switzerland. Or so we thought.

'So am I,' Gérard admitted. 'What's wrong with being Swiss?'

'You are not permitted to go to Enarotali. *Salamat jalan*.'

178

He was dismissed. What did East Timor have to do with all this? And a whole file compiled on us. Wow!

We subsequently learned that a Swiss pilot flying for a missionary group had run guns to the OPM before fleeing to Australia. Since then, all new pilots were rigorously screened. The combination of being Swiss, having a private plane, having been to East Timor and wanting to visit Enarotali was too much for the authorities. We were clearly trouble-makers!

So we headed for Wamena, climbing easily to 7,500 feet, up over the forested mountains, following a muddy road that cut a path of destruction up to prohibited Enarotali. We had imagined the Freeway to be a broad valley. Instead, it was a claustrophobic chasm between various mountain peaks, topping between 10,000 and 13,500 feet, on either side. To the south lay the spectacular Maoke Mountains, where snow-covered Puncak Jaya soared to 16,500 feet. Over the last 8,000-foot pass, we swung into the broad Baliem Valley where Wamena lies on a plateau. Rows of gleaming corrugated iron roofs indicated unwelcome Javanese transmigration. The local tribesmen lived in round, thatched huts in neat fenced-off compounds. Their ditch-digging farming technique was not to irrigate but to drain the soil for their staple crop: sweet potatoes.

Explorers first reached the Baliem Valley in 1938, discovering an astonishing stone-age people who were meticulous farmers. Then it was forgotten until a reconnaissance aircraft crashed there in 1954. A rescue mission traced it, and returned with tales of a last frontier, a primitive society which had survived intact into the mid-twentieth century. Despite the outward tranquillity of the agricultural villages, however, tribal battles of great violence were a regular occurrence.

Wamena was still not connected to the coast by road. All the town's building materials, vehicles and foodstuffs were flown in. Beyond the airport fence, rows of naked Dani tribesmen, their penises scrunched up inside penis gourds attached round the waist with string or sashes, gazed at the aircraft. The fact that some gourds were long and thin and others short and fat was, apparently, unrelated to the equipment inside. Dani women wear flouncy grass skirts, like row upon row of petticoats, which swayed pleasingly as they walked. They all carried multi-purpose string bags called *asali*, usually filled with sweet potatoes and their tiny babies, on a padding of hay, lying on top. Once able to sit, the babies are promoted to the back of the neck.

On a trek into the countryside, we passed numerous Dani tribesmen headed to Wamena market. Everyone stopped to shake hands with us, beaming. The village compounds are fenced off by wooden planks upon which thick mulch is laid to protect the wood from the weather. The sole entrance puts any intruder at a disadvantage. It entails climbing up a rickety rung ladder over the fence at the same time as crouching low to pass under an arch. Inside a compound, the arena is surrounded by round sleeping huts and two corridor-like huts, one for cooking, the other a stable for pigs at night. Pigs, to the Dani, are like buffaloes to the Toraja or horses to the Sumbanese. They are a sure way of obtaining wives, and are loved like one of the family. When carrying them suspended between two poles, the Dani do so gently, the right way up, cushioned in raffia, not upside-down and squealing like elsewhere in the world.

In Pugima village, we were taken to meet the chief, Make Itlay, a muscular man who had donned a pair of shorts, though his fellow villagers wore penis gourds. We were invited to crawl through the low entrance into the male hut, which opened into two storeys. The upper one, with a slatted floor for sleeping, was kept warm at night by a smouldering fire below, which also kept bugs away. The chief, upon hearing that Gérard was a pilot, became ebullient and presented him with a valuable stone axe blade, as a vital reminder of our trip to Pugima. Stone axes are much revered and used as gifts to a bride's parents. They are elongated, flat stones smoothed and shaped by a special process of heat and water. Make kept shaking Gérard's hand and embracing him. The Dani had the warmest handshakes we had ever come across. They exuded such apparent joy, despite the simplicity of their lives, that we felt duly humbled.

Our Indonesian visas were about to expire. We flew to Jayapura to clear Immigration and refuel for the long flight to Australia. Departing early one morning, we climbed back over the mountains to Wamena and followed the Baliem River through Southern Gap down spectacular gorges. The muddy torrent, liberally dosed with waterfalls, drops 5,000 feet in fifty kilometres. Whole mountainsides collapsed into it as it plunged to the steamy jungles below.

Suddenly, the Maoke Mountains were gone. Before us spread an endless swampy plain, flat as a pancake and densely forested, streaked by a web of rivers. It was an area still inhabited by uncontacted, cannibal tribes. The coastal village of Agats was the second place (besides Dili) at which Jakarta had prohibited us from landing. Michael Rockefeller, son of the former vice-president of the USA, had gone missing, presumed lunch, near there in 1961.

It was above the double row of huts at Agats that the greenery ended. A blue expanse spread before us: the Arafura Sea.

18 'No bloody photographs, mate!'

The excitement of reaching Australia was so great that we forgot the perils of a long water crossing, six hours over the Arafura and shark-infested Timor Seas. We would be able to make ourselves understood again, without worrying about unwittingly offending another culture. No need to ensure our lodgings, which would have showers and flush toilets, were not beside rowdy mosques. After months of eating *nasi goreng* (fried rice) and *mie goreng* (fried noodles) from breakfast to dinner, we longed for juicy steaks, salads and a good bottle of wine.

When Gérard went to the back for a pee and to eat up all the choc chip biscuits so they would not be confiscated by quarantine, I discerned a low brown outline ahead.

'Land ahoy!' I yelled with childish glee.

He struggled back through the narrow passage to see for himself. Yup! There it was! Valiant little *Romeo* had brought us all the way from Brazil to Australia. It was unbelievable.

The Coburg Peninsular was the arid Australia I had envisaged. A dirt road coming from nowhere, going nowhere, wound through the scrub. It looked indeed like *terra nullius*. We scrutinised it with the binoculars. For some time, we had been in contact with the efficient controller in Darwin. We could even understand what he said! But only thirty miles out, the city was still invisible, couched in thick smoke from bush fires. The First Officer of HMS *Beagle*, who named Darwin Harbour in 1839, probably found it more easily than we did. The tower directed us to the customs area, instructing us not to open the doors until the fumigator arrived. A plump, middle-aged Australian, looking like a schoolboy in tight shorts and a bush hat, waved us in to park. He passed a spray-can through the storm window.

'Squirt this about in there, mate,' he instructed.

As we waited the statutory five minutes for stowaway foreign insects to die, a troop of similar schoolboys in beige shorts assembled. One clutched the leash of a golden Labrador. Two young ladies in overalls waited nearby. Things really were upside-down in Oz. Shouldn't the girls have been wearing the tight shorts and the men those baggy blue overalls? When permitted to open the door, we emerged beaming into the Australian sunshine. Our hellos were ignored. No one smiled or proffered a hand as they had in every other country we had

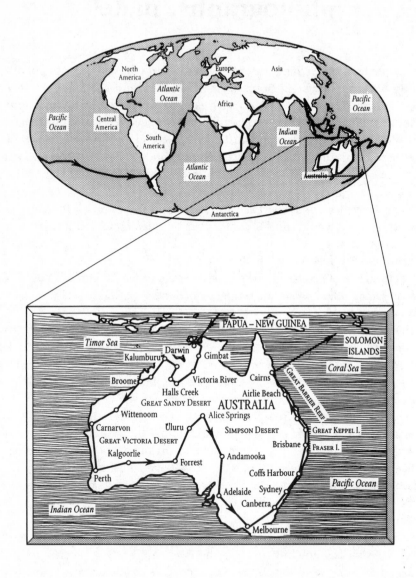

visited. Instead, questions were fired at us. Wher'vya come from? Whatchya carrying on board? Fill in this form. Sign here. Our spirits were too high to be quashed by such a reception, and we thought their uniforms would make an amusing photo.

'Do you mind if I take a picture?' Gérard asked.

'No bloody photographs, mate!' came the brusque reply.

The two women tackled me, demanding to inspect the luggage. Gérard contended with the men, who instructed him to remove the engine cowling. They thrust the dog's nose against the red-hot engine.

'Be careful!' Gérard yelled. 'You'll burn him!'

The handler glowered suspiciously. Why did he not want the dog to sniff the engine? Ah hah . . . These Aussies were no fools. They had looked up the registration of the aircraft. Brazilian, eh? A bloody Brazilian aircraft so far from home could only be carrying one thing: cocaine. 'We'll get these bastards!' their expressions said. The quarantine officer demanded all foodstuffs. We knew Australia was strict about plants, animals and foodstuffs, but we had not expected such rudeness. They poked in every corner of the plane like maggots in a dead body. The Labrador's nose was shoved against every nook of the hull, and then he was unceremoniously thrown into the cabin. He scrambled everywhere, sniffing furiously, finding nothing. Disappointment clouded the face of his handler, as if he was the addict. The two ladies, a petite blonde and a recent Chinese immigrant, were to search the luggage. *All* of it. I laid the bags outside on the hot tarmac, and in they delved. What's this? What's this? What's this? They began to irritate me. When the Chinese girl turned her attention to the cabin, the blonde distracted me with nonchalant questions: How many countries have you visited? Really, how nice . . .

'Uuuugh!' the Chinese girl ejected. 'What's this?' Disgust further compacted her eyes. In her hand was the pee bottle, its lid off and her nose an inch from the rim.

'It's piss!' I replied, not embarrassed this time, but with ill-disguised pleasure. 'Uuuugh!'

'Who asked you to smell it?' She gave me a withering look and pointed at the second pee container with an enquiring glance.

'Yes, more piss. As you see, there's no loo on board. Be my guest. Have another sniff.'

She scowled. The blonde fired more questions.

'Ah haaaah!' the Chinese girl exploded. 'You got an animal in here,' she accused, pointing at the hairs on the carpet.

'Indeed, there was one. Your dog. Remember?' I retorted. But she was implacable, and continued her frenetic search.

'So what's in here?'

This time, she had found a Tupperware full of white powder. She swelled with pride. She had outdone that useless cur. She had found the cocaine. It was a moment I had always dreaded, being caught by disbelieving customs officers.

'It's fat-free milk powder,' I said lamely.

She sniffed and tasted it. Foiled again.

'Forget it, luv,' the blonde called out. 'The dog's been in there. There are no narcotics.'

Defeated, they sent us to the office to complete the paperwork. The Chinese girl carted off a booty of milk powder and an *asali* string bag ('because it stinks') from Wamena. I was instructed to carry the pee bottles to quarantine, where I was pragmatically allowed to pour the contents down the toilet. The quarantine officer added the milk powder to the rice he had confiscated (perhaps he loved rice pudding), but returned the 'stinking thing', and presented a bill for A$35. I felt he should have been paying us.

Once landside, we stared in dismay at the milling crowds of white people, grotesquely overweight. Beer bellies bulged over shorts. Women wore drab dresses like cleaning-ladies uniforms. It was the first 'white' country of our trip. We had simply forgotten what it was like! Rather a shock after the petite figures of Asia.

Modern Darwin, capital of Northern Territory (known as the Top End) is a characterless monument to shopping malls. Its outback charm was swept away by Cyclone Tracy in 1974. Drooling vampirishly, we sought out a steak restaurant, ordered medium-rare, and waited . . . and waited . . . until a shrivelled piece of leftover firewood was put before us.

'Excuse me, we asked for medium-rare,' Gérard said.

'Yup. That's it,' the waitress replied and stalked off.

It was impossible to put a knife through it. Gérard went to the counter.

'We ordered medium-rare. You call this medium-rare?'

'Yup. Most people have it charcoaled. Take it or leave it.'

We left.

'I don't like it here. Let's go back to Indonesia.' I was crushingly disappointed with Australia. Robert Louis Stevenson's words kept coming to mind: '*It is a better thing to travel hopefully than to arrive.*' Where were the jovial Crocodile Dundees that supposedly populated the continent? Had we flown 100,000 kilometres for this?

It is said that since the white man arrived in Australia just 200 years ago, more species have been made extinct there than on any other land mass. This is a remarkable achievement considering that still today, Australia ranks with Iceland and Mauritania among the least populated countries on earth.

We flew to Cooinda, on the banks of the South Alligator River in the much vaunted Kakadu National Park, in the hope of seeing some kangaroos. All over Australia they are shot as vermin, because they compete with the cattle for grass. Dingos do occasionally take a calf, but one excuse for shooting them is 'they're not really native animals'. They've been in Australia for 4,000 years. That makes them 3,800 years more native Australian than the heavy-footed cattle which now devastate the environment.

A nature walk revealed not even a wallaby. The camp was filled with rowdy drunken teenagers – a bun fight compared to the serenity of African game parks. Disillusioned, we departed to a bush strip at Gimbat, recommended by a young pilot we met.

'There's a creek nearby, and you can walk up to the old homestead,' he had said.

This indeed was Crocodile Dundee terrain: eucalyptus woods bathed in dappled beiges and ochres, tufts of yellow grass. Footprints of roos and monitor lizards dotted the sand by the cold, clear creek. To the chatter of pink galahs and the mournful laugh of Australian magpies, we pitched the tent under a gum tree. A blue-winged kookaburra watched us with a disconcerting yellow gaze. Happiness. Just the two of us, and *Romeo*, at peace in the Australian bush.

Until, later, a jeep approached warily down the strip and stopped beside *Romeo*. Gérard went to greet the driver who stared unblinking at the plane.

'Hi!'

'You right?' In Australia, right means all right. Correct is rendered by 'not wrong'. 'Looks like you've been here a couple of hours.'

It was not a question. It implied he had not heard us land so his accuracy was surprising. Was he guessing from the grains of dust which accumulated on the wheel tracks?

'Yes, we landed at about three.'

'Got permission to land here?'

'Permission from whom?'

'From the director of Kakadu National Park. This is a private strip, mate. Gotta have permission.'

Oh no, not again!

'Well, a pilot at Cooinda recommended we stop here. We're touring from Brazil. We didn't know we were still in the park.'

He muttered into his walkie-talkie. 'John, seems they're a coupla tourists. Haven't got permission. Say they've flown in from Brazil. Setting up camp for the night. Over.'

185

'They gotta have permission, Mick. Get them to move on. Where they headed? Over.'

Mick looked enquiringly. We played ball. 'Headed for Katherine, John.'

'Well, suggest they move on, Mick, unless they're adamant about staying the night. Over.'

'Okay. Roger.'

'We're adamant about staying the night,' Gérard interjected.

Mick dropped his policeman's stance and became chatty. The land had been a pastoral lease and was recently acquired by the park.

'We have to be careful, y'know. There've been a lot of snoopers around – reporters n'that. We like to know who's where.'

He left us to camp in peace. It was a sensitive area because of a dispute over nearby Coronation Hill, stuffed with uranium. The Aboriginals had declared it a sacred site and managed to prevent mining, to the fury of many Australians who conveniently blamed them for a decline in the economy by hindering development. Abo-bashing is a favourite Australian sport. For 50,000 years, the Aboriginals had survived foraging for food and creating a sensitive web of spiritual oneness with the rocks, rivers, plants and animals which shared their hostile environment. No cares, no diseases. Then came the dregs of British society, riddled with influenza and syphilis, who shot them, stole their lands, disrespected their souls, and introduced alcohol. Like tribal peoples everywhere, their way of life was destroyed. Now they are criticised for taking advantage of the dole system and spending their money on drink and junk food. There is nothing peculiar to Aborigines in that: plenty of white Aussies do the same. The difference is that the Aboriginals find it all so daft they call the dole 'sit-down money'.

Doomed Wittenoom, a former asbestos mining centre, lies in the spectacular iron-rich Hamersley Ranges of Western Australia. The government was applying fierce pressure for all inhabitants to leave the area, and the population had dropped from 1,500 to forty-five. From the air, we had seen the cement foundations where houses once stood. A few hard-core Wittenoom residents, a friendly bunch strengthened by solidarity, were determined to stay.

Pete and Ali Dawson, Wittenoom-lovers from the south, befriended us and invited us to join them on a trip to Hamersley Gorge where exposed layers of red iron-rich rock bear witness to subterranean forces. White gum trees gleaming against the crimson cliffs are reflected in the still creek waters. A bright blue sky moulded the edge of the red mountains, coated with metallic grey-green spinifex grass which grows in thick clumps. Novices who make to sit on a treacherously inviting fluffy clump rise hastily with a yelp for each leaf blade ends in a sharp point.

The following day, we were trapped by violent storms. Pete and Ali thought it amusing, for it proved what the tenacious residents said about Wittenoom: it gets a hold on you. Our old tourist map had a special section on Wittenoom and the Hamersleys, but the town is no longer marked on new maps, so intense are the government's efforts to obliterate it. We laughed to think that our favourite place in Australia did not exist!

From Perth, the Great Eastern Highway slithered ahead, leading to the Eastern Goldfields over endless fields showered with sheep. Further on, the scrub stretched grey-green into the distance, a threadbare carpet over the red earth. From Kalgoorlie, Australia's best preserved gold rush town, we were unsure how to proceed across a great void: south to the Great Australian Bight, where the empty Nullarbor Plain drops over dramatic cliffs into the sea, or due north-east to Ayers Rock.

'Where are you headed?' the Briefing Officer asked.

'No idea. Have you any suggestions?'

He thought this was some Pommie joke until we explained our dilemma. There were 1,000 kilometres of featureless land between Kalgoorlie and Ayers Rock, he warned, suggesting it was better to follow the railway across the bare Nullarbor Plain and rest overnight at Forrest, a meteorological and rail maintenance station. Forrest sounded appealing. It was some name for a place in the middle of the Nullarbor (No Tree) Plain.

For 400 miles, we followed the monotonous straight line of the railway track, piercing the distant horizon ahead. The sun scorched the totally treeless expanse which spread out on all sides, coated with hardy grasses and occasional stunted bushes. No sign of life. Not even a kangaroo. After passing several abandoned railway maintenance stations, Forrest surprised us with its substantial tarred runway. A little girl peeped round the doors of a hangar by the patio. Her parents, Craig and Margaret, materialised, saying that we could sleep in the transit house for A$42.

'And I'll cook for you if you like,' Margaret ventured.

'That's kind but we do have food. We'll manage.'

'Well, I don't mind at all. I'll be making dinner for the three of us anyway,' she insisted.

'Well, thanks very much. Can we contribute something, maybe?'

'Don't worry, we have everything. It'll be a pleasure. Dinner's at seven.'

She explained that supplies arrived once a week on the Tea and Sugar Train from Port Augusta. The total population of Forrest was ten adults and eight children. They were divided into distinct settlements, the met people beside scraggy trees they had planted, and the railway people 200 yards down the track. Despite the isolation, they were not buddies. Margaret admitted she liked her immediate neighbours but not the other met family.

'The wife, well, she's American, y'know . . .'

Even in distant Forrest! So many Anglo-Saxon Australians seem to be xenophobic. They hate not only the Abos and the Chinks, but disparage the communities of Italians, Greeks and Portuguese, and nurture a particular dislike of newly-arrived Englishmen, or Pommie bastards. Anyone not born in Oz is considered a 'bloody immigrant'. How quickly they have forgotten they are all merely offspring of earlier bloody immigrants.

'And the railway people?' I asked.

'We don't see much of them. They're different. One of the guys, y'know, he's always drunk by sunset.'

Since she declined my offer to give a hand with dinner, I left to write up the diary. Gérard went to the hangar to fix the HF fuse that had blown. By 18:45, he was still not back, so I went ahead armed with a box of wine for dinner.

Craig answered the door. 'Hi! I was just going to bring your dinner over. We've just finished,' he announced.

'I thought we were having dinner together,' I stammered, taken aback.

'Never thought of that,' Margaret mused. 'Suppose we could've. Anyway, Craig'll bring it over – just stick it in the microwave to warm it up.'

So it had not been an invitation! What naivety to think an Australian couple living in a five-family outback station might be interested enough in the outside world to invite some foreigners to dinner! Presumably she was going to charge us then? I had interpreted her 'Would you like me to cook you dinner?' as an Aussie version of 'Come to dinner'. Keeping a firm hold of our wine-box, I retreated.

'Did you realise that dinner is to be paid for?' Gérard asked when he came in.

'So it would seem. How much?' I asked, peeved.

'Well, out at the hangar, Craig suddenly said, "The government gives us the money for the food." I didn't get what he was on about, so he added, "The dinner will be ten dollars each." By then, it was too late to refuse.'

The issue was not the cost of the dinner, but we had hoped for the company of an Australian family. Instead of the dull school food – tinned pea soup, tinned spaghetti bolognese, packet cake and packet custard – that had been sent round, I could have made a decent meal from our own supplies.

The next day, the railway track continued to Port Augusta without us. We swerved north-north-east across the Great Victoria Desert, leaving the 'civilisation' of Forrest for Ayers Rock, that splendid hump in the middle of Australia. Now referred to as Uluru, as it is known by the Yankuntjatjara and Pitjantjatjara tribes who revere it, it soars impressively above the plains, its bumps and undulations forming a playground for the sun's tilted rays which enhance it with mysterious shadows.

Our problems were with outback Australians or civil servants. In Perth, Adelaide, Melbourne and Sydney, we were warmly welcomed by old and new friends alike. Helen Walford, a dear schoolfriend from Kenya days who put us up in Melbourne, attributed the unfriendly treatment we had received to our English accents. Is that a valid excuse? Judi Breed, a vivacious Australian we had met at Victoria River Downs, a vast cattle station in the Top End, warmly offered us a room when we reached Sydney. She and her husband Trevor welcomed two virtual strangers and piles of luggage into their house for almost a month. Their young daughters, Marissa and Nicole, accepted us as lodgers and let us share the room with their forty-six Barbie dolls.

Since meeting Thomas Casey in the briefing room at Karachi, we had been intrigued by his route across the North Pacific to the Aleutians, an arm of islands extending out from Alaska across the Bering Sea. From northern Japan, it was 1,500 nautical miles over inhospitable waters to Shemya US Air Force Base on Semichi Island, and another 1,500 island-hopping miles to Anchorage. We contemplated taking this route back to the Americas. Looking for advice, Gérard phoned Shemya and spoke to a US captain who, as a private pilot himself, did not recommend it.

'A certain Thomas Casey is lucky to be alive,' he said. 'Last week, he was plucked out of the water by a fisherman after his engine stopped.' Even in his floatplane, Casey had run into problems. He landed at Attu, in the Near Islands, and picked up car fuel. His engine failed sixty miles further on. No doubt Compton's objective was to deter us. He succeeded, adding that most of the year a complete overcast hovered at 200 feet. South or south-westerly winds of thirty to forty knots were standard, but these could increase to eighty knots without warning. The 'best' time of year was September or October when the sun might appear for an hour in the afternoon and the ceiling rose to 500 feet.

So, back to Mapa Mundi. Our eyes roamed the vast South Pacific Ocean – half a globe of unadulterated blue. Cairns to Santiago spans 130 degrees longitude – 7,800 nautical miles of ocean, thinly sprinkled with archipelagos in the western half. After Polynesia, there is a vast gap until solitary Easter Island, and then an even larger one to South America. With a larger fuel tank and no luggage at all, we could conceivably make it from Easter Island to South America, with the option to stop at the precarious airstrip on Robinson Crusoe Island, 400-odd miles before Santiago. The winds, at least, should be behind us. Navigating with the GPS, which provides exact geographical co-ordinates at all times, it would be possible to avoid the mistakes made over the Atlantic.

For the long haul across the Pacific, everything had to be serviced, checked and re-checked. The auto-pilot, which had given up the ghost before reaching Australia, was one of the essential items to have repaired. To increase our autonomy to eighteen hours and our range to 2,450 nautical miles, Gérard acquired a second-hand 340-litre ferry tank and strapped it in beside the smaller tank, so as not to shake free in heavy turbulence. He also added a dump valve, so that the tanks could be emptied in an emergency. Full of air, they would theoretically keep the plane afloat, giving us more time to escape. Serious thought had to be given to survival gear. This meant facing the fact that we might actually have to use the life-raft. Such a notion had always been pushed to the back of our minds when undertaking other sea crossings. But zigzagging across 18,000 kilometres of Pacific Ocean to occasional island refuges was another story. Could *Romeo*'s solitary engine manage all that way? Our regulation inflatable raft was cramped for two. It had no roof and was not intended for long-term survival: it presumed that an engine failure would be reported immediately and help would be on the way. We knew that if we fell into the Pacific, we would probably be on our own for some time. If, after a crash, we were going to bother climbing into a raft at all, it may as well be one that would stay afloat for longer than half a day. We obtained a sturdy four-man marine raft. It looked like an overgrown tractor tyre with an orange roof and, although it was cumbersome, at twenty-three kilos, if splutter came to splash, it would be worth it.

The Fédération Aéronautique Internationale, based in Paris, informed us that the first and last time such a flight was made in a piston-engined aircraft was in 1954 – in a twin-engined Catalina flying boat! For almost forty years, no one had flown the route with a piston engine. No doubt, the isolation of Easter Island had something to do with it. If we made it, it would be the first crossing from Australia to South America in a single-engine.

Our first leg was to be across the Coral Sea, from Cairns to Munda, in the Solomon Islands. Although Brisbane–Nouméa would have been a more direct route, we did not want to miss these unusual islands. A host of intriguing names beckoned us up the New South Wales and Queensland coasts, over the spangled glory of the waters of the Great Barrier Reef: Coffs Harbour, Maroochydore, Noosa Heads, Great Keppel, Whitsunday Passage, Cape Upstart, Cape Bowling Green, Magnetic Island . . .

By the time we reached Cairns, the auto-pilot was playing up again. Gérard spent hours on it. He removed both fuel tanks, executed a painful, fiddly job, re-installed them and made a successful forty-minute test flight. Five minutes before landing, it went on the blink again.

'This could take weeks,' he fumed. 'It could be one faulty prong in the network of all the auto-pilot connections with the rest of the aircraft. Each component tests okay. I can't understand what the problem is.'

He was determined not to leave without an operational auto-pilot and contemplated returning to Brisbane, a five-hour flight. I was averse to turning back and reminded him how pioneer aviators flew slower planes across remoter routes without auto-pilot, battling the joystick for twenty hours at a time. But, after grim hours of finicky work, he announced at last that it seemed to be fixed. That meant it was time to leave.

For over two years, we had been constantly on the move – new places, new cultures, unfamiliar beds. The truth was, we had begun to weary and long for home. This, above all, helped to propel us out over the Pacific.

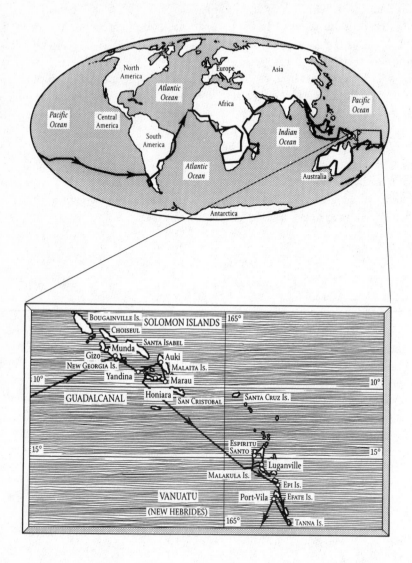

19 'How big is your island?'

The departures board listed an unscheduled flight: PT-RXE: 06:45.

'Which country's PT the registration of?' the customs officer asked.

'Brazil.'

'Brazil? Oh yeah?' He flipped through the passports. 'Bet they gave you a tough time in Darwin?' he chortled.

The sun was just up. A row of leaping kangaroos on the red Qantas tails lined the terminal building in Cairns. Our 18,000-kilometre trans-Pacific flight was about to start with a six-hour flight across the Coral Sea to the Solomon Islands.

'Cairns isn't a bad place. Perhaps we could stay here after all,' I said, chickening out as usual before a long water flight.

'C'mon baby, you want to go home, don't you? Well, it's just across this patch of water! Let's go.' Gérard put a strong, encouraging arm around me and drew me towards the white bird.

How come he's never frightened? I thought.

We climbed easily in the cool dawn. The sun glinted off golden ripples on the bay as we aimed at a splatter of low cloud on the horizon. The Great Barrier Reef, a last foothold of land, slipped away and moments later we plunged into a moist band of cloud. For two hours, all went white. An occasional break revealed a raging grey sea below.

When the gloomy curtain was finally swept back, we burst into brilliant sunshine over a ruffled indigo sea. Australia was gone, its red dust washed off *Romeo*'s fuselage. Below, an exquisite array of coral reefs and atolls – the Louisiade Archipelago, part of Papua New Guinea – then a silvery millpond ocean, gleaming back immaculate reflections of tufts of cloud.

'Good place to practise water landings,' I remarked.

'That's funny. I was just thinking the same thing.'

'Ah hah! Gotcha!' I thought. 'So he does think about these things sometimes!'

When two islands finally appeared ahead, we were elated. After the modernity of Australian towns, it was like starting a new adventure. The forested bulk of New Georgia grew and grew, until we skimmed a bay studded with palm-fringed isles to approach Munda village, a cosy collection of leaf and thatch bungalows tucked under the trees. A vast gleaming-white crushed-coral strip stretched out welcomingly. It had been craftily built by the Japanese in 1942 under a network of suspended palm tree tops. Despite messages sent by the islanders to tip off the Americans that an airfield was being built, the reconnaissance aircraft could not find it until, ready for use, the palm top disguise was pulled aside.

We parked beside an Aero Commander, a large twin-engine. A jet-black uniformed Melanesian handed the regulation aerosol through the window and asked us to wait two minutes.

'Hallo. I'm Robert from Customs,' he said, extending a hand, when we disembarked. How unlike Darwin!

'Hi, Robert. It's lovely to be here.'

'Oh, really? Thank you.' He seemed surprised, and pleased. He had no idea how his simple, natural greeting filled us with warmth and delight.

The verandah of the wooden terminal was filled with rows of black faces. We asked Robert if a flight was due. No, they had come to see us! Word had spread that the first ever direct flight from Cairns was coming in. Munda, they thought happily, had finally made it onto the map. They had expected a real plane full of big-spending tourists, not a fly driven by two scruffs. The faces under frizzy mops stared at us in disillusioned silence, but when we waved, they grinned.

The phone in the office rang indignantly. Honiara Control was in a panic. Had we landed safely? They were nervous because days earlier, a Solomon Airlines Twin Otter had smashed into a mountain in bad weather, killing all on board.

'I suppose, in your country, it no matter if plane crashes, if so many people dead,' Robert said. 'In Solomon Islands, is too much sorrow, all together, fifteen peoples dead in one day.'

Despite this sombre note, we felt we had landed in paradise. The sun shone cheerily on lush tropical vegetation and the inviting blue lagoon dotted with islets. Time stood still.

'If you go to Munda, you'll never want to leave!' Gary Clifford, a Solomons-based pilot we met in Sydney, had remarked. We could sympathise with that. Relaxing on the terrace at Agnes' Lodge, we gazed across Roviana lagoon at Rendova Island and celebrated with piña coladas.

The pilot of the Aero Commander arrived for a beer. It was Gary Clifford! Conversation inevitably turned to engine failures over water. He had once made a forced landing in the sea with a full Islander after an engine failure on take-off. He had yelled at the passengers to open the rear door and jump into the water, but they all just sat there, immobile, smiling blankly. They thought they were dead. Only when he opened his door did they realise they were still alive, and made a frantic scramble to climb out! Light, low-wing aircraft with retractable gear are best for water landings, he agreed. To reduce impact, he suggested touching first with one wing on the downside of the wave so the nose would swing round to face the oncoming swell. It sounded easy but, Jees, I hoped we wouldn't have to try it out.

Solomon Islands became independent from Britain in 1978. A cluster of large, forested tropical islands, they are an enclave of calm with a laid-back way of life still dominated by tribal tabus. Japanese, Malaysian and Indonesian loggers are tricking naive island chiefs into signing away the timber on their tribal lands. The wood is already a steal, but they are also cheated on the royalties. A discrepancy of forty per cent had been found between the number of logs supposedly loaded in the Solomons and the number off-loaded in Japan. Clear-cutting whole mountainsides before conservationists interfere, the adverse effect is immediate. Rain washes soil down exposed slopes into the lagoons, killing corals and fish.

'I'm a killer,' Alfred, a local chief, announced disconcertingly as he joined us for a drink. 'Yeah, I kill plenty Japanese. I have gold teeth, from Japanese. Why not, I say? Maybe, some day, I sell them.'

The Solomon Islands had copped it badly in the Second World War, first occupied by the Japanese and then pounded by the Americans. The former built a powerful base at Rabaul, in Papua New Guinea, and established various camps in the Solomon Islands. In 1942, the Americans fought bitterly to retake Guadalcanal, and seized Munda in August 1943.

'Sometimes, we kill Japanese,' Alfred continued. 'Sometimes, not so lucky. They kill us. Many 'Mericans dead. Thousands Japanese dead. Terrible. 'Mericans carry back dead ones, bury them. Japanese, no. Leave in the bush. When now we heard on BBC about new war in that place–'

'Iraq?'

'Yes, him. Iraq. We shaking. We think another war coming soon. But no, finished! So we very happy.'

Yandina, the least mountainous of the Russell Islands, is a vast coconut plantation belonging to Lever. David Friend, the managing director, a svelte man with sophisticated grey hair, made us welcome and billeted us in the rambling house of the commercial manager, Adjit, an Indian from Kerala. It had been built in 1965 on an elevation surrounded by young coconut trees by the then-managing director, whose wife warned him that when the palms grew tall enough to block the sea view, she would leave him. Some years later, the situation became critical and the MD had to seek approval from the board in London to chop down 105 trees to restore the sea view. An empty band ten metres wide still leads the eye down to a solitary line of palms hugging the shore.

The tale of the MD's wife clearly impressed me. That night, I dreamt of a mad English botanist who was plotting a garden round the house. She suddenly decided to move the house to make way for a golf course. The bulldozers moved in with a tremendous roar, setting my bed shaking like a pneumatic drill.

'Bloody nutter! She really is moving the house,' I thought as I woke. The room was shuddering violently. 'Earthquake, chéri!' I yelled, having experienced one before, in Peru, in a twelve-storey building.

I heard Gérard leap out of bed and stagger round the dark room, groping at the walls.

'Perhaps we should get under the bed,' a dazed, bodiless voice suggested.

'Best place is under the doorway,' I told him earnestly, while enjoying the rocking motion of the bed as the rumbles of Mother Earth's belly-ache filled the darkness. 'Wow! Feel that! It's great, eh? Why not come and lie down! You can really feel it move!'

It was not exactly a sexy invitation to bed, more like a trip to the funfair. Gradually all went still. Gérard was still at a loss in the middle of the room. He returned dazily to bed. Several more tremors followed. Each time, he rose and staggered about like a drunk. In the morning, I asked him what he was doing.

'I thought the house was going to fall down, but I couldn't find the door. I just wanted to get out but I was too sleepy.'

'Gee, thanks for leaving me behind!'

The Solomons lie on the New Britain fault. Tremors occur frequently, but this had been the strongest – 7.3 on the Richter scale – Adjit had experienced. The epicentre, the radio confirmed, was forty miles away on Santa Isabel.

It was into the sombre mountains at the end of Guadalcanal that the Twin Otter had crashed. We raced to reach the airfield at Marau before rain obliterated it. As we swooped towards Wood House Passage and Conflict Bay, two yachts pinpointed the idyllic anchorage that had inspired so many yachties we had met to rave about Tavanipupu Island. In the fast-falling dusk, we had failed to notice Marau village tucked under the trees and were surprised, as we taxied back down the grass strip, to find an audience of over a hundred people who came to laugh at the 'so little plane'.

A canoe took us across to Tavanipupu. We rented a small, A-frame cottage beside the delightful home of Charles and Mefanwy Humphries, overlooking a lawn dotted with hibiscus which sloped down to translucent shallows of coral gardens. The Humphries had first arrived in the Solomon Islands thirty years before to work for the British Colonial Service. Retired onto a remote paradise island, their social life revolves round visiting yachtsmen, who autograph the several volumes of scrapbooks they have collected.

'Please list all the places you've been, just like the yachties do. That'll show 'em!' Mefanwy said, thrilled to add a photo of a circumnavigating aeroplane among so many yachts.

I noticed, with a cold shiver, that several yachts bore a subsequent postscript: LOST AT SEA. I hoped it would not be our epitaph.

Honiara, the capital of the Solomons, may be a dingy, unattractive town, but it is unpretentious and the people are friendly. Together with Juan and Luna from the yacht *Borromeo*, whom we befriended at Tavanipupu, we lunched with seventy-one-year-old Father Bill Meese, a colourful Australian naturalised Solomon Islander. A Peter Ustinov lookalike with a goatee beard and a front row of gold teeth, he was a lively soul in baggy shorts with an extensive belly stretching out the fibres of a T-shirt. A hearty eater and drinker, he amused us with his old-timer tales and, after several brandies, insisted on taking us for a drive in his ancient sedan.

'Do you know what they call hair in Pidgin?' he asked as he drove. 'It's grass. Ha ha.' He pointed to his moustache. 'This is nose grass. And pubic hair? Shame grass! Ho ho ho!'

In the back seat, Gérard, Luna and I laughed heartily, but Juan, who sat nervously in the front beside the priest, had his eyes transfixed on the road. We were speeding towards a stationary truck in our lane and an oncoming car in the other. Without taking his foot off the pedal or ceasing the flow of jokes, Father Bill swerved onto the grass verge and passed on the inside.

We were all relieved when he headed off the main road into the hills behind Honiara to where a Japanese war memorial had been built in 1981. The bitter fight for Guadalcanal had left heavy losses of life on both sides and the bay, full of sunken ships, was subsequently named Iron Bottom Sound. The dusk air was thick with the perfume of frangipani trees. A white block in front of the cross-shaped memorial read, in Japanese and English: 'At this place repose all the spirits of those who sacrificed their lives in World War II at Guadalcanal and the entire Pacific area. This represents a requiem for their souls and serves to remind us all of the patriotism which they dedicated to the mother countries. We pledge here to establish eternal peace on earth.'

Frail sunshine filtered through the haze. We were headed for Espiritu Santo, Vanuatu, formerly New Hebrides, flying south-east along the mountainous Guadalcanal coast and aiming for the gap between Guadalcanal and Makira Islands.

At 3,000 feet, we had trouble maintaining sight of the coastline. The Twin Otter disaster came to mind. A huge Cb blocked our path a few miles before Marau. Fully laden, we were reluctant to face bad turbulence and decided to go under, through rain if need be. We circled down in decreasing visibility. The GPS had a fit of amnesia, refusing to collect data. I struggled to keep track of our position on the chart.

'Am I safe going north-east?'

'Yes, but not for long. Malaita's ten minutes away. We're surrounded by mountains.'

We bounced round in a tight white circle, without seeing anything, lower and ever lower, believing we were over the sea but knowing the islands rose all around. We had to be over the sea, or we would have already crashed into a hillside.

'Let's just go back to Honiara.' I was scared.

'Hell no! We'll have to do all the paperwork again.'

When we broke free into patchy rain, the sea was 500 feet below us. Gérard suggested crossing the mountains to the south-west coast. I studied the map. Sure, there were passes between various peaks at 8,000, 6,000 and 5,000 feet. And the cloud? We swung back towards Guadalcanal Island, where forested mountainsides rose to meet us in thick haze. There were no roads, only an occasional leaf village below. Would these people come to rescue us if they heard a loud bang? What the hell made me think we would survive?

'I thought the whole point of our trip was that we had no schedule,' I sniped acidly. 'If the weather's bad, we don't have to go. It's like setting sail in a storm.'

'It's brighter here. Look, blue sky ahead,' Gérard said cheerily, ignoring my hysteria, determined to go on.

'Over the clouds at 10,000 feet.' His reluctance to turn back just because of a little bureaucracy infuriated me. It was petty and dangerous. Everything was against us: an overloaded aircraft over unfamiliar mountainous terrain in bad weather. I nagged and moaned and sulked and pouted until he agreed to land in Honiara.

On the tarmac, in watery sunshine, I felt a fool. The tremendous relief to be back on the ground metamorphosed into a secret fear that I could not take a whole Pacific Ocean of flying. Was I cracking up? Was I going to make his life hell for the next four months? Would he ship me off to an asylum?

Gary was on the tarmac, also forced back by bad weather. 'This is the beginning of the monsoon,' he said. 'Must be the ITCZ. Have you seen the Sat picture?'

When Gérard had asked the met office for the weather in Santo, he was told it was not available. No mention was made of a Sat screen in the room next-door.

'What a classic!' Gary exclaimed, as we went in. There, on the screen, was a perfect cyclone with a gaping eye. We scrutinised the outlines of the land mass beneath it. Phew! It wasn't us. The poor Philippines were about to cop it again. We moved the image down. The ITCZ ran right across Guadalcanal, but all Vanuatu was clear. We opted to fly north round the top of Guadalcanal and down the south-west coast, so as not be wedged between mountains and be able to fly safely through the bad weather.

In due course, we reached Vanuatu, joining the south-west coast of Espiritu

Santo at Remarkable Point. Its mountain tops were lost in cloud, their bases falling out into steep valleys or plunging directly into the sea. At the southern tip, we rounded Cape Lisburne and swooped down the Segond Canal where Luganville's half dozen streets spread in lethargic limbo. It also had a coral wartime airstrip with neat grass verges. A hundred thousand Americans had been stationed here during the war. A short distance from Luganville is Million Dollar Point where, after the war, they built a ramp and dumped vehicles, supplies and even foodstuffs into the sea rather than leave them for the islanders.

At the northern end of Espiritu Santo, a single track road leads down an escarpment to Big Bay, where the Spaniard Pedro Fernandez de Quiroz had begun a settlement in 1606, believing he had found the great southern continent of *terra australis*. Disease and local resentment drove him away within three weeks. Now, beside its black beach, lies the village of Matantas. The village chief, Moses, gave us *carte blanche* to wander at will. Children ran to and fro wearing custom (traditional) dress. For the boys, this meant a cloth suspended on a band over their private parts. Girls wore an astute arrangement of leaves which covered both front and back from the waist down. Several families, in custom attire, lived in one section of the village beside a malodorous pig sty. Mangy dogs, in varying stages of starvation, scuttled and scratched with the semi-naked children. The Seventh Day Adventists lived apart, in proper houses.

The Ni-Vanuatu people suffered miserably at the hands of ruthless blackbirders who, between 1860 and 1900, forcibly recruited labour here to till Queensland. Then, in 1906, the Anglo-French New Hebrides Condominium was formed, creating a confusing system of simultaneous French and British colonial rule whereby each government competed to foist its own civil servants on the local population. This complicated the independence process, because the French were unwilling to relinquish a colony (as in the case of New Caledonia to this day). But, on British insistence, Vanuatu became independent in 1980.

In Tanafo, a group of Ni-Van live in strict accordance to their custom ideals. Half a dozen men with coarse features, long fuzzy beards, bushy hair and complexions varying between jet to chocolate, chatted under the trees. They wore loincloths suspended on belts made from bark, and beads of seeds round their necks or in their hair. They greeted us warmly. We struggled to understand Bislama, the Ni-Vanuatu version of Pidgin. Its name derives from a corruption of *bêche de mer*, much sought after in the area by nineteenth-century traders. One man who spoke a little English, explained that custom ways spurned the use of modern tools like axes and knives. They made their own machetes from bamboo and lived entirely off the land, rejecting the paraphernalia of white man's civilisation.

Since we knew that in the Solomons and Vanuatu tribal chiefs charged 'custom money' to visitors, Gérard offered a contribution. It was declined with great dignity. They had no use for money, they said, and felt sure we would not charge them if they came to visit us one day. We felt comfortable sitting on the grass, chatting to these dignified people, rich in hope and belief. There was nothing we could give them, nothing they wanted from the twentieth century.

Tanna's grass airfield looked more like a ski-slope. We halted beside a bunch of kids who, accustomed to tourists, had an aggressive nature we had not encountered on other islands. No aircraft overnighted on Tanna, so it was a dilemma where to park safely. We chose a corner opposite the terminal beside some leaf huts where a ragged old man, Johnson, introduced himself. He was the only adult around and, I think, a little mad. He jabbered incessantly at us in rapid Bislama and gesticulated wildly. To be on the safe side, we agreed with all he said.

'No gud. No gud. Luk.' He play-acted a thief breaking into the plane. 'Johnson luk plen. Then yufela glad. Then yufela unpack samting. Then mi glad.' He flashed a toothy grin and rolled his eyes, looking quite wild and threatening. Then he clapped us on the back and roared with laughter. We felt he made a better friend than enemy.

A communal taxi pick-up took us to White Sands, beside Yasur volcano, which we wanted to climb in the afternoon, staying on till dark when the lava glowed dramatically. But by the time we reached it, after the taxi made numerous social stops, the sun was setting. We resolved to climb before dawn. Roy, the taxi-driver, offered us a room in his house in Yaneumakel village. He sent his two daughters scampering to organise space for us before departing for a *kava* drinking session. Popular throughout the Pacific, *kava* is made from the root of a certain pepper plant, which is either ground or preferably chewed to a pulp, to which water is added before sieving. The resulting dark brown gravy, drunk primarily by men, is served in half coconut-shell cups and downed in one. It numbs the tongue and throat and induces such a sense of relaxation, that it is best taken lying down. However, the flavour is so unappetisingly medicinal, we never swallowed enough to succumb to its tranquillising effects.

'Papa drinks the *kava*, then he goes dreaming,' little Saloki explained as she showed us round the simple, three-roomed cement house where we were to sleep. Despite our protests, someone was moved out of a double bed to make way for us.

We were starving by this time, and set about cooking spaghetti before a chattering audience of tiny black faces with bright white eyes. These were Saloki's girlfriends. They played lovingly with my hair, enraptured by its length and softness.

'How big is your island?' they asked.

'Very, very big. So big you can't imagine it.'

'Did you go to school in your village?'

'No, in the neighbouring village.'

'Ohhh. We have a school in our own village.'

Once the food was ready but before we could offer them any, they vanished and silence reigned in the household. We bolted down our dinner, fearing it was bedtime in a village with no electricity, but no sooner had we finished than they all reappeared, bounding with joy. They were only being discreet. They announced we were going to a party. Seven little girls, speaking French or English, depending on which school they attended, led us through dark forest to another village. A crowd was gathered beside a huge pile of wood for a bonfire, singing spiritual songs and dancing to guitar music. The girls also sang along in full voice. When the crowd turned silent and the preacher began, we noticed periodic explosions, like gunshots. Firecrackers, perhaps, from the party? Or a tribal war? We were puzzled until, turning round, we saw the volcano peak shimmering orange in the darkness. Yasur's tremendous glow at night serves as a lighthouse for ships at sea. After the Bislama sermon had droned on for some time, we tried to sneak away but the girls insisted on accompanying us. As we reached the village, they spoke in whispers so as not to wake sleeping neighbours.

We dragged ourselves out of bed at 04:00 trying to make no noise as we gathered up torches, water bottle, biscuits and jumpers. A clear starry night greeted us with a chink of moon and a refreshing ocean breeze as we left the village for the ashy plain at the base of the volcano. The steep sides loomed heavenwards towards the red glow which roared periodically. In the velvet darkness, it was impossible to find the path. We started to climb straight up the side. Sinking up to our ankles in volcanic ash, sliding one step back for every three forward, it became apparent that unless we found the proper track, we would make very slow progress. Within moments, we were smothered with grit. Occasionally, the volcano roared angrily. The higher we climbed, the angrier it became, and the more pronounced was the trembling of the whole mountain. I was sure it was going to explode. The eastern horizon turned pink. We would obviously never make the summit in darkness. I wondered if I would make it at all. Our route was threaded with ravines. What looked like rock shredded underfoot, sending stones scampering down the sheer sides and serving as a sharp reminder of what a missed foothold would mean.

Gérard struggled manfully, encumbered with camera and video bag. I dawdled like a wimp, contemplating defeat, hating that dirty noisy mountain. Higher up, the ash became softer and nauseous sulphur fumes pervaded the air. Gérard went ahead in the half-light, sending showers of French curse words down to me each time he stumbled. He bawled at me to find a different path while Yasur bellowed with rage. He was almost at the rim, stuck beneath a ridge that jutted backwards. Seeing him in that situation, I wanted to yell such useless advice as 'Be careful'.

In my mind's eye was the troubling image I had of Yasur from the air. The crater edge was extremely fine. It was only made of compacted ash. My God, what if it gave way and he fell inside? Petrified, I couldn't concentrate on my own footsteps and kept looking up to see how he was managing. I wanted to tell him to come back, but he would never hear me. My ankle twisted over in a chasm and I almost fell. When I looked up again, he had disappeared. A mini avalanche of stones clattered down the slope. Oh, my God! I didn't know whether to rush up to see if he was clutching to a ledge inside the crater, incinerating in bubbling lava, or to go immediately for help. I bawled *yoohoo* again and again, desperately, my throat dry from ash and fear. No answer. My heart pounded. What the hell should I do? It would take ages to reach the village for help. Why on earth didn't he answer?

He suddenly strolled into view, not above but way below me, where he had been obliged to descend to find another route. Better not let him see I'd been panicking. He soon overtook me and bounded up to the rim.

'Woooow!! It's fantastic. Listen to that. Come, quick,' he called excitedly.

I staggered on up and lay down to peer over the edge. There was a terrific roar and the whole mountain shook, sending vibrations through every capillary. Round blow-holes boiled and hissed, spitting molten red lava high into the air like geysers.

'I'm going. I don't like it,' I whined.

'Don't be silly. It's been doing this for hundreds of years!'

'I don't care. I don't want to be looking inside when it blows.' I gathered up my water bottle and rucksack.

'C'mon baby. It's not going to blow now, right now, just when we're here. Let's go over there, where the edge is wider.'

Admittedly, on the rounder crater lip, I felt safer and dared to peer down at the lava bubbling up from the bowels of the earth. Nevertheless, I stuck close to Gérard. Perhaps he had a hidden knack of stopping volcanoes from erupting, a special trick he had never told me about.

20 'The hurricane season started yesterday'

Jack Snow, a New Zealander working for the CAA in Nadi (pronounced Nandi) contacted the Fijian Ministry of Tourism, Civil Aviation and Energy in the capital, Suva, to have our domestic flights approved.

'From an Operations point of view, there is absolutely no problem,' he told the assistant minister over the phone. 'They just want to visit a few islands, spend some money, and come back to Nadi before leaving for Tonga.'

'So we'd better send a local pilot with them to show them the way?' the voice offered.

'I don't think it's necessary. They've flown all around the world for two years and managed to find Nadi. I'll brief them on local airport conditions.'

A fax had to be sent to formalise the request. The next day, we called Jack for news. No reply had arrived from Suva.

'Just be on your way,' he advised. 'The worst that can happen is I'll have to summon you back here and give you a bollocking on your return. Have fun!'

We traced the line of the Yasawa islands, dotted with idyllic beaches, before crossing to Vanua Levu over Bligh Water. It was here that Fijian war canoes had given chase to Captain Bligh and his men as they passed through the Fijian Islands in 1789, having been cast adrift by the *Bounty* mutineers in Tonga. Labasa (pronounced Lambasa), capital of Vanua Levu, is a predominantly Indian town and heart of a sugar-growing region. There were few native Fijians in the streets. Sixty thousand Indians had arrived in Fiji as indentured labour between 1879 and 1916 in a scheme devised by the country's first governor, Sir Arthur Gordon, who wished to protect Fijians from exploitation on the plantations. A large majority of them opted to settle in Fiji, resulting in the uncomfortable racial ratio which exists today. Melanesian Fijians account for only forty-nine per cent of the population, while the Indians run a close forty-six per cent. In Labasa, women in garish saris and men wearing Muslim caps filled the streets. Towering over them, huge Fijian policemen strolled by in *sulus*, a monochrome skirt like a pleatless kilt, worn with more comfort than trousers in the hot climate.

Fiji (a corruption of Viti Levu, the name of the main island) became independent in 1970. Due to the modern-day conflict of interests between native Fijians

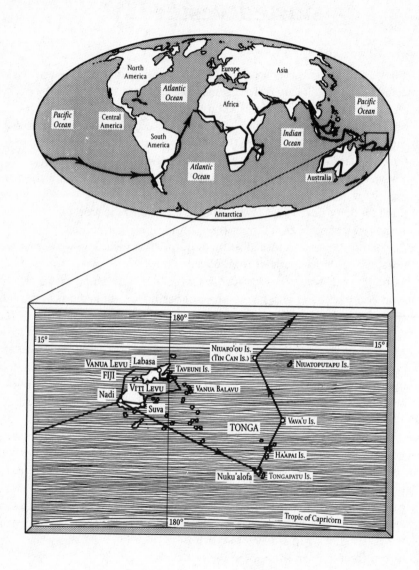

and Indians, a democratic system in which the Indians are victorious is unacceptable to the former. The result has been two easy military coups in 1987. The armed and police forces are heavily dominated by native Fijians, making Fijian-led uprisings a predictable success.

In nearby Savusavu, at the dilapidated Planters Club, a drinking-den for the remnants of the non-tourist white community in the area, old timers were downing pints of Fiji Bitter.

'What do you plant?' I asked one planter, a tall grey-haired man with sun-baked ruddy complexion. He looked at me blankly. 'I mean, what do you farm? Copra?'

'I run a few cattle,' he nodded. 'We manage to survive, in spite of everything, heh.' I had expected him to whinge about hard work and useless labour.

'Is it hard work then?' I set him up.

'My dear,' he said, taking a deep breath to give him patience, 'we live like in the good old days. We don't work, we supervise. Aaah yes, we still supervise, thank God! Do this, do that. Not like in New Zealand. Ho, ho. We'll supervise for a few years yet.' His buddies murmured their agreement. 'We just sit on the tractor, drink champagne and supervise. Ho ho.' His eyes twinkled.

Steep green hillsides plunge into a cobalt sea along the north-west coast of Taveuni where small villages of neat houses and churches dot the seashore. We came in gently on the grass strip, parked by the tower and switched off. A tall elegant lady appeared at the window as I was putting on my shoes.

'I've come to meet you,' she said. 'I'm Do Cammick.'

Ric and Do Cammick were handsome New Zealanders who had been in Taveuni for eighteen years. They had set up Dive Taveuni on a heavenly spot at the edge of a cliff offering magnificent views across Somosomo Strait to Vanua Levu. Six luxurious *bures* dotted the lush garden. Having suffered various calamitous hurricanes over the years, Ric was an avid listener to weather bulletins.

'The hurricane season started yesterday,' he announced with aplomb as we entered reception.

'How can a season start on a definite date?' I chortled.

'Don't laugh,' he replied. 'One is brewing east of the Solomons, moving this way. Last year, the first one came through on 27 November.'

It was 16 November.

'It'd be fun to experience a hurricane,' Gérard piped in.

'You're kidding!' Ric said gravely. 'It is an utterly nerve-racking, devastating and expensive experience. Particularly if you've got buildings and boats on your hands.'

Gérard had been joking, really. We had *Romeo* to worry about.

The next morning was sparklingly perfect. Breakfast was laid on a long table, decorated with hibiscus and frangipani, on an open-air deck overlooking the sparkling sea. There were half a dozen fellow guests, mostly American doctors.

'I'm going to have a lazy day,' seventy-five-year old Bill Senior announced. He settled on the cliff-top terrace to contemplate the idyllic surroundings while his son, a grumpy radiologist, went on the morning's diving expedition.

It was such a clear day, we resolved to make a sight-seeing flight of Taveuni. On our return, the aura of calm had been replaced by hushed panic. Bill Senior had taken a stroll down to the beach and broken his leg. Fortunately, two of the doctors had stayed behind. They put the leg in splints, and six beefy Fijians had carried the patient to his *bure*. A radio message had been passed to the dive-boat, and Junior arrived in due course, stony-faced.

'I knew he'd do this,' he muttered furiously.

Gérard repeatedly offered to fly them to Nadi.

'He's perfectly all right. He can just stay in bed till our flight in the morning. It's his own fault.'

William, the neurosurgeon who had made the splint, advised that the leg would swell enormously in the night. Due to the patient's age, he strongly recommended proper treatment. Junior begrudgingly accepted to go to Nadi. Gérard and I rushed ahead to prepare *Romeo*. Most of our luggage had to be removed, for both men weighed over a hundred kilos each. Since the right leg was broken, Bill Senior could sit in the only rear seat, his leg stretched between the fuel tanks. The patient arrived on a PVC sunlounger in the back of Do's Land Rover. We set him on the tarmac as we unloaded the last of the baggage. He was in remarkably high spirits, joking with the small crowd of curious Fijian children that had gathered, and constantly thanking us. Do returned with sour-faced Junior and four large bags. It was a tight fit.

'He doesn't need that,' Junior remarked curtly as I tied a lifejacket round his father. 'If we come down, he'll die anyway with that leg.'

'That's precisely why I'm putting it on him now.' I was astounded by such filial callousness and showed his father how to open the door in an emergency.

Gérard landed back in Taveuni just before sunset. On arriving at the hotel, he received a round of applause from the guests, who wanted to know how it went.

'Well, it wasn't an easy flight,' Gérard told us. 'There was a solid cloud layer at 3,000 feet. Since Junior had been deep-sea diving, I couldn't risk climbing high and ending up with two patients on my hands. So, sometimes, to stay visual, I was forced down to about 500 feet, with rain all round. "How the hell you gonna find land again?" he asks me. I was really pissed off with him by then, so I just told him I knew what I was doing. Know what he says? "I can't believe you flew all the way from Brazil in this thing!" Never muttered a word of thanks, not even when we landed safely at Nadi and the ambulance I had asked for on the radio was there waiting on the tarmac.'

'I wouldn't be surprised if they sue us,' Do whispered to me.

'I was thinking the same thing. You do all you can to help someone and then receive notice of a lawsuit.'

'Well, I'd like to see them get anywhere in Fijian courts,' she said contentedly. 'In Fiji, you're old at fifty. They are amazed if people survive to seventy-five, and would feel it is quite reasonable to break a leg. We've got twenty staff members as witnesses that he could not walk well, and that he had a weak spot for alcohol. So they can try to sue if they like.'

Vanua Balavu, home island of the then Prime Minister, Ratu Mara, is a thin hilly island in a dog-leg. The grass airstrip on a steep gradient only receives a weekly flight from Suva. A kind-faced middle-aged man in a grey *sulu* approached. He introduced himself as Josateki and advised that there were only four vehicles on the island. To reach Lomaloma, the main village, we would just have to wait. A fish truck duly picked us all up, stopping along the roadside to sell its catch: huge parrot fish, coral trout and sweetlips.

'Fijians very lucky,' Josateki stated, as we bounced along with the fish. 'We just plant something, it grows. Eating easy – taro, potatoes, cassava, mangoes, chickens, pigs. We need little money to buy sugar sometimes. So we sell some vegetables. Indian, he has one store, makes lots of money. Keeps it, always making more money for self. Not same Fijian. Fijian only little money. Then, when visitors come to village, he spend money, make big feast.'

Fijians spend their money and energies on feasting. It is their way. Any family member in need of food must be fed. No Fijian can stay rich for long. Poor relatives, no matter how distant, soon show up on the doorstep.

Lomaloma, the largest village, consisted of school buildings, a small hospital, the Prime Minister's extensive seafront house, a tiny post office and half a dozen shops including a Hot Bread kitchen. The neat houses, separated by green lawns and decorative plants, were made of wood or straw and corrugated iron, in varying combinations, some on piles, some not. The only rest-house was a wooden *bure*.

'But you haven't booked,' said the buxom proprietress, a Tongan called Mele. 'I'm expecting the Australian ambassador and his wife tomorrow for the school prize-giving. Sorry, but I am preparing the *bure* for them.'

In effect, it was freshly painted and all the furniture was spread on the lawn.

'We'll only stay one night, Mele. We'll leave early in the morning, promise.'

She ceded, and carted off the coral trout we had bought from the fish truck for our dinner. 'I'll make curry,' she decided.

We winced as she smashed it to pieces with a machete. We would have preferred it gently grilled, served with lemon and hollandaise sauce. Never mind.

Under a large tree, where women peeled vegetables on woven reed mats, five young pigs lay trussed up on their sides, destined for the ambassador's feast. Our sleep that night was disturbed by their grunting and indignant squeals as they struggled, against all odds, to get free.

Suva, with a population of only 200,000, is the largest Pacific island city after Honolulu. It has a laid-back small-town atmosphere, where the variety of races is clearly apparent. Mundane concrete Indian stores mix with the Doric pillars of colonial buildings, part of a proud heritage still surviving in Suva's curvaceous streets. The small museum, tucked in the botanical gardens, was a vignette into Fiji's fascinating past. It included a scaled-down model of the formidable thirty-five-metre double ocean-going warring canoes. Reed matting sails were fitted to masts and such heavy steering oars were used as rudders that four men were needed to lift them into place.

Cannibalism had been a fact of life. Death, rather. Fierce tribal battles had been frequent. After a massacre, so much meat was available that hands, heads and thoraxes were thrown away. Brains were a delicacy, usually given to the gods by smashing the head on a stone near the temple. When no battle victims were available, a passer-by would be snatched or a luckless slave or low-class tribal member would do. There appeared to be no preference regarding age or sex. In the cabinet exposing the pronged forks used for eating human flesh were the botanical prints of the plants that accompanied as vegetables. Only the recipes were missing. A number of Europeans were eaten in the years of first contact. Nevertheless, they still successfully depleted the islands of sandalwood, *bêche de mer* and whales throughout the 1800s. All manner of conmen and crooks were attracted to Fiji. The confusion became such that the Great Chief Cakoban, unable to control the domain any longer, voluntarily ceded it to Queen Victoria in 1874.

Back in Nadi for a fifty-hour service, we bumped into Jack Snow.

'Just as well you went on your trip,' he laughed, 'the ministry still hasn't replied to your request!'

In the centre of Nuku'alofa, capital of the Kingdom of Tonga, the white walls, russet roof and turret of the King's Palace, unchanged since 1882, rose imposingly beyond a large green football field where an Oriental was teaching kung fu to

Tongan soldiers. Large women sat under parasols on the nearby jetty selling sea urchins and clams in palm-leaf woven baskets. They feasted as they awaited customers, smashing open the live urchins to get at the soft yellow starfish intestines clinging inside the shell.

The town was not picturesque, its older buildings being replaced by characterless new ones along dusty streets strewn with rubbish. But the imposing size of the Tongans, with their honey-coloured skins and large, oval faces, gives the place a special feel. Men and women alike are huge, and proud of it. In Talamahu market, the stalls were piled high with sweet potatoes, yams, cassava, taro and kava root. Both men and women wear long black skirts and *ta'ovala*, the traditional Tongan raffia mat, wrapped round their waists. Looking hot and uncomfortable, the *ta'ovala* stretches from a crumpled band at the waist, tied with rope, to down below the knees. With general usage, it cracks and frays. Some are so old they are no more than a tangle of rats' tails, but being hereditary items, they are passed with great pride down through generations.

We had almost finished our meal at the Seaview restaurant when a smiling Tongan couple sat at the table opposite. One of the lady's fingers was bandaged awkwardly.

'What did you do to your finger?' Gérard broke the ice.

'Well, you aren't going to believe me if I tell you,' she said coyly in immaculate English. 'A fish bit me!'

'A fish? What fish?'

'Well, it was one from my own fish trap, the one just out there . . . ' She pointed seawards, as if we must know the trap she meant. 'It was one of those big round ones, with spikes-'

'A porcupine fish,' her husband added.

'Well, I'd finished gutting it . . .'

'You mean it was dead?'

'Yes, that's the funny thing. The guts were out. I wanted to put it into the pan, so I decided the easiest way was to put my finger inside the mouth to lift it – and it bit me!'

We all laughed. But it had been a serious bite and the nail had gone black.

'So I got angry, and threw it in the boiling water. Do you know, even then, it carried on snapping! I couldn't bear the sight of it any more, and gave it away.'

'So I didn't even have the chance to taste this adventurous fish. Only a dead fish would dare to bite my wife's hand!' her husband laughed. 'What do you do in Tonga?'

'We don't live here. We're just passing through. We're travelling around the world in a small plane.'

'That's great! I'm Cecil Cocker, the Minister of Finance. This is my wife, Tu'ifua.

Come and drink your coffee with us.' They were both garrulous and had nine children.

'That's proof how much we love each other,' Tu'ifua chortled. 'We're both half-breeds, so we're a bit different from Tongans. But we love Tonga, and the Tongans' way of life, always having fun, talking in riddles, never saying what they mean so that the other has to guess. It's a game. We Tongans like that.'

Cecil proudly told us about Tonga's record pumpkin exports to Japan, excelling all previous years' general exports. Tonga's biggest exchange earner had always been remittances from family abroad.

'The Japanese love pumpkin. Next year, I intend to triple exports,' he announced proudly. 'Tonga cannot rely on remittances from abroad. We are 100,000 people. We need to find new sources of income.'

Cecil explained Tonga's kingship to us. No one wanted change, he said. The nobility knew their place, the commoners knew their place, and both accepted it like that. The current monarch, King Taufa'ahau Tupou IV, was famed for his vast size. His mother, six-footer Queen Salote, had won the admiration of the British public by waving ecstatically from her coach, in the pouring rain, during the parade for Queen Elizabeth's coronation in 1953.

On Lifuka Island of the Ha'apai group, we stayed in a bungalow at Niu'akalo Beach hotel. A fellow guest, a Scotsman called Bob on contract from Australia, had been installing shipping lights in the harbour under the direction of the harbour-master. To his consternation, he had discovered that a huge coral head, completely exposed at low tide, lay in the middle of the channel. He protested. The harbour-master was unconcerned. The fishermen knew it was there. They did not need lights to show them into the harbour. Bob pointed out how visiting yachtsmen would interpret red and green lights to mean a safe passage.

'They silly. They should smell reef like us,' was the most sympathy he could raise.

Captain Cook had aptly named Tonga the Friendly Isles. Seletuti, the hotel proprietress, was a warm-hearted, big-bosomed lady. She soon found out we had a plane, as it was a small island, and rushed off to see her husband in hospital.

'I tell my husband: Dear, we have at our hotel one pilot and his wife, they came to Ha'apai in small plane from far away. And they stay at our hotel! My husband, he make the eyes open big. Really, Seletuti, they come with a small plane? I tell him yes, they are in our hotel. And I see the other peoples, they are listening, with the ears big, because they don't know the small plane only for two peoples. But the doctor, he tells them yes, he has seen it at the airport, one small plane. So I tell them, "They come from far away in so small plane. And when the pilot, he tired, he sleep and his wife she fly the plane." Their eyes, they making bigger, but their hearts don't believe.'

She stopped for a breath before continuing.

'I have seen before the small plane. In United States. I go there one time. And I see the very very big plane, so big like so many houses. But I don't like United States. I tell to my son and my daughter, let's hurry to do everything, so we can go happy to Ha'apai again.'

'But, Seletuti, why didn't you like it?'

'I frightened. Too many, the very big planes, the very small planes. And the – how you say? Highway? Too many cars. They smash together in the back, the peoples dead. And the policemen, with the guns, shooting the people. I don't like it. I pray God, "Back to Ha'apai, quick!"'

On departure day, Seletuti had tears in her eyes as she gave us three cowrie shells. 'This is for you, my son and daughter, for you to remember your Tongan mother who loves you. You put in your house, you remember Ha'apai, you back again. Last night, I am thinking by myself, me, I can give them nothing, only I can pray to Jesus, He go with them in the plane, just three of them together. He taking care, flying with you in so small plane to a safe place.'

Off Ha'apai lay the sharp cone of Kao volcano, with a crown of wispy cloud, beside Tofua Island. It was here that Captain Bligh and his men were cast adrift from the *Bounty*. Tofua was ringed with steam issuing from volcanic vents beside the bowl in which lay an intriguing crater lake where, we had been told, a crazy American had once landed a seaplane. To the north Vava'u, an archipelago of fifty islands, spread spectacularly before us as we approached down the Pulepulekai Passage. Rocky outcrops, islands, bays and caves dotted sapphire water which smashed in a white ribbon over the reef and turned topaz. Lovely villages nestled on the headlands. Neiafu, the main town, cuddled up on various bays before a small party of yachts. As we parked, a man in customs uniform approached.

'Hallo. Mrs Moss? I'm Vili. Mr Cecil Cocker asked us to meet you. Mr Lava is waiting.'

Good old Cecil – he had promised, but we thought he would forget. Mr Lava was Collector of Customs, Postmaster-General, Harbour-Master and Sub-Treasurer for Vava'u. He invited us to stay in his hundred-year-old colonial house overlooking the Halaevalu wharf. In the garden stood a monument to the first European visitor to Vav'au, the Spaniard Francisco Antonio Mourelle, who stopped in Port-of-Refuge on *La Princesa* in March 1781. Indoors, Lava's wife, Tagikina, and daughter Agnes welcomed us with fresh pineapple juice.

'Thank you, all. You're being so kind. Vava'u's certainly a very beautiful place. We had a wonderful view from the air.'

'Some people,' Lava said gravely, 'pray to God to take them to heaven.

Not me! I pray to God *not* to take me to heaven. I prefer to live in Vav'au!'

Later, by the post office, we bumped into Peter Goldstern the crazy American who had landed a plane on Tofua lake. He invited us to dinner and regaled us with flying stories. He was a ferry pilot with 6,000 hours in his log book when he went down in a brand-new Mooney off Greenland on 22 December 1979. After the engine failed, Peter called Mayday, gave an approximate position, and took twenty minutes to struggle into a survival suit, no easy feat in a cramped cockpit. He had no life-raft. Nevertheless, he was the first pilot to survive an engine failure over the glacial North Atlantic. He jumped into the icy swell, feeling futile and foolish clutching an ELT. After two and a half hours in the freezing water, he was convinced he would drown when a Canadian Argus aircraft buzzed over and dropped him a life-raft. It was his lucky day. He was rescued six hours later by a Russian meteorological ship.

The blue sky was flecked with scurrying stratocumulus. North-north-west for Niuafo'ou, 210 miles away. After an hour, the weather changed. Bulging stratocumulus forced us down to 1,000 feet over rough, grey seas.

Niuafo'ou is a pure volcanic island with no beaches and no port. Seas pound the ragged black rocks. It also has a crater lake where megapodes, a kind of jungle chicken, lay their eggs near thermal pools to be hatched by the heat. The nickname of Tin Can Island derives from the fact that, for many years, mail was dropped off into the sea in cans for retrieval by the islanders in canoes. In 1946, when there was an eruption, all islanders were evacuated and not allowed home until 1958. The population stands at 780. In the main village, the end-of-term ceremony at the school was taking place. Teenage boys and girls, festooned with leaves and leis, sang heartily and danced the *lakalaka*, leaping up and down with impressive concerted arm movements and clapping. Three girls, constantly smiling, performed the *tau'olunga*, caressing the air with their hands while the other children sang.

'Why do rich people like you spend money to visit Niuafo'ou, so poor?' a man on horseback asked us. We said we loved unspoiled islands like his.

'East or west, Niuafo'ou is best,' he agreed. 'Tourists very difficult to come to Niuafo'ou.'

The well-cropped grass airstrip was only a disguise as an airport. It was really part of Old MacDonald's farm. When we had landed, a herd of goats darted onto the terminal patio where a large pig and string of piglets ran for cover. Dogs and chickens roamed the spongy grass at will. We asked King, the airport manager/tractor driver who cared for the strip, if we could pitch a tent. We were perfectly happy to camp, but he felt we should be treated better and chivvied his wife, Savieta, to prepare the Royal Tongan check-in office for us. In moments, she had produced foam mattresses, armchairs and a plateful of bananas and water-melon, and invited us to shower at her house. Meanwhile, King and three friends reclined on raffia mats, preparing *kava* in the tractor shelter. The evening air was filled with their gentle murmur as they chatted over their *kava*, with occasional low guffaws, until long after dark.

Waking early, we watched the sky slowly lighten from our bed on the floor. There were already several majestic cumulonimbus about. But the speedy cloud base was high, so it looked good for the flight to Apia, Western Samoa. Across the lawn, *Romeo* stood at peace, as if building up strength for what lay ahead.

The farm came to life: various pig families trotted resolutely about their business and a harem of white chickens clucked along behind a cock. Sosefina, Savieta's five-year-old grand-daughter, arrived giggling with a platter of bananas and boiled eggs.

'Hallo gu'morning'owareyou?' All came out in one breath.

By the time we were ready to leave, a small crowd had gathered respectfully behind the fence to watch. We bade farewell to yet another Tongan family who had overwhelmed us with generosity and affection, and gave them all our food supplies.

'Oooo,' said Sosefina when I produced a Scottish doll for her. 'Crismas!'

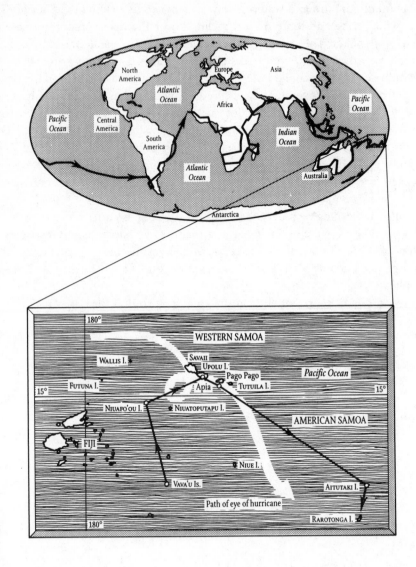

Path of eye of hurricane

21 'No chance of a cyclone'

Although the 180th meridian cuts through Fiji, the International Date Line kinks back so that Wallis and Futuna, the Kingdom of Tonga, and New Zealand's outlying islands fall west of it. On the flight to Samoa, we slipped back in time from Friday 6 December to Thursday 5. The 6 December is a date we will never forget, not only because we had to live it twice.

The flight to Faleolo, Apia's international airport, was the smoothest we had experienced for a long time – gentle sunshine filtered through cirrostratus onto placid blue seas. Small stratocumulus collected in family groups. There were the usual twenty-knot easterlies but no buffeting gusts. As we approached a towering cloud formation to the north, we guessed it must conceal 6,000-foot Mount Silisili on Savai'i Island, the largest of the Samoan group. There was no reason to suspect foul play: rainclouds habitually accumulate around prominent islands emerging suddenly from the seabed. At Faleolo on Upolu Island, sudden thirty-knot crosswinds whipped the water-logged runway. Gérard managed a smooth landing, one wheel first, fighting to keep the centre line until the wind blew us off to one side, dragging all three tyres on the ground roll. In a trice, it was raining torrentially, trapping us inside.

When the rain eased, a truck approached. A portly Samoan, who introduced himself as Heini, offered us a place in Polynesian Airlines' 727 hangar. We accepted gratefully. In the hangar, he mentioned the vague threat of a cyclone some 800 kilometres to the north-west, dismissing it as 'far away from here'. At worst, it might spoil the beach weather for the weekend. Reports suggested it was moving at nine knots. That gave us two days' margin to get away if necessary. Heini insisted we could stay in the hangar as long as we wanted, reassuring us that it had withstood Cyclone Ofa, the worst in Samoa's history, in January 1990. Unaccustomed to cyclones, we failed to realise that the ominous clouds over Savai'i could be part of the system, or that the thirty-knot gusts already pummelling the corrugated iron roof were the precursor. The rain slackened into a shower, and we accepted a lift into town in the staff bus. Passing through numerous villages with neat colourful houses, open-sided thatched *fales* and countless churches, we were struck by the beauty and tranquillity of the place. Frangipani, breadfruit, mango, banana and coconut trees abounded. On verdant lawns, horses grazed placidly among pink-and-black pigs.

Aggie Grey's Hotel, the Raffles of the Pacific, sat serenely on the far bend of Beach Road, staring at the ruffled ocean. Our room overlooked a patio with a breadfruit tree, a spindly Norfolk pine and a fish pond with water lilies. All was calm. We phoned Peter Goldstern in Vava'u to ask him to chase up a file we had left at the control tower. He asked if we realised a cyclone was brewing, giving the co-ordinates he had copied down from the radio. The seriousness of the situation still failed to sink in.

Friday 6 December : Day One

The howling wind woke us at dawn. Gérard groped for the radio, seeking reassurance that Western Samoa did not lie in the cyclone's path. There were gale warnings, and the news that Tropical Cyclone Val would pass to the north of Upolu that night, causing heavy seas. Despite our curiosity, we had no intention of hanging around for a hurricane. The advantage we had over a yacht was that of moving quickly and efficiently out of range.

The skies were overcast. There was heavy-duty soul searching to be done. Should we leave? If we did, where would we go? Where would be safe? What were the alternatives? Niue or Wallis? Cyclones unpredictably change course at any moment. What if we had an engine failure? No one would search for us in such seas. South to Rarotonga was a good option, but Cyclone Val could follow us there. A second cyclone, Wasa, was headed for Polynesia. How about back to Tonga? The safest destination was probably Fiji, well west of Val's track, but it could mean flying through horrific weather.

I was happy for us to be safe on the ground, with a good roof over our heads. Gérard, more concerned about *Romeo*, was in favour of moving on. In the end, Polynesian Airlines' 'cyclone-proof' hangar tempted us to conclude in favour of staying in Apia. At breakfast, all hotel guests seemed completely carefree. We felt neurotic, sitting in the dining *fale* in gentle sunshine. The wind ruffled the tablecloth, sending butter papers flying.

'Must be the beginning of the cyclone,' I commented to the waiter who retrieved them.

He forced a smile, condescending to my alarmism. 'Don't worry, there's no chance of a cyclone. We had one last year,' he said, moving away on bare feet.

'But seriously, we heard on the radio–'

'No way! I told you, we had one last year.'

By lunch, however, the hotel was all a-twitter. The local radio station had announced that Cyclone Val would pass alongside at Upolu at 19:00. The concern was contagious. We left immediately for the airport to ensure *Romeo*'s safety. The winds had increased to a light gale and the seas, already violent, pounded yellow waves onto the reefs, sending spray high into the air. In the villages, households prepared for an invasion, battening roofs down with rocks and banana tree trunks. Those who lived in *fales* were roping their furniture together and weaving palm leaf screens around the poles supporting their roofs.

Our priority was to see the weather picture in the control tower where, to our surprise, everybody was bubbling with good humour. The met report from Nadi was eight hours old and showed Cyclone Val, still classified as a Tropical Storm, 480 kilometres away. Winds were forecast to reach seventy knots, less than during Cyclone Ofa, when waves had crashed over the runway and covered it with debris. Winds are considered gale force from thirty-four to forty knots (+61 kph), storm force from forty-eight to fifty-five knots (+86 kph) and hurricane (cyclone) force at over sixty-four knots (115 kph). The tower staff jovially admitted they would abandon their posts when the glass blew in. In the same breath, they reassured us of the strength of Polynesian Airline's mighty hangar where *Romeo* was tucked into a corner beside the only cement wall. Their Twin Otter was still out flying. Gérard inspected the hangar and was impressed by its sturdy steel structure.

'No worries, mate. Just go back to town and have a beer. It'll be right,' Heini insisted. 'The nightwatchman will take care of everything.'

We looked down from his office at *Romeo*'s perfect, gleaming-white form, alone in that vast hangar. A wave of tenderness welled over us. It was impossible to imagine anything would destroy that angelic bird. However, by the time we reached town, the wind had become a steady gale force with powerful gusts.

'I'm going back to the airport to sit it out,' Gérard said. 'I can pull *Romeo* out if necessary. I can't just wait here.'

If the hangar fell down, I didn't want him to be in it but all my efforts to dissuade him were in vain. And he didn't want me there. The worst was expected for 19:00. By 20:00, it was still gusting strongly, but if this was a hurricane, it wasn't so bad. Nevertheless, I was delighted when Gérard walked in at dinner time. Upon reaching the hangar, he had found it deserted. The Twin Otter had been backed in and left without chocks. The hangar doors had been closed, but not secured. The wind had already lifted the eastern tip of the corrugated iron roof, which grated horribly on the steel girders. He had tidied away all loose objects – tools, paint tins and ferry tanks – left carelessly lying around. When the power failed, and he could no longer see the flying objects, he realised there was nothing more he could do and was only putting himself in danger. He spent a sleepless night, bounding up at each gust, imagining the worst. I could not muster the same concern. A fierce bout of food poisoning had clasped me, so that between excursions to the toilet, I slept fitfully, not hearing nor caring about the cyclone. How heartless I must have seemed. Gérard spent hours sitting on the cast-iron benches in front of the hotel, watching the five boats trapped in Apia harbour as they frantically fought wind and churning seas. They were caught unawares with

217

insufficient time to make it to Pago Pago, the Pacific's safest hurricane harbour only seventy miles away.

Saturday 7 December : Day Two

'If it maintains its present course, Tropical Cyclone Val will pass alongside Upolu at 13:00,' the radio announced.

It was supposed to have passed by already. There seemed little logic in the information broadcast: the position of the eye of the cyclone became increasingly ambiguous. The local radio station, which relied on Nadi meteorological office, announced that it was thirty miles north-east of Savai'i, while the New Zealanders insisted it was thirty miles south-west.

All day, we lived under Val's spell. It rained torrentially, while the sea boiled like witch's soup. Filthy brown waves crashed along the sea wall of Beach Road, flinging lava rocks ashore. Bent double, the trees valiantly defied the winds, periodically ceding branches or giving up altogether. Still sick, I continued running from bed to bathroom and back, not giving a damn about the weather. Despite the roaring winds, I slept all afternoon while Gérard, tormented by fears as to *Romeo*'s fate, stalked the lobby. The road to the airport had been cut off by fallen trees and power lines. Extensive damage was reported. The Samoans seemed unperturbed by Nature's wrath and strolled along the seafront, completely drenched, taunting the waves. The colourful umbrellas, so omnipresent on sunny days, had vanished.

When awake, I tried in vain to dial England to reassure my mother. From the violent centre of our little universe, we imagined the whole world was worrying about Samoa. In the evening, New Zealand radio warned of 'phenomenal seas' and winds of ninety to a hundred knots (160–180 kph), gusting 150 knots (270 kph). The cyclone had changed its course to south-west and was threatening Niuafo'ou and Niuatoputapu. We blessed our luck that we were not there, with no protection for *Romeo* at all.

Gérard spent another sleepless night, springing up at every gust. He clutched the radio like a lifeline, but the local station had become sporadic. The island's electricity had failed. Aggie's, of course, had its own generator. The banshee battering of the wind cut out all other noises, including the crash of a coconut palm we found on the roof of our room in the morning.

Sunday 8 December : Day Three

The winds were a steady 100 knots. The boats moored just 500 metres away were barely distinguishable through the horizontal rain squalls. Mammoth waves crashed against the shore, strewn with trees, branches and rocks. The old courthouse had lost most of its roof. Sheets of corrugated iron flew noisily down the street, followed by other projectiles. Trees bent at impossible angles, their shredded leaves whipping wildly in the wind.

Hordes of expatriates moved in to the hotel, fleeing the leaking roofs of their hillside mansions. They arrived with their computers, videos, TVs and washing machines. No Samoan families sought refuge. Suddenly, Aggie's had to provide 250 meals thrice a day. The waiters were smiling and courteous, despite their own worries about their homes and families. The well-to-do fretted about airline connections, missed meetings, the lack of a telephone. We too were guilty, egotistically obsessed about an aircraft, while the islanders fought to save their houses and even their lives. But *Romeo* was part of our soul, part of our family, our home for the last two years, our lifeline.

Monday 9 December : Day Four

The winds were calmer, perhaps only fifty knots, a mere breeze after all we had been through. The rain had stopped. Relief that the hurricane was over left deep apprehension as to what we would find at the airport. In three days, we had time to accustom ourselves to the idea that *Romeo* could have been destroyed. But deep down, neither of us could accept such an ignominious end to a valiant plane.

We decided to try to drive to the airport. In town, Samoans were out viewing the damage and clearing fallen trees to open the roads. The devastation was dramatic: everywhere twisted sheet metal flapped like paper in the wind. No sooner had we left the residential areas than the wind resumed full force from the other direction, driving rain with such venom across our path that visibility shrunk to a few feet. We were aware of acres of banana trees bent double; not uprooted, just quietly folded in the middle. Fallen power and telephone lines, hanging low, whip-lashed the road.

The hurricane was definitely not over: the winds had simply swung 180 degrees, returning with more force than ever. The lull had simply been the fringe of the eye. The fronds of the coconut trees, having billowed westwards like fields of windsocks for three days, snapped backwards and broke in the west wind. Most trees were already defoliated. The soft-top Suzuki took a battering, swinging dangerously across the wet roads between huge trees which had fallen. We expected it to take off at any moment and contemplated turning back. Anxiety for *Romeo* drove us on.

The solid terminal building still stood proud in lashing rain. Two lonely figures in yellow oilskins stood like stranded goldfish at the entrance. In a desperate hurry to reach the hangar, we waved and raced on passed the administration buildings transformed into a scrapyard. Sheets of roofing iron decorated the lawn like modern sculpture. We approached the hangar from the rear, eyes straining through the rain in search of reassurance. We found none. The hangar roof had been ripped off. As we rounded the corner, a horrifying scene greeted us: the massive sliding doors were wide open. Four had been flung to the ground. The remaining two leaned, cock-eyed, on the girders that supported them. Wind and rain blasted through. We strained frantically to discern the awful truth. *Romeo* was tucked behind the Twin Otter, which was dancing diagonally across the hangar.

'Hell! The roof of the fuselage is smashed in.' I clutched Gérard's arm. Our hearts were racing, our throats dry with grief. He pulled up alongside the hangar.

'No, you're wrong! It's just the outside cover that's ripped. *Romeo's* fine!'

Disbelievingly, we peered through the driving rain. The torn canvas gave the impression of an ugly rent in the fuselage. *Romeo* was intact.

'It's a miracle. An utter miracle,' Gérard stammered dizzily. 'But hell! Watch the Otter!'

Buffeted by the winds, the Otter was bouncing on its fat tyres like a yo-yo, perilously close to *Romeo*. Its tail was mangled aluminium from hitting the roof girders, and both wing-tips were severely damaged. The Otter's nose was beginning to hammer into *Romeo's* fibreglass engine cowling. By pure luck, because of the angle of the blades, the propeller was untouched.

The wind and rain intensified. A strip of corrugated iron caught round one of the Otter's wheels screeched ominously. Two steel girder frames supporting the doors were leaning on a yellow crane which had tilted until jammed against a third girder. Everything hinged on the crane. Gérard instructed me to take the driving seat, and rushed into the hangar. The gusts must have been 150 knots. Bent double against the wind, he manoeuvred *Romeo* away from the Otter's onslaught. Each time the wind intensity increased and the wail of twisting metal echoed horribly, he would rush back to the car in case the hangar caved in. After several such dashes, he had placed chocks on the Otter and cajoled *Romeo* into the safest spot by the base of the yellow crane, nose to the elements, upwind from the Otter. As long as the hangar would hold . . .

We were surprised by the arrival of another vehicle – a white police Landcruiser. It contained an Australian army sergeant and a Samoan police officer. In a concerted effort to stop the Otter from sustaining more damage, the three men secured it to a side pillar with some thick rope. It took three attempts. When they finished, the Otter danced again and the rope snapped. They gave up.

We all drove back to the terminal building. The goldfish in oilskins turned out to be the Senior Air Traffic Controller, head of the CAA, and two other staff who had been on duty for three days. They were in remarkably good humour. Gérard was determined to remain at the airport with them, insisting I return to Apia with the police. Nothing could make him change his mind. He was drenched, but the happiest I had seen him for four days. I felt wretched and prayed his survival instincts would take preference over *Romeo*.

All night, the hurricane hammered. Stomach problems over, it was my turn to lie awake and worry as the rain drove through the closed louvres, drenching the carpet. This time, Gérard did not return. I only learned his full story days later, from his diary:

Drenched to the bone, I spend the rest of the day in the leaking Suzuki by the hangar, occasionally sprinting out to clear away an obstacle that could hit either plane. I harvest a pile of iron sheets, and secure them under a metal bench at the back of the hangar. My principal concern is the two-metre swing of the first two sections of the hangar which have lost the stability of the doors. They keep bending back towards the aircraft. I muse how far they will bend before collapsing on Romeo.

I become increasingly disheartened. After the initial surge of relief at finding the plane intact, and the subsequent effort to move it to a safer spot, I imagined that all was well. But the hangar comes ever closer to capsizing, and the hurricane still rages. I have an impulsive urge that I must get Romeo *out. With my friends at the terminal, Alfred the Airport Manager, Pita the Senior Controller, Roy the Maintenance Manager, and Fala the Civil Aviation man, we stand in front of the hangar, deciding on the best way out.*

The wind must be a constant eighty knots, gusting 120. With the aid of their Landcruiser, we position three heavy cargo trailers, ready to act as tie-downs. I tie ropes to the aircraft. With a plan of action in mind and everyone in position, ready to start, a cold chill runs down my back. 'You're about to make a big mistake,' an inner voice nags. Can we feeble men prevent the wind from flipping the plane over? If we find we are unable to guide it in the right direction, we will certainly not manage to manoeuvre it back to its present position in the hangar.

'Stop! Wait!' I yell above the roar of the wind. I agonise in silence, trying to make the right decision. This move could mean Romeo's *loss or salvation, and ultimately it will have been my choice, not Nature's handiwork. I appeal to Fala. He, too, is doubtful.*

'The most critical moment is the beginning, as we leave the shelter of the hangar. The funnel effect could send the aircraft flying into the roof in the far corner, on top of the Otter. We won't be able to stop it.'

He is right.

'Okay. Forget it, guys. Thank you all. Let's get the hell out of here.'

They return to the terminal. I stay, forlorn and beaten. Utter helplessness swamps me. I can only wait, and wait, and wait, giving thanks for every minute that passes without the collapse of the hangar. The cyclone is reported to be moving east, good news in terms of wind intensity and direction, for Romeo is protected from south-westerlies, if the hangar stands.

By 19:00, the constant wind speed has decreased and the gusts seem less frequent. I inspect the two front sections of the hangar every ten minutes. The structure continues to sway dangerously. Perhaps the third section, on which everything depends, will hold. The crane, increasingly entangled in the roof sections, single-handedly supports the hangar. For the first time since discovering Romeo in one piece in the morning, I manage to relax slightly. Cold and starving, I venture into the hangar to collect dry clothes and cooking gear.

Back at the terminal, I find Alfred, Roy, Pita and Fala in one of the last intact rooms. Lit by the Landcruiser headlights directed through the window, they are sipping Vailima beer. To their amazement, I propose to cook for them, their first meal in four days. Vegetable soup, followed by mie ayam and two tins of Solomon Tai-yo First Grade tuna. Hot coffee to wrap up the feast. Snug in a dry set of clothes, life improves.

Radio bulletins advise that the eye is only sixty miles away. The gusts, still very frequent, seem over 100 knots. At 22:00, I return to the hangar, fearing the worst. By torchlight, I note with relief that the two front sections have not budged. Two aluminium ferry tanks are aquaplaning on the flooded floor.

I retrieve a sleeping bag and return to the terminal. Fala has laid down a door in the radio room for me to sleep on, to keep me off the soaked ground. I am busy installing myself when a powerful gust whistles through the terminal. Will the hangar have withstood this one? Jumping into my dripping shorts and T-shirt, I race back to the hangar for the hundredth time.

A new threat has developed. The constant swaying of the roof has loosened the cross-section angle-irons, each about six metres long. One already lies on the floor in front of the Otter. Others dangle dangerously close to Romeo. They could pierce the fuselage like an arrow or write-off a wing. With this new worry, I find it impossible to relax and stay at the hangar to see the storm through.

Tuesday 10 December: Day Five
At 04:00, a second angle-iron crashes down. Two more are held by a single bolt. The inner voice returns: 'Romeo must come out now,' it tells me. I estimate the winds to have dropped to a steady seventy knots with occasional 100-knot gusts. It seems comparatively like a sea breeze, perfectly manageable.

I return to the terminal for help and find all four men asleep, their first night's rest since the cyclone began. I cannot bring myself to wake them. It dawned on me that it would be best to drive the plane out of the hangar, a quicker operation, leaving Romeo less exposed to the wind tunnel. The cargo trolleys are already in position, the ropes attached to the plane. I point the jeep's main beams into *the hangar, and place my torch between the trolleys as a target to aim for. I manoeuvre Romeo by hand into a clear exit path. Luckily, there is little fuel in the tanks, otherwise I could not have done this alone in such winds. All set, I sit in the cockpit, waiting for a respite. The engine is only too happy to spring to life: with a healthy dose of throttle, we shoot out into the hurricane.*

It was the wrong moment, for I find myself sideways to the wind, frantically applying full left rudder and more power to turn the nose towards the trolleys. The plane is shaken like a leaf, and the tyres scrape along the cement. If I release the down pressure on the elevators, we will find ourselves belly-up or airborne over the hangar. Somehow I hold the right direction. I cannot see the wings, but have marked out a path and know if I keep to it, the wings will be clear. I reduce power right on top of the torch and cut the engine during a lull. Hand brake on as hard as possible. I leap out, pleading Romeo to stick around, as I race to tie the ropes to the trolleys. It feels like a gymkhana event. I push and secure a third lighter trolley to the tail. With what uncanny foresight had we bought so much rope in Fiji two weeks ago?

I collect the car and see in the headlights, to my horror, that the plane's wheels are lifting off the ground. If the wings were not weighted down by the trolleys, Romeo would already be upside down. The gusts are violent again, straining the ropes. I park upwind, just in front of the propeller, and attach a line to the front gear. Driving the car forward, the line becomes taut, restricting Romeo's movements to a fluttering of wings, like a young bird learning to fly. I flop inside the car, sodden, exhausted but happy, firmly believing we have beaten Cyclone Val. Cosy in the Suzuki, my safe house, I doze, waking hours later to a pale sky. The winds have weakened. For the first time in four days, clouds are visible, travelling at a dizzy speed.

I pass a hand through my hair, matted from all the salt water borne on the wind. Puzzled, I contemplate bloody fingers. Then, I remember. While manoeuvring Romeo, I had felt a hit on the top of my head, followed by a bang. Otherwise involved, I had forgotten about it. The inch-long cut was presumably caused by a flying bolt. It could have had the effect of a bullet, but my name wasn't on it. I release the car from its new vocation as an anchor, and drive past the hangar. On the very spot where Romeo had cowered for two days lies a steel girder. That inner voice was right. Romeo too has beaten the bullet! I'm covered in goose-pimples.

Fala is the only one awake at the terminal. I tell him my good news. 'At least the runway appears to be usable, even though all nav aids and communications are down,' he comments.

I duly drive onto the runway to check it out. Although waterlogged, it is remarkably free of debris. Back at the plane, I re-secure the nose, check the wing lines, and repair the antenna severed by flying debris. Then I switch on the engine for power and summon a distant world on the HF radio.

'*Nadi, Nadi, this is PAPA-TANGO-ROMEO-XRAY-ECHO calling on the ground in Faleolo.*'

'*Say again call sign and location.*'

'*PAPA-TANGO-ROMEO-XRAY-ECHO, on the ground, Faleolo, Western Samoa, how do you read?*'

A moment's stunned silence.

'*PAPA-TANGO-ROMEO-XRAY-ECHO, confirm your location Faleolo, Faleolo.*' *The incredulous voice quivered.*

'*Affirmative. Please relay following message to relevant authorities, ready to copy?*'

'*Go ahead.*'

'*One: ground winds thirty to forty knots, weather clearing. Two: runway fully operational, I say again, fully operational. Three: negative VOR, negative NDB, negative DME. Tower has negative HF, negative VHF. Four: relief operations may start immediately.*'

It is 05:30. This is the first contact from Faleolo in forty-eight hours, the first message out of Western Samoa to advise that the five-day purgatory is over. I repeat the message, received with disbelief, various times. All other air traffic remains respectfully silent.

'*PAPA-TANGO-ROMEO-XRAY-ECHO, please remain this frequency for further contact.*'

'*Regret unable stand-by. Back with you at 18:00 Zulu.*' *I can only operate the HF radio when the engine is running and cannot sit indefinitely in the cockpit on the off-chance of a message.*

'*Roger, call you 18:00 Zulu.*'

At 17:55 Zulu, as soon as I have the radio switched back on, I hear Nadi calling.

'*PAPA-TANGO-ROMEO-XRAY-ECHO, PAPA-TANGO-ROMEO-XRAY-ECHO, Nadi 8846. Come in please.*'

'*Nadi, this is PAPA-TANGO-ROMEO-XRAY-ECHO. Go ahead.*'

'*Please copy following message. A Royal New Zealand Air Force Orion to arrive Faleolo approximately 00:30 Zulu. Please provide following details. One: frequencies available to aircraft. Two: your type of aircraft. Three: confirm state of runway. Four: times of radio stand-by. Five: other details if any.*'

I fail to see the relevance of my aircraft type in this emergency context. The New Zealanders apparently disbelieve me. I could imagine the High Command in New Zealand analysing the situation, and saying, 'But who is this guy? Should we trust him? Our boys at the High Commission haven't said anything. What the hell

is a Brazilian single-engine doing in Faleolo in a hurricane? How has it survived?'
I reply to all points, reconfirming that the runway is fully operational.

'Confirm only radio contact with Faleolo airport is through PAPA-TANGO-ROMEO-XRAY-ECHO?'

'Affirmative. Next contact 19:00 Zulu.'

At 1900 GMT, I advise that the tower's HF was expected operational by 20:00 Zulu and that aircraft refuelling was available. The emergency generator is working, but the tower's radios were damaged by the deluge when the windows blew in.

'KIWI 463 inbound for aerial inspection, ETA Faleolo 22:40,' Nadi informs me.

So the Orion will not land. A runway assessment by a humble single-engine pilot is not to be trusted!

The hurricane was over. I had tormented myself all night for letting Gérard stay at the airport, visualising him lying wounded in the hangar. As the morning dragged on, my pangs increased. Why had he not come back? In desperation, I rushed to Polynesian Airlines' town office in case they knew anything.

'Are you Mrs Moss?' a bouncy young girl asked. 'Well, your husband's fine. I just left a message for you at the hotel.'

My legs trembled. 'Thank you. Thank you . . . errr . . . dare I ask about our plane?'

'The plane's fine too.' She beamed.

In a disbelieving daze, I strolled through a maze of destruction back to the hotel, and received the following written message: DON'T WORRIED. HIS ALRIGHT SO AS THE PLANE. Gérard returned at lunch time. He was utterly, utterly exhausted – but a happy man.

Eighty per cent of Upolu's houses were ruined. But that very day, the Samoan people were out collecting up their scattered possessions and roofing iron. They wasted no time fixing and cleaning up their houses and gardens. Outside each household, clothes were strung out like Christmas decorations, putting a touch of colour back into the burnt landscape. The forested hills looked as if the American Army had been through with Agent Orange. Who would have thought wind and water could make so much damage? The banana plantations were already doctored, the trunks chopped off where they had bent so new shoots could emerge. But they would take eight months to bear fruit. Bunches of green bananas, rescued from where they had fallen, filled the market along with breadfruit, mangoes and coconuts. But, in a month's time, there would be nothing to harvest. Then the problems would begin.

Romeo's fuselage was dented in various places and the nose-wheel door damaged. A replacement closing mechanism for the nose-wheel hatch was required. Telephone lines were still down so Gérard contacted Peter in Vava'u on the HF for help. Peter never hesitated for a moment. He tracked down the mechanism in Florida. A friend of his in Boston air-freighted it to Fred Sorensen, a Hawaiian Airlines DC-8 captain in Honolulu flying the Pago Pago route, who organised its safe passage on Air New Zealand's inaugural Hawaii-Apia-Auckland flight.

A couple of days later, with all repairs made, we departed wistfully from Aggie's, our home for ten traumatic days, and drove one final time through the villages where shiny new sheets of roofing iron made a patchwork pattern with rusty ones that had resisted Val. Elated at being airborne again, we followed Upolu's salt-scorched south coast. The wreck of an Australian cray-fishing boat, washed up during the hurricane, was a sobering sight. We knew the crew members were lost. I graphically visualised the horror of spending a cyclone in a yacht. It served as a justification, as if any were needed, for having refused to go sailing.

Inexplicably, I felt a sudden dread, similar to when we had left Fernando de Noronha to cross the Atlantic. Yet this flight to the Cook Islands was only half that distance. A bellicose slate-coloured ocean sloped off towards a hostile horizon. Gérard suddenly turned the nose and headed back to land.

'What's the matter?'

'I don't know. Engine sounds rough. Don't you think so?'

The engine sounded the same as ever to me. Depending on the state of my anxiety, it was more or less rough most of the time.

'Perhaps it's my imagination. Or the buffeting wind,' he conceded.

On my flimsy reassurance, he resumed course across the great ocean. All engine instruments read normal. We pressed on.

The engine continued to sound rough: it was just purring happily.

22 'You'll go down in a blaze of glory!'

Crinkled folds of mountains, draped in green forest, rose sharply out of the sea, pointing rocky fingers at the threatening skies. We were always delighted to spot land ahead, but the dramatic outline of Rarotonga came as a surprise after the flatness of its idyllic satellite atoll, Aitutaki.

The Cook Islands consist of fifteen main islands scattered on almost two million square kilometres of ocean. Avarua, the capital, no more than a neat village with half a dozen streets, was a-bustle with Christmas shoppers. The Rarotongans seemed to have completely assimilated Western ways. Apart from occasional women wearing a crown of *tiare*, Polynesia's highly perfumed white flower, only their burnished complexions distinguished them as Polynesians. They even spoke English amongst themselves. More Cook Islanders reside in New Zealand than on the islands. It only takes an hour to cruise round Rarotonga on a tree-lined road that passes petite cyclone-proof cement houses in bright colours, which look out over gentle turquoise water inside the wall of reefs. Each garden is a colourful perfumed jumble of hibiscus, *tiare tahiti* and frangipani.

We received a fax from Stan and Rosie Haynes, our dear neighbours in Rio who had been our lifeline with Brazil for the last thirty months, keeping us informed of the entangled intricacies of the economic measures dreamed up by the government. This time, it included a harrowing story that had appeared in a South African paper. A twin-engined aircraft, piloted by two South Africans, had come down in the Atlantic between Brazil and the West African coast. It would appear that the flight plan was correctly filed in Recife for the flight to Abidjan, where it was only received some days later. When a plane is late arriving at its destination, a search normally begins two hours later. In this tragic case, no action was taken for two weeks. It was only after the pilots' families, in despair, put pressure on the South African government, that it was discovered that Mayday calls had been heard by Dakar and by Recife Control, but not acted upon. The aircraft was outside both their respective areas, and Abidjan did not even know an aircraft was supposed to be arriving there. How naive we had been when crossing the Atlantic to think that anyone might have come to our rescue. The eastern half of the Pacific, away from traditional shipping or aircraft routes, was even more isolated. As we approached Polynesia, the watery distance to Easter Island began to fill me with horror. After Stan's fax, I was increasingly tempted to persuade Gérard to forget the whole thing. After all, what was this burning

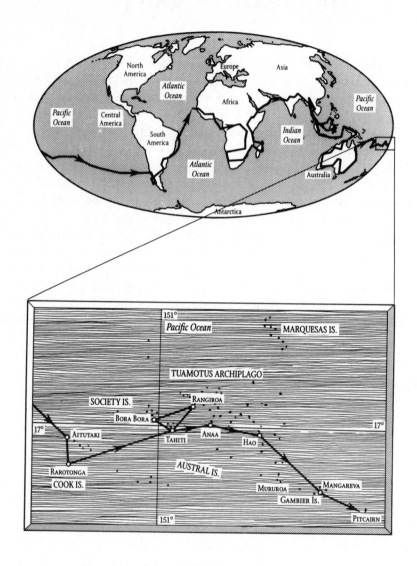

compulsion to go on? So what if we didn't complete the full circle? Did we have to go on just to say we had done it? Our lives were more important. If he had confessed to similar doubts, I would have played the devil's advocate. The fact that *Romeo* had survived the hurricane proved our guardian angels were hard at work. Surely they would not have bothered to save us just to crash into the sea further on?

We realised it was essential to have someone who cared keeping track of our movements. When dining with Peter Goldstern in Vava'u, we had been introduced over the airwaves to Arnold Gibbons, an amateur radio operator living in Rarotonga. Arnold, or ZK1DB, is a boat-hold name for yachties in the Pacific. He provides them with a weather service, transmitting daily at 04:00 GMT for half an hour and tracking their positions. Despite referring to himself as 'we', implying that other people are involved, he voluntarily collates the weather information and prepares the broadcasts. Rosie, Arnold's wife, invited us to join them for Christmas lunch. They lived in a small house tucked behind *tiare* hedges near the airport. Being a lapsed private pilot, Arnold enthused boisterously about our trip and led Gérard away to his radio room to look at weather patterns.

'Do you know, I used to hate this hobby of his,' Rosie confided to me. 'We were both working, you see, and when we'd come home in the evening, he'd just have time for a cup of tea before rushing to the met office. Then he'd spend an hour plotting out the weather, and another transmitting. We never had an evening to ourselves. I had to do everything: make dinner, clean the house, put out the rubbish, cut the grass, while he talked to those damn yachties.'

'So what changed your mind?'

'Well, I began to read some of the letters they send him. Then, one day last year, there were twenty boats in the harbour. They all wanted to meet Arnold. They brought loads of food, and even their dishes and cutlery. They filled this house and all of the garden. It was such a happy day. I realised how much he meant to them and I was proud of him. When I think of all the lives he has helped to save . . . do you know, if there's a yacht missing, he can't sleep. He calls and calls until he knows it's safe.'

'It's very admirable what he does, Rosie.' Here was a humble, self-sacrificing individual who deserved recognition for his years of silent service. But awards like OBEs tend to go to ambassadors, company chairmen or prominent personalities who are already well paid for what they do.

Arnold was so enthusiastic about our flight to Easter Island and Chile that he immediately offered to stay by the radio on the appointed days to cover our crossings. We were embarrassed, asking only that he listen in when he could, but he insisted he would back us up all night long. The empty 3,400 miles that awaited us beyond the Gambier Islands

229

became less formidable, but I was afraid what Rosie would say when she found out.

On the day we left for Papeete, in the chilly pre-dawn, two figures huddled beside *Romeo*. They were Guntram and Tekura, who owned the only ultra-light in the Cook Islands and had pulled it onto the dewy grass for us to see.

'Well, at least you'll go down in a blaze of glory!' Guntram remarked at the sight of our internal fuel tanks. He admitted to being too afraid to fly out to sea in his machine which was excessively well-equipped for flying circles over Rarotonga. 'I'm one of those people,' he confessed, 'who sees a seed of wheat growing in the garden and rushes out to buy a combine harvester, a flour mill and a bulk carrier.'

At last, we distinguished the prickly volcanic outline of Moorea and the impressive bulk of Tahiti emerging in the haze beyond it. The fabled Society Islands. We came in low over dreamy sunlit waters. Halfway across the Pacific!

A visiting aircraft was not a common occurrence at the Aéroclub de Tahiti. The club president, Léon Chanel, chastised us for giving no warning so that we could have been welcomed in fitting traditional Tahitian manner, but it already was the most enthusiastic reception we had ever received. A grand dinner was arranged in our honour.

After a tour of Bora Bora, Huahine, Rangiroa and Tekihau, we returned to Papeete to organise the continuation over the Pacific. Fuel was available at the military airport of Hao, an atoll halfway to Mangareva in the Gambier Islands, our last stop in Polynesia. Special permission from the French Army was required to land there. Two 200-litre barrels awaited us at Totégégie airport in Mangareva, to top us up for the 1,420-mile haul to Easter Island. There would be serious weight problems when all tanks were full, so our luggage, bar one rucksack, the cameras and laptop, was freighted to Santiago courtesy of Lan-Chile, the only airline flying between Polynesia and South America. We asked Philippe, Gérard's stepfather, to fly to Santiago. Philippe lived in Peru for thirty years and speaks fluent Spanish. He agreed to monitor the flight from Easter Island to the continent. Thus, if we went missing, he could help mobilise Chilean search and rescue services, help that the unfortunate South African pilots did not have.

Apart from the reassuring back-up from Arnold and Philippe on the critical flights, we wanted to know what services were available from the Polynesian side. Loïc Moisan, head of Search and Rescue operations, was impressed with the precautions we had taken ourselves, facing up to the possibility of an emergency with realism and responsibility. The thirty-minute reporting procedure to Arnold by radio was best. In addition to the obligatory ELT (Emergency Locator Transmitter), we had purchased a Marine VHF radio and a solar panel to recharge it, since rescue was more likely to be in the form of a ship than an aircraft. Moisan said the rescue aircraft, a Falcon 10, would search only in daylight hours, flying as far as the Papeete FIR boundary. He agreed it was even technically possible for it to fly on and refuel in Easter Island. This was good news.

We subsequently sought out a Lan-Chile 707 flight crew at their hotel. The captain, Patrício Toro, clearly thought us mad but gave us an invaluable en route chart used by Lan-Chile, which included all reporting points and distances on a single page. He reassured us about the excellence of the Chilean Search and Rescue Hercules, because Easter Island is an alternative airport for the Challenger. We doubted they wanted to practise on us and Philippe would be in Santiago, precisely to chase up on our behalf.

A telex to the aviation authorities in Santiago advised of our intention to depart Mangareva for Easter Island on 17 January, a date chosen specifically because Lan-Chile had a flight that day, which meant extra radio coverage for us. Out of the question, came the reply. Two aircraft are not permitted to converge on Pascua at the same time because if one crashes on the runway, there is no alternate airport for the other. This was irrelevant in our case: if we crashed first, our scraps could be swept aside; if they crashed, we could land on the grass. But we duly modified our departure to 16 January.

It was only thirty-seven engine hours since the 100-hour service in Fiji, but we were about to face our most critical flights. Air Moorea offered the use of their hangar for a thorough fifty-hour inspection: oil change, new filters, new plugs, general lubrication, clean-up and check-up. The evening before we left Papeete, the Aéroclub organised a farewell champagne cocktail party in our honour, and announced that the fuel we had loaded that morning at the club pump was a *petit cadeau* to send us on our way. We were profoundly moved and embarrassed by this generosity. Tahiti had given us the warmest welcome and departure we had received anywhere.

Early next morning, Loïc Moisan arrived as we loaded up. He apologetically presented a document for us to sign. It was a disclaimer relieving the French of responsibility for us beyond Papeete FIR. To see it in black and white came as a shock. Embarrassed, he said his boss had instructed him to obtain our signature, but that nothing had changed and they would search for us as far as Easter Island if necessary. After that cold shower, the leis of flowers and shells showered on us by umpteen well-wishers brought morbid thoughts to mind. 'Feels like they are sending us to our deaths!' Gérard remarked once we were strapped in the cockpit.

The lagoon of Anaa atoll is famous for the verdant hue it reflects into the clouds

231

above, acting as a lighthouse for Polynesian sailors. It now has 400 inhabitants, but had once been the *chef-lieu* of the area of some 12,000 people with cannibalistic tendencies. It was our first stop in the Tuamotus, a cluster of islands which curve down towards the Gambiers.

Tobia Tane, the controller, welcomed us with an invitation to lunch at his pink house under casuarina trees overlooking the lagoon. His wife, Titine, greeted us warmly and rushed away to open tins of corned beef, Vienna sausages and sardines. All over the Pacific, the islanders have given up fishing and rely increasingly on tinned foods. As we sat under the casuarinas, the sea breeze dusted off the stress of the last few days.

'*Voilà notre chambre d'amis,*' Tobia said, pointing to a tiny bungalow twenty yards away. 'If you like it, stay here with us.'

How could we refuse an offer to stay on in paradise? Like insatiable blotting paper, we soaked up the tranquillity of the bungalow for two days. As the critical flights drew closer, each happy moment became increasingly important. We derived enormous pleasure from the simplest things: the wind blowing through the mesh windows from the coconut plantation; lying on the mattresses on the floor looking out of the open doorway at the luminous green water just feet away. At dawn, the lagoon was a pale aquarelle until the sun rose behind the palms, intensifying the colours into vivid daytime hues. The men fished for *paaihere* which we barbecued or made into *palu ore*, the delicious Tahitian dish of raw fish, marinated in lemon juice and coconut milk. We dined under the stars and chatted late into the night. An atlas was produced because they wanted to know everywhere we had been.

According to the South Pacific Handbook, Hao has been out of bounds for non-French ever since the *Rainbow Warrior* affair in 1985. A special visa is required. *Romeo* had a clearance: we hoped it included permission for us to be there.

Hao's lagoon is sixty kilometres long, narrow at one end and branching out till approximately a kilometre wide. As we flew across the outer rim of *motus* and reefs, the whereabouts of the military base were no secret. Massive hangars rise beside the 3.2-kilometre runway which incongruously straddles the northern end of the atoll. DC-8s carrying the *coeur* of atomic bombs arrive here from France before proceeding to Mururoa. Polynesia is usefully considered France by the French, so that nuclear testing is in effect carried out on home ground, conveniently on the far side of the globe from Paris. If there is absolutely no danger, as the French government tries to make out, then why, all the Pacific islanders want to know, aren't the bombs tested in the Bois de Boulogne? Hao had once been a nuclear research station, and though bombs were not tested, much material was stored here in block-houses. Up to 3,000 Frenchmen had then resided at Hao. The structures had been dismantled in 1972, when Mururoa took over as the centre of subterranean nuclear experiments, leaving Hao with just 350 soldiers serving as a back-up for Mururoa.

On the patio, a handful of army personnel awaited us. They were all smiling and eager to please. After refuelling, *Romeo* was invited into a hangar at the end of the patio. It was the largest we had ever seen and brought back a flood of memories of the final state of the last hangar *Romeo* had been in. Would this one have withstood Cyclone Val? Marc Texeire, *le Commandant de l'Aérodrome*, a tall gentleman with a trim beard, cordially invited us to go diving the next morning and then lunch at the Officers' Mess. We smiled to think how we had been sent packing without lunch from the base on Iles Glorieuses, exactly half a world away!

Upon landing at Totégégie, the airport serving Mangareva, Carlson, the portly, long-haired controller, greeted us with flower leis and set about hand-pumping the two barrels of fuel into the tanks. Henri Blomme, the resident gendarme, had come over from Rikitea, the main village, to collect us in the police launch, a battering half-hour ride across the lagoon on metallic waves.

There was a Scottish feel to the green hills and sharp mountains of Mangareva, the largest of the Gambier Islands, known as *les Iles Oubliées*. Rikitea crouches under the shadow of impressive Mount Duff and the murderous towers of a disproportionately huge white cathedral built in the late 1830s by Père Laval. This mad obsessed priest had arrived like a cyclone in the Gambiers, casting over the islanders' idols and so enslaving them into arduous forced labour to build his churches that he succeeded in killing over 5,000 in the space of twenty years. Rikitea consists of a clutch of tidy houses arranged in neat gardens on each side of the single street. It exuded the quiet calm of a graveyard. We stayed *chez* dusky Hélène, who prepared us wonderful meals and presented me with a black pearl, for which the Gambier Islands are famous.

Arnold had told us of an English amateur radio operator called Ron who temporarily resided on the outer island of Taravai. Ron had lived a beachcomber's life, pottering from one Pacific island to another on a beat-up yacht with his wife and two children. He agreed to give us back-up coverage for the flight to Pascua because, as we moved east, we feared losing contact with Arnold, who was already over 1,000 miles away.

So that Gérard could check the engine, Henri dropped us back at Totégégie airport the evening before our pre-dawn departure for Easter Island. We checked the survival gear in its waterproof bag: six days' dried rations; a vital hand-pump water-maker; ELT beacon; marine VHF radio and solar panel; two hats, T-shirts and sun-screen. From the tales of shipwreck survivors which we read with morbid curiosity, we learned that food became a major problem. They had all been well-equipped with line and hooks, but when fish were pulled alongside, they simply escaped with the hook. To avoid this, Gérard had devised a spear which dismounted into four sections, with which we intended to haul the catch on board.

We had rehearsed leaping out of the plane with our respective loads. I would climb out of the back door with the waterproof bag, which had its own life jacket tied around it because it was very heavy, heavy enough to pull me under. It would be disastrous if it escaped. The very thought filled me with dread – I felt sure it would whoosh out of my hands before I could get round to the other side of the plane where (hopefully) Gérard would be waiting with the life-raft in the water. His job was to manoeuvre its twenty-three kilos out of the front door and make sure it did not sail away in the wind. Attaching a raft to a sinking aircraft has been done before! Dwelling on such issues, we slept fitfully on the hard benches in the tiny terminal building. When we rose at 02:30, the starry night was loaded with the precious scent of Mother Earth, a poignant smell of land, which mingled with the salt on the breeze.

Carlson arrived in his speedboat from Rikitea at three a.m. with the latest weather report from Papeete. It was not heartening: the winds were favourable, but a thick north-south trough hung over Pitcairn and Henderson Islands. We dithered. Were conditions good enough? Shouldn't we wait for an improvement? Unaware of our dilemma, Carlson went to light two flares on the runway. Then he hung shell leis round our necks, bade farewell and vroomed away. As if to say, get a bloody move on!

23 'That's the last land you'll see till Easter!'

We taxi to the threshold, trying to avoid the hermit crabs immobilised by the headlight which beams down the white coral runway and fizzles out against the barrier of darkness where only one flickering flare is vaguely visible. It's 04:30. Gérard revs the engine, scrutinising the instruments. Will its vibrant pulsating keep up all the way to Chile?

Romeo lifts off eagerly, surprisingly easily, despite the fuel load. What a marvellous little plane! Flashing red and green, the harbour lights tug at our heart strings, but we rudely ignore them and wing away towards a distant dawn. The glow of the panel lights reminds us of another flight, long long ago, across the Atlantic. I had vowed never again. Yet here we were.

There's a new noise, though. A whooshing sound. Damn! I haven't shut the door properly. How foolish! It is impossible to rectify this in flight because of the pressure built up inside. Tough. Icy air will blast us for the entire flight.

We climb sluggishly, painfully. Too sluggish for full power. Something's amiss. Gérard realises the wheels are still down. That's two silly mistakes in as many minutes. We can't afford any more.

We maintain 3,000 feet, just above low, skittish clouds for some time. Arnold is with us from the start, soothing us every thirty minutes as we report our co-ordinates, which he is mapping on a chart. He's 1,400 nautical miles the other way, as far away as our destination.

The dawn, as usual, brings relief, but our speed is not good: 105 knots on climbing, 110 to 117 knots levelled off. Head winds are stronger than anticipated, but with the GPS, this time we know exactly what progress we're making. Gérard is in quiet, calm control, serious with responsibility. I feel less afraid this time. Perhaps because of the exciting rendezvous ahead: we are heading towards the Pitcairn Islands, a group of four scattered isles under British administration since 1902. Oeno and Henderson lie on the direct route to Pascua, but we are deviating in order to overfly Pitcairn, the only inhabited island, lying 287 nautical miles from Totégégie.

The *Bounty* mutineers had meandered the Pacific for nine months in search of a bolt-hole until Fletcher Christian remembered mention of this island. They arrived in 1790, found the island uninhabited and promptly burned their boat

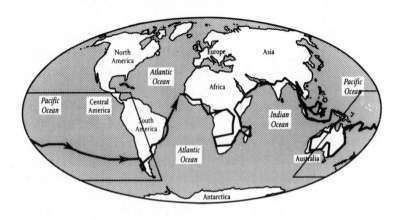

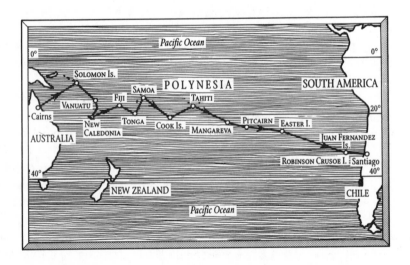

236

to avoid detection. They remained undiscovered for eighteen years. We find their descendants after two hours and forty minutes. Meralda Warren, an amateur radio operator and wife of the Justice of the Peace on Pitcairn, knows we'll pass over the island at about seven a.m. She's loud and clear over the radio. We feel exhilarated as the haughty lump of Pitcairn rises ahead, silhouetted on a glaring silver sea. We skirt its wild, eroded southern coast where sheer cliffs drop from an undulating green plateau into pounding surf.

'OK, Gérard, we've spotted you. We're on the north-east point, high on the cliff, on the peak above town. Half the island is up here with me waiting for you,' Meralda says excitedly over the radio.

We swing round, heading towards a clutch of rooftops.

'That's it! You're coming straight for us. We're waving!'

About thirty tiny figures are waving from the top of a pinnacle above Adamstown, where they have climbed to watch us fly past. Pride and gratitude well up inside us.

'We're really honoured to have all you guys here to meet us, Meralda. It's great. Thank you for your wonderful welcome.'

'It's a pleasure. Everyone's yelling for you to come lower. It's really exciting for us, you know, something that never happens on Pitcairn. We're really appreciative, Gérard.'

There seems to be no wind. We swing round again, buzzing right over their heads. The noise must be infernal, but they clamour for more! The night before, we had overheard a radio conversation between Meralda and Arnold. She had expressed concern that we might try to land.

'Negative, Meralda. I don't think Gérard will feel tempted to put his wheels down on Pitcairn!' Arnold had replied.

We do feel sorely tempted, but there is no plausible stretch of flat ground. The islanders had recently voted not to have their island flattened for an airport. There is not even a safe harbour: Bounty Bay and Western Harbour are vague refuges requiring constant vigil, depending on the winds. Occasional supply ships drop off provisions and mail and the odd cruise ship stops for a couple of hours; their more daring passengers are ferried ashore in the islanders' aluminium long boats.

Adamstown, a handful of houses among the trees on the northern coast, sits on a convenient shelf above merciless Bounty Bay. It is named after the last of the mutineers, John Adams, who survived till 1829 with nine women and nineteen children. The other mutineers and the Tahitian men they brought along had wiped each other out in brawls. We zoom over the heads of the welcoming committee one last time.

'Sadly, we have to head off now, Meralda. We've a long way to go. To all of you down there, thanks for the wonderful reception.'

'It's thanks to you for the excitement here today. We wish you a safe touchdown on Easter Island, Gérard and Margi.'

It must be a lonely, windswept life down there. What tenacity they have. With immeasurable regret, we pull away east over the empty expanse of the Pacific that surrounds them.

An hour later, we call Papeete. There is an interruption.

'PAPA-TANGO-ROMEO-XRAY-ECHO, this is Pascua, Pascua. Easter Island. How do you read?'

Pascua! The word has the power of a friendly hand pulling us to safety.

'Pascua, ROMEO-XRAY-ECHO. Loud and clear. Go ahead.' What joy! Contact established so early. We adopt a thirty-minute reporting procedure with Pascua as well. Eight hours to go.

We pass abeam Ducie Island, its pretty lagoon surrounded by a circular string of *motus* with tenacious scrub. Not a bad place to end up in the life-raft, I muse. Pascua still lies 850 nautical miles away.

'Well, that's the last land you'll see till Easter!' Arnold announces. I hope he means Easter Island, and not the date. It's only January . . .

Neither of us is hungry, but eating is a diversion. We only had a cup of Nescafé before leaving. Hélène had given us a packed lunch. We have a chunk of New Zealand cheese, boiled eggs, bananas and some *firifiri* doughnuts she had made, though cockroaches at Totégégie had eaten most of them. It made a great change to our usual menu of boring biscuits.

The speed picks up to 140 knots. Gérard makes a new estimate of five hours thirty minutes to Pascua. Can it be true? So close already? We are light-hearted. The visit to Pitcairn has broken the monotony. Six hours have flown past.

Arnold warns of a trough of bad weather across our path, reassuring us that it clears to the east. We are already flying beneath cirrus and above scattered stratocumulus. For the rest of the day, we fly through his trough.

'You will fly through a long band of Cbs . . .' Arnold is advising us when interference cuts him off mid-sentence. Swirling bulges of cumulus challenge dark grey seas ahead. Cones of rain and ice fall from altocumulus and evaporate mid-air.

'Arnold recommends a heading of 080 degrees,' Ron bridges for us. So he's been there all the time, listening in silence. Good old Ron! In fact, we are on a course of 081, trying to avoid the worst, and are amazed that from 2,000 miles away, Arnold can pinpoint so precisely the heading we should take.

'Ron, tell Arnold it's as if he's up here flying with us!'

Will we ever be able to tell him what a difference it has made to clutch at the security blanket that his voice over the radio is to us? Feel like hugging him.

We have no wish to be pounded in turbulence if it's avoidable. We deviate to a brighter heading of due east for thirty minutes till, with the stormscope flashing energetically, we are forced down to 1,000 feet and resume the correct heading through heavy rain. All around, dark sky and rain press down on us in a succession of downpours, as if trying to smack us into the gloomy seas. At times, we are forced as low as 200 feet. *Romeo* perseveres stoically, but grim images of Peter's story of an engine failure over the North Atlantic creep through my mind like a rampant virus. I analyse the swells and wonder unhappily how they'll look from the flaps of the life-raft.

We battle on and, at 120 degrees west, cross the Papeete FIR boundary. This is officially as far as the French will come to our rescue. Our guardian angel materialises, and starts cleaning up the horizon. Relieved, we climb back up to 9,000 feet and chug on until, at 112 west, all clouds have vanished. A summer blue sky, a winter blue ocean.

We have been shivering for hours because of the damn draught blasting through the unclosed door. Nevertheless, we feel prematurely victorious and dream of hot showers, a meal and a cosy bed loaded with blankets. I salivate at the thought of hot coffee and can even imagine the smell. Amazingly, it's just one hour to Pascua. The pee bottles are dangerously full – we'll have to control ourselves better on the leg to Chile!

A hundred miles short of Pascua, Arnold has become so faint that we rapidly thank him and bid farewell before he's lost. Then, at thirty nautical miles, the island looms pale-green and unimaginably lovely in the evening sunshine. GPS has brought us in spot on target. The houses of Hanga Roa, the only town, are tucked in gardens under trees. It could be a shanty town for all I care, to me it looks the most friendly, homely place on earth.

'ROMEO-XRAY-ECHO on the ground at 01:10 (20:10 local time). Congratulations and welcome to Pascua!' An unexpected burst of humanity from a controller, so stoic by profession. He directs us to the Chilean Air Force patio where a portly gentleman in civvies guides us to a halt.

'*Felicitaciones! Soy Juan Edmunds,*' he announces, extending a large strong hand. It's Juan who has arranged the importation of our Avgas. Good man! 'Señor Felipe (he means Philippe, Gérard's stepfather) is very worried, but I've told him you are safe.'

A crowd gathers. Unsure on our feet, we cling together, shivering uncontrollably in thick tracksuits despite the warm evening sunshine. They call out *felicitaciones* and *bienvenidos*, shaking our heavy hands. We feel exhilarated and utterly drained. After the formalities, carried out by the Chilean officials in a kind, unobtrusive manner, Juan shows us to a small hotel overlooking the sea. We open a bottle of Australian champagne chilled in flight by the icy blast. Pensively, we watch the sun set over the empty ocean whence we had come. It's wonderful to be here, on magical Isla de Pascua, the most isolated island on earth.

But another, longer, lonelier journey still lies ahead.

Oscar Medina, the airport manager, had asked us to pay him a visit. He announced we would have to sign a disclaimer before a notary public relieving the Chilean government of any responsibility for us. Not again! Did that mean no emergency rescue? He reassured us this was not the case. The authorities were also against our landing at Robinson Crusoe Island in the Juan Fernández Archipelago, 370 nautical miles from the mainland. Apart from being a welcome break to the 2,000-mile flight, we wanted to visit the island, but they claimed the airstrip was too precarious. We were still determined to try.

We could go nowhere in Hanga Roa without the villagers asking if we were the crazy ones from the *avioneta*. Beyond town, Pascua stretches out like a great barren plateau punctured with volcanic cones. The roads are dusty tracks, even in town where a layer of tarmac would improve dust levels enormously. But the Chilean Government, having annexed the island in 1888 with impractical designs for a naval base, has shown little interest in investing in its infrastructure.

The Rapa Nui people refer to their island as *Te Pito o te Henua*, the Navel of the World. Having slogged across 1,400 miles of ocean to reach it, we could identify with this bellybutton notion. The great Chief Hotu Matu'a is said to have occupied it at an undetermined time arriving with his retinue from the motherland of Hiva. Whether Hiva lies to the east or to the west is still a matter of debate. European explorers first began to visit the island in the 1720s. Jacob Roggeveen left twelve Rapa Nui dead during his brief visit on Easter Sunday 1722, when he named the island. Unexplained upheavals and vicious internecine strife took place in the subsequent years. In 1862, Peruvian blackbirders kidnapped half the population, mainly the learned classes, taking them to work as plantation slaves and to mine guano. Only fifteen survived to return. Contact with the outside world brought smallpox and leprosy. French plantation owners from Tahiti also collected a labour force, so that by 1870, there were only 110 pure-blood Rapa Nui still alive. Now, there are none. The nation's memory banks were annihilated, leaving the *raison d'être* of Rapa Nui civilisation unexplained.

All around the rim of this enigmatic island are stone *ahus* or altar platforms upon which once stood *moais*, massive stone busts. For reasons yet unelucidated, these were wretchedly cast from their pedestals. Numerous